# CASIODORO DE REINA

*Spanish Reformer of the
Sixteenth Century*

Portrait reputed to be of Casiodoro de Reina in the Old Folks' Home
of the Niederländische Gemeinde Augsburgischer Confession
in Frankfurt am Main.

A. Gordon Kinder

# CASIODORO DE REINA

*Spanish Reformer of the
Sixteenth Century*

TAMESIS BOOKS LIMITED

LONDON

Colección Támesis
SERIE A — MONOGRAFIAS, L

© Copyright by Tamesis Books Limited,
London, 1975

ISBN 0 7293 0010 2

Designed and Printed by
The Compton Press Ltd.
Compton Chamberlayne, Salisbury, Wiltshire

for

TAMESIS BOOKS LIMITED
LONDON

*To Silcoates School, near Wakefield, Yorkshire,
where, when Sidney H. Moore was Headmaster, my interest
in the Continental Reformation was kindled*

# Contents

|     | List of Abbreviations | xi |
|-----|------------------------|-----|
|     | Preface | xiii |
| I   | Introduction | 1 |
| II  | From San Isidro to his Flight from England | 18 |
| III | From his Flight from England to the Publication of his Bible | 38 |
| IV  | From the Completion of his Bible to his Arrival in Antwerp | 57 |
| V   | From Antwerp till his Death in Frankfurt | 67 |
| VI  | Some Consideration of his Theology and Learning | 82 |

### APPENDICES

|      | | |
|------|---|---|
| I    | Request for a Spanish Church in London 1560 | 93 |
| II   | Corro's Letters to Reina from Théobon and Bergerac | 95 |
| III  | Depositions concerning Reina laid before the Bishop's Commissioners | 99 |
| IV   | Two Letters of Jean Cousin concerning the Affair of Reina | 113 |
| V    | The Offence of Sodomy in England and the Case of Casiodoro de Reina | 119 |
| VI   | Reina's Letter to Diego López | 121 |
| VII  | The Letters of Casiodoro de Reina | 123 |
|      | Bibliography | 126 |
|      | Index | 138 |

# Abbreviations

| | |
|---|---|
| *BH* | *Bulletin Hispanique* (Bordeaux) |
| *BHR* | *Bibliothèque d'Humanisme et Renaissance* (Geneva) |
| *BSHPF* | *Bulletin historique et littéraire de la Société de l'histoire du Protestantisme français* (Paris) |
| *Bataillon* | Marcel Bataillon, *Erasmo y España*, second Spanish edition, (Mexico, 1966) |
| *Bib. Wif.* | E. Boehmer, *Bibliotheca Wiffeniana – Spanish Reformers of Two Centuries from 1520*, 3 volumes, (Strassburg/London, 1883-1904) |
| *Col. doc. inéd.* | *Colección de documentos inéditos para la historia de España* (Madrid) |
| CSP | *Calendar of State Papers* (London) |
| Frankfurt docts. | Frankfurt City Archives, Sammelband Kirchendokumente B, Französisch-reformierte Gemeinde 195, fols. 589$^r$-634$^v$ |
| *HSP* | *Proceedings of the Huguenot Society of London* (London) |
| Hessels | John Henry Hessels, *Ecclesiæ Londino-Bataviæ Archivum*, 3 volumes, (Cambridge, 1889) |
| *Heterodoxos* | Marcelino Menéndez Pelayo, *Historia de los heterodoxos españoles*, 2nd edition, (Buenos Aires, 1945) |
| Lehnemann | Johannes Lehnemann, *Historische Nachricht von der vormahls im sechzehnten Jahrhundert berühmten Evangelisch-Lutherischen Kirche in Antorff* (Frankfurt, 1725) |
| MacFadden | William MacFadden, 'The Life and Works of Antonio del Corro' (unpublished Ph.D. thesis, Queen's University, Belfast, 1953) |
| *RAE* | *Reformistas Antiguos Españoles*, 20 volumes, edited by B. B. Wiffen and L. de Usoz y Río, (London/San Sebastián/Madrid, 1848-70) |
| *Returns* | R. E. G. Kirk & E. F. Kirk, *Returns of Aliens dwelling in the City & Suburbs of London*, 4 volumes (Aberdeen, 1902-8), Volume 10 of *Huguenot Society of London Publications* |
| S. & V. | Ernst H. J. Schäfer, 'Sevilla und Valladolid: die evangelischen Gemeinden Spaniens', *Schriften des Vereins für Reformationsgeschichte*, 78 (Halle, 1903) |
| Schäfer | E. H. J. Schäfer, *Beiträge zur Geschichte des Spanischen Protestantismus und der Inquisition im sechzehnten Jahrhundert*, 3 volumes, (Gütersloh, 1902) |

Schickler       Fernand de Schickler, *Les Eglises du Refuge en Angleterre,* 3 volumes, (Paris, 1892)

Tollin       Nathaniel Tollin, 'Cassiodore de Reina', *BSHPF,* 31, 386-97, & 32, pp. 289-98 (Paris, 1882-3)

*ZHT,* 50 (1870)       Eduard Boehmer, 'Cassiodori Reinii epistolæ tredecim ad Matthiam Ritterum datæ', *Zeitschrift für die historische Theologie,* 50, pp. 285-307 (Gotha, 1870)

# Preface

When mention is made of Spanish Reformers, a common reaction is a startled enquiry regarding their very existence, and no less an authority than the *Enciclopedia Universal Ilustrada* dismisses the subject of the Reformation in Spain by saying that its influence was hardly felt because of the reforms instituted by Cisneros, especially those concerned with the morals and training of the clergy; because of deeply-rooted faith; and because of the Inquisition, which quickly moved in to extinguish the first two early centres in Seville and Valladolid.[1] Notwithstanding the work of those mentioned below, the rather facile view seems to be generally held that the movements and influences which produced the Reformation elsewhere in Europe had no counterpart or parallel in Spain.

In the middle years of last century, two Quaker gentlemen collaborated in an attempt to rescue from oblivion the works of Spanish Protestants of the Reformation period, and to reissue them together with some rather random facts about their lives. The partnership between Luis de Usoz y Río in Spain and Benjamin Baron Wiffen in England was very fruitful, and resulted in a series of twenty privately-printed volumes called *Reformistas antiguos españoles* (1847-1865), now almost as rare as the original editions. As it happens, Casiodoro de Reina does not feature very largely in this series, since what little he published was in Latin, with the exception of his Bible-translation, and even his extant letters are almost all in Latin or French. (His one letter in Spanish was published by Boehmer in 1880.) Wiffen had projected a work which would give biographical and bibliographical material about Spanish Protestants more systematically and in more detail, but he died before he was able to carry out his intention, and it fell to a friend of his, a professor at the University of Strassburg, Eduard Boehmer, to bring out the work. Boehmer acquired all Wiffen's papers and put these out in a rather higgledy-piggledy manner as a memorial to Wiffen in three volumes entitled *Bibliotheca Wiffeniana* (London/Strassburg, 1883-1904). Afterwards, the manuscript material and Wiffen's books went into a special collection in Wadham College, Oxford. In addition, Boehmer pursued investigation into the Spanish Reformers independently, and published in particular numbers of letters he was fortunate in unearthing, and notably the one in Spanish by Casiodoro mentioned above.[2]

[1] *Enciclopedia Universal Ilustrada*, L (1923) entry under 'Reforma'.

[2] 'Cassiodori Reinii epistolæ tredecim ad Matthiam Ritterum datæ', *Zeitschrift für die historische Theologie*, 50 (Gotha, 1870), pp. 285-307; 'Ein Brief von Cassiodoro de Reyna', *Romanische Studien*, 4 (Bonn 1880), pp. 483-6; *Q.F.F.Q.S. Viro summe venerando Ioanni Friderico Bruch . . . Primo rectori diem natalem octogesima vice . . . Insunt*

Another German, Ernst H. J. Schäfer, investigated most thoroughly the records of the Spanish Inquisition as they concern Protestants, publishing the results in his monumental three-volume *Beiträge zur Geschichte des Spanischen Protestantismus* (Gütersloh, 1902), and in sundry articles, the most important of which was 'Sevilla und Valladolid : die evangelischen Gemeinden Spaniens im Reformationszeitalter', in *Schriften des Vereins für Reformationsgeschichte*, Vol. 78 (Halle, 1903).

At the early age of twenty-four, Marcelino Menéndez Pelayo drew extensively on the foregoing when he prepared his *Historia de los heterodoxos españoles*, 3 vols. (8 books), (Madrid, 1880-81), of which the fifth book is of particular interest to us here. He was a brash, if talented, young man, and in this work he was less than careful in his references, but his monograph is nevertheless valuable – if only because it draws together so many sources.

All works on Spanish Reformers must rely heavily on the work of these five men, and, although there has been considerable modification of what they report, in the main what they wrote remains an indispensable source, and a good foundation on which to build more detailed work.

The remarkable *magnum opus* of Marcel Bataillon, a professor at the Institut de France, *Erasme et l'Espagne*, 2 vols. (Paris, 1937),[3] and his other studies of the period, seemed to give an impetus to a number of studies of Illuminism, Erasmianism, and the Reformation in the Peninsula. The painstaking and detailed work by William MacFadden, *Antonio del Corro* (unpublished Ph.D. thesis, Queen's University, Belfast, 1953), brought to light much new material in this field, much of it quite directly relevant to the present study. More recently still, the last ten years have produced an appreciable amount of work by North-American scholars in the field of Spanish Protestantism. Particular mention ought perhaps to be made of *Three Spanish Heretics* (Geneva, 1967) by Paul J. Hauben, which deals with four, not three, Spanish Protestants : over half the space is taken up by a consideration of Corro, derived directly from MacFadden's thesis, and the rest is a rather sketchy consideration of Reina, Cipriano de Valera, and Adrian Saravia. Nevertheless, it introduces new material on Reina.

Concerning Reina specifically, there are many works and articles which mention his activity in one place or another. Wiffen's work dwelt largely on the Genevan and English periods, and on Reina's subsequent connexions with those places. A long article by Nathaniel Tollin in *BSHPF* 31 & 32 in 1882-83 took notice of documents held in Frankfurt City Archives, but without going into them in any detail.[4] Interesting material to do with the production of Reina's *Biblia del Oso* in Basle was given by Adolf Fluri in 'Die Bärenbibel',

---

*Epistolæ quædam Ioannis Sturmii et Hispanorum qui Argentorati degerunt.* (Strassburg, 1872).

[3] First edition in French, *Erasme et l'Espagne* (Paris, 1937); second edition in Spanish corrected and enlarged, *Erasmo y España, estudios sobre la historia espiritual del siglo xvi* (Mexico, 1950); third edition in Spanish further corrected and enlarged (Mexico, 1965).

[4] 'Cassiodore de Reina', *BSHPF*, 31 (1882), pp. 386-97 & 32 (1883), pp. 241-5, 289-98 (hereafter Tollin).

*Gutenbergmuseum* 9 (Berne, 1923). Various writers have dealt with Reina's period in Antwerp and Frankfurt, beginning with Johannes Lehnemann, whose *Historische Nachricht* (Frankfurt, 1725) gives extracts from Reina's letters to Matthias Ritter the Younger dealing with Reina's time in Antwerp, and goes on to tell how he led his congregation into exile in Frankfurt. The Antwerp period has been further elaborated in articles by Johann W. Pont in the early 1900s, and by Floris Prims in the 1950s.[5] A number of writers in Frankfurt have given information about the final five years of Reina's life: amongst these stand out Hermann Dechent (*Kirchengeschichte von Frankfurt am Main seit der Reformation*, 2 vols. (Leipzig/Frankfurt, 1913)), Alexander Dietz (*Frankfurter Handelsgeschichte*, 3 vols (Frankfurt 1910) and 'Cassiodorus Reinius', (*Frankfurter evangelisch-Lutheraner Kirchen-Kalendar*, Jahr 1894, Frankfurt, 1894)), and the anonymous *Franckfurtische Religions-Handlungen*, 2 vols (Frankfurt, 1735-45).

The fact remains that, since the work done in *Bibliotheca Wiffeniana*, which, because of its pioneer nature, was very incomplete, nobody has attempted a full biographical study of Casiodoro de Reina, although several people have pointed out that one was needed.[6] The work here presented is in the main a response to the need thus expressed, and represents, with some revision of detail, a major part of the thesis presented by me for the degree of Ph.D. at the University of Sheffield in 1971.[7] An attempt has been made to gather together all the known facts and extant material concerning Reina. Research has revealed considerable unpublished material relating to this man, who was a product of the abortive Reformation movement which began in Spain in the 1540s and continued through the 1550s, but was completely stamped out by the Inquisition in the early 1560s. This movement had its origins both in native currents of evangelical thought and anti-Roman feeling, and also in ideas imported from Erasmus and main-stream Reformers through literary and political contacts with more northerly countries. Some consideration is therefore given to these phenomena to account for the presence of Reina and others like him in sixteenth-century Spain.

The life of Casiodoro de Reina presents an interesting subject for study if only for the fact that he was one of this little-known group of Spaniards who became Protestants, all too few of whom managed to escape the Spanish Inquisition, but, beyond that, several aspects of his activity are interesting for

[5] Johan Wilhelm Pont, 'De Belijdenis van de Luthersche Gemeente te Antwerpen over de Erfzonde 1579', *Nieuwe Bijdragen tot Kennis van de Geschiedenis en het Wezen van het Lutheranisme in de Nederlanden*, 1 (Schiedam, 1907), pp. 119-64; 'De Luthersche Gemeenten in de Zuidelijke Nederlanden (1536-1585)', *Nieuwe Bijdragen*, 3 (1911), pp. 395-436; 'De Catechismus van Franciscus Alardus', *Nieuwe Bijdragen*, 2, (1909), pp. 1-146; Floris Prims, *Register der Commissie tot onderhoud van de Religionsvrede te Antwerpen 1579-1581* (Brussels, 1954); 'Een incident uit de Religionsvrede 1580', *Bijdragen tot de Geschiedenis* 3rd series, 5 (Antwerp/Ghent, 1953); *De Groote Cultuurstrijd*, 2 volumes, (no place or date).

[6] Jorge A. González, 'Valera's Method for Revising the Old Testament' (unpublished Ph.D. thesis, Emory University, U.S.A., 1967), pp. 10f; MacFadden, p. 193.

[7] A. Gordon Kinder, 'Three Spanish Reformers of the Sixteenth Century: Juan Pérez, Cassiodoro de Reina, Cipriano de Valera' (unpublished Ph.D. thesis, Sheffield University, 1971).

their own sake. His production of the first complete Bible in Spanish to be translated from the original tongues was no mean feat, whilst the tenacity of purpose he exhibited in carrying out his enterprise in spite of difficulties and privations deserves praise, and the fact that the translation, with few revisions, remained the standard version of Spanish-speaking Protestants for four centuries speaks much for his achievement. His refusal to give up in the face of heaped-up accusations, true or false, his pursuit of the Christian ministry, his refusal to be a parasite when the latter was denied him, the way in which he led his congregation from Antwerp to Frankfurt and there laid the foundation of a charitable work which is still in existence, and much more, reveal a strength of character which is out of the ordinary. His importance can be judged from the interest in him shewn by such leading Reformers as Johann Sturm, Oporinus, Beza, Bishop Grindal, Zanchi, Olevianus, Matthias Ritter the Younger, and Renée de France, besides a host of minor personages, and the very interest of the Spanish Inquisition, which burnt his effigy at the stake, and tried in vain to engineer his return to Spain, is significant. Added interest is provided by Reina's remarkable mobility, for, besides his activity in certain well-defined centres : Seville, Geneva, London, Antwerp, Basle, Strassburg, Frankfurt; his name appears in many other intermediate and unexpected places. Amidst the tensions and disputes of his rather violent age, his eirenic spirit provides a calm contrast. Some attempt has been made to analyse Reina's theology, although it was not intended that this should be primarily a theological study; and, in view of their very scattered provenance, a systematic indication of the sources of Reina's many letters has been undertaken.

No one can undertake research such as that now presented without the help and encouragement of many people, and I should like here to register my thanks to those who have made the task possible. Besides various relatives and friends who have followed with interest its various stages, the major thanks must go to Professor Frank Pierce of the Department of Hispanic Studies of the University of Sheffield, for his guidance, continual help, enthusiastic encouragement, and tireless co-operation in ways great and small, as he supervised the original thesis from its rather vague inception to its completion. Special thanks must also go to the Prior and brethren of St. Michael's Abbey, Farnborough, for providing a Methodist with facilities for writing in the early stages, and to Cheshire County Council Education Committee and the Governors of Sale County Grammar School for Boys, for permitting my secondment, and to the President and Governing Body of Corpus Christi College, Oxford, for the Schoolmaster Studentship which helped in its later stages.

To the following additional persons I record my thanks for various forms of help, guidance and encouragement : Professor Marcel Bataillon of the Institut de France; Bruce Boucher, Esqr., of Magdalen College, Oxford; the Delegitoj Esperantistaj of Antwerp and Frankfurt; Madame Monique Droin-Bridel of Geneva; Monsieur le Pasteur F. Dubois of the Eglise Réformée Française of Soho Square, London; Dottore Luigi Firpo of Turin; Rev. Professor Jorge A. González of Berry College, Georgia, U.S.A.; Professor Paul J. Hauben of the University of the Western Pacific; Herr Georg Itzerott of Frankfurt; J. J. Roberts, Esqr., of Sale Grammar School; Dr R. Rosenbohm of Frankfurt University Library; and to Professor Edward M. Wilson of Emmanuel College, Cambridge, who has been particularly helpful.

The following institutions have willingly and generously allowed me the use of their facilities and materials, or have provided xerox copies or microfilm of items in their collections: *Antwerp*: City Archives; Stadsbibliotheek; *Basle*: Offentliche Bibliothek der Universität; *Belfast*: Library of Queen's University; *Frankfurt am Main*: City Archives; Stadt- und Universitätsbibliothek; Theologisches Zentralbibliothek des Evangelischen Gemeindeverbandes; *Geneva*: City Archives; Bibliothèque Publique et Universitaire; Musée Historique de la Réformation; *Halle*: Universitäts- und Landesbibliothek Sachsen-Anhalt; *London*: Library of the British and Foreign Bible Society; British Museum (Reading Room and Manuscript Room); Eglise Réformée Française, Soho Square; City of London Guildhall Library; Library of Lambeth Palace; *Manchester*: John Rylands Library; Library of Victoria University; *Oxford*: Bodleian Library; University Archives; Library of Corpus Christi College; Library of Wadham College (Wiffen Collection); *Paris*: Bibliothèque Nationale; *Sheffield*: University Library; *Strassburg*: City Archives; Bibliothèque Publique et Universitaire; *Zurich*: Zentralbibliothek.

The portrait of Casiodoro de Reina reproduced as the frontispiece hangs in the Old Folks' Home of the Niederländische Gemeinde A. C. Augsburgischer Confession in Frankfurt am Main, and thanks are due to that institution and to Dr Paul Majer for providing the photograph.

The publication of the present study has been facilitated by a subsidy from the Twenty-seven Foundation of the Institute of Historical Research, whose aid is gratefully acknowledged.

A. GORDON KINDER

*Sale, Cheshire.*

# I

# Introduction

As in other countries, the movements in Spain which pressed for reform of the Church derived from both indigenous and foreign sources. Spanish interest in the Bible during the fifteenth and sixteenth centuries was genuine and extensive, and this culminated in the great Complutensian Polyglot version commissioned by Cardinal Don Francisco de Ximénez Cisneros, and finally issued in 1521, after nearly twenty years' work. Furthermore, the extent of this interest can be judged as much by the ready sale of works of popular piety which incorporated portions of the Bible as by the academic interest in and study of the Bible by humanist scholars such as those of Alcalá de Henares.

Cisneros, from 1485, when he became Archbishop of Toledo and Primate of Spain, till his death in 1517, encouraged devotion in the clergy, especially amongst Franciscans and Dominicans. Far from hindering the appearance of the Reformation :

> . . . las tendencias evangélicas que constituyen el vigor de la reforma franciscana o de la reforma dominicana se encarnan en una minoría monástica entregada a la espiritualidad. Esta minoría simpatizará con Erasmo y aun llegará algunas veces a hacerse sospechosa de luteranismo.[1]

He founded the University of Alcalá de Henares in 1508 to improve the education of the clergy, some at least of whom must have begun to compare Biblical fundamentals with ecclesiastical reality, and, in thought and prayer, in speech and writing, would begin to strive towards an ideal which more nearly approached the evangelical norm. He also encouraged the writing and translation from Latin of devotional writings, and the publication of partial translations of the Bible. "In matters of doctrinal dispute and heretical ideas, Cisneros was open-minded and tolerated ideas and men who were in fact charged with heresy. Thus his attitude and impulse gave to many courage to hold their own religious ideas, which, although not completely heretical, at least caused fermentation in later days. Criticism of the biblical text was also unopposed by Cisneros".[2] Indeed, it is perhaps as well to remind ourselves that in the Church of the early sixteenth century much more latitude was allowed than was possible after the Council of Trent (1545-1563), and many people who would not have considered themselves Protestant held, for example, a belief in justification by faith.

Jewish and Muslim New Christians may also have played their part, as vari-

---

[1] Bataillon, p. 10.
[2] José C. Nieto, *Juan de Valdés and the Origins of the Spanish and Italian Reformations* (Geneva, 1970), p. 54.

ous recent writers have pointed out. The devotion of both those religions to a holy book is well enough known. Ex-Muslim and ex-Jew together would find many features of Roman Catholicism uncongenial, whilst the evangelical interpretation of the Christian faith would be much more in tune with their religious bent, particularly because of its devotion to Scripture. We shall find émigré *marrano* merchants in later chapters of this book.[3]

From about 1512, the movement known collectively as illuminism began to play its part in the preparation of Spain for Erasmian, and, at a later date, Protestant, ideas. As Bataillon says :

La crisis religiosa de la época de Carlos V se explica mucho mejor cuando se sabe que el alma español, desde principios del siglo, estaba familiarizada con el Evangelio. Sin embargo, el testimonio de ello no ha de buscarse precisamente en el movimiento de Alcalá, movimiento erudito, condenado, por la altura misma de sus miras, a no ejercer sino una influencia restringida.[4]

The adepts of illuminism, called *alumbrados* or *dejados,* claimed to experience a direct and personal contact with God, which led them to feel a great spiritual liberty, especially in the face of religious formalism, which they denounced. Opinions differ widely as to whether their doctrines could be said to have a Protestant origin, or whether they arose independently. In any case, they were sufficiently similar for *alumbrados* to be prosecuted by 1534 as heretics and Lutherans, and for contemporaries to accuse them of Lutheranism. The great desire of *alumbrados* was to abandon themselves to the love of God, and by this experience to purify the passions and the desires. They were given to ecstatic states and visions, and recognized no authority but the Scriptures. In their freedom of judgement with regard to the monastic life, indulgences, fasts, the reverence paid to saints, etc., their position shewed great affinity with the later pronouncements of Erasmus and Luther.[5] The leading lights of this move-

---

[3] E. Asensio, 'El erasmismo y las corrientes afines', *Revista de filología española,* 36 (1952), 45, 52, 59; A. Domínguez Ortiz, 'Los conversos de origen judío', *Estudios de Historia social de España,* 8 (1915), p. 79. Antonio Márquez, whilst rejecting strongly any idea of doctrinal influence by Jews or Muslims directly on the *alumbrados* (*Los Alumbrados* (Madrid, 1972), pp. 86-94), nevertheless says, 'En cambio, si del terreno doctrinal pasamos a niveles más hondos y elementales – el propio género de vida a que se ven sometidos los conversos – las posibilidades de que éstos actuasen como substrátum o fermento revolucionario es bastante plausible' (p. 92).

[4] Bataillon, p. 44.

[5] The *alumbrados*' beliefs do not seem to have been reduced to a doctrinal system, but A. Selke de Sánchez, 'Algunos datos nuevos sobre los Alumbrados', *BH,* 54 (1952), p. 126, gives a list of forty-eight propositions from which some of their beliefs can be deduced. They are prolix, imprecise, and full of qualifications. She discerns Lutheranism in them, and quotes in evidence Juan Maldonado, *De felicitate christiana* (Burgos, 1541), who said of the *alumbrados,* 'redolebant certe Lutherum', and that the outbreak of illuminism in Toledo was 'una chispa Luterana que de no haber sido apagada de la Inquisición, hubiera podido causar un gran incendio'. B. Llorca, *Die Spanische Inquisition und die 'Alumbrados'* (Berlin, 1934), pp. 29f, on the other hand, is definite in declaring the doctrines of the *alumbrados* to be quite independent and different from Luther's, a view which is supported by M. Serrano y Sanz, 'Pedro Ruiz de Alcaraz, iluminado alcareño del Siglo XVI', *RABM,* 7 (1903), pp. 1-16, and reinforced emphatically by Nieto, *Juan de Valdés,* pp. 59-68.

ment often came from the Tertiaries of the mendicant orders, of whom many were women; not a few were aristocrats, and the New Christians also played a great part in spreading their devotions.[6] In fact, the similarity of many of their practices and tenets to those of the Muslim Sufis has been noted.[7] Many of their adepts were young clerics and monks. Noble houses often sheltered them. These enthusiasts, who at first seemed over-zealous pietists, by preferring their own conventicles to churches made the authorities suspicious, and so at Toledo on 23 September 1525 the Inquisitor-General, Alonso Manrique, Archbishop of Toledo, condemned the whole movement.[8]

Thus, by the time the first works of Erasmus began to appear in Spain, there was a considerable number of people with analogous ideas, ready to take to him with enthusiasm. The first book of Erasmus to appear in Spanish was *Tratado o sermon del niño Jesús y en loor del estado de la niñez* (Seville 1516), translated by Diego de Alcocer.[9] The *Enchiridion* came out in 1526, in the Spanish version of Alonso Fernández, Archdeacon of Alcor. It was published with Inquisitorial approval, and was immediately sold out, and a second edition followed in the same year, dedicated to no less a person than the Inquisitor-General. This is not to say that Latin editions of Erasmus's works had not entered Spain in quantity earlier than this. In fact, Erasmian ideas had become quite important in the religious life of Spain well before the appearance of the *Enchiridion*. The essential strains of Erasmianism are two : one is realistic, down-to-earth satire of what he considered ecclesiastical abuses; the other a strong moralistic pietism. Very rapidly, many Erasmian humanists began spreading these ideas in Spain. Some had met Erasmus in Charles V's dominions outside Spain, and many of them held positions of influence in academic and ecclesiastical life. Erasmus had his admirers and protectors at the court of Charles V, and Spanish versions of his works appeared regularly between 1527 and 1535, and often went into several editions. Bataillon asserts that they enjoyed a popularity in Spain unequalled in other European countries, and that at first they met with no obstacles.[10] This is not to say that Erasmus had no opponents in Spain : one indication of such opposition is that in 1527 the Emperor's agent in Rome, Juan Pérez, obtained a letter from the Pope to the Archbishop of Toledo which was meant to protect Erasmus from attack in Spain,[11] whilst some of the mendicant orders, smarting under the repeated criticism from the Erasmians, pressed for a national debate to decide whether his works were heretical or not. This meeting was finally held at Valladolid in March, 1527. It broke without coming to any firm decision, and this failure to censure

[6] Serrano y Sanz, as note 5; Bataillon, pp. 179-82; J. C. Longhurst, 'The Alumbrados of Toledo', *Archiv für Reformationsgeschichte*, 45 (1954), pp. 234f.

[7] G. H. Williams, *The Radical Reformation* (London, 1962), pp. 5f; A. Castro, *Aspectos del vivir hispánico* (Santiago de Chile, 1949), p. 74; Nieto, *Juan de Valdés,* p. 57; Idries Shah, *The Sufis,* 3rd edition, (London, 1971), p. 245.

[8] Selke de Sánchez, as note 5.

[9] F. J. Norton, *Printing in Spain 1501-1520* (Cambridge, 1966), pp. 12, 176; Desiderio Erasmo, *Tratado del niño Jesús y en loor del estado de la niñez.* Ahora fielmente reimpreso en facsímile con un estudio preliminar de Eugenio Asensio (Madrid, Editorial Castalia, 1968).

[10] Bataillon, p .279.

[11] *Bib. Wif.* II, 58; Bataillon, p. 264, note 4.

3

it really set the seal on Erasmianism in Spain. Official approval was emphasized by a personal letter from Charles V to Erasmus on 13 December 1527, assuring him that he need feel no concern. With the Crown, the Inquisition, and the majority of the Spanish Church on its side, Erasmianism was in a strong position in Spain, but this was to be undermined fairly soon by the suspicions engendered by illuminists and Protestants.[12] In fact, the auto de fe in which Pedro Ruiz de Alcaraz and Isabel de la Cruz were punished for illuminism on 22 July 1529 at Toledo, was the same one at which Diego de Uceda had to do penance for Erasmianism.[13]

In about 1526 a number of *alumbrados* and Erasmians made an abortive attempt to found a group of twelve apostles in Medina de Rioseco, whose aims, so the Inquisition reported, included a plan to reform the world by spreading their new gospel everywhere and by linking up with Luther in Germany. This and similar activities by the two groups triggered off a campaign against them by the Inquisition, which was apparently convinced that they represented native forms of Lutheranism. Numbers of arrests and trials took place in the 1520s and 1530s, and punishments and flights from the country effectively wiped out open expression of this form of activity for some years. The purge was by no means so severe as that which was to take place in the late 1550s and early 1560s.[14]

Amongst the sympathizers with this movement were the brothers, Alfonso and Juan de Valdés.[15] Alfonso carried on a correspondence with Erasmus, of whom he was a great admirer, and at one time managed to use his influence as Charles V's Latin secretary to thwart a plan to get the Inquisition to ban Erasmus's works in Spain. Some time before 1528 (although it was not printed till 1529), Alfonso had written the *Diálogo de Lactancio,* in which he defended the Sack of Rome and introduced many Erasmian ideas, and shortly before his death from plague in Vienna in 1532, probably in 1531, he wrote the *Diálogo de Mercurio y Carón,* in which he criticized the ruinous condition of the Church.[16] His death saved him from the Inquisition, although moves had already been made in 1531 against both his work and that of his brother Juan. Juan had been a member of the illuminist conventicle organized by Pedro Ruiz de Alcaraz in the home of the Marquis of Villena, and he was already compromised with the Inquisition when he published the *Diálogo de doctrina christiana* (Alcalá, 1529), in which he spoke most favourably of Erasmus. This prompted Manrique to order his examination.[17] Charged with unorthodoxy at Alcalá in 1529, Juan was quickly cleared, but was soon under attack again. He

[12] H. Kamen, *The Spanish Inquisition* (London, 1965), pp. 7of.

[13] J. C. Longhurst, 'Alumbrados of Toledo', p. 243.

[14] J. C. Longhurst, 'Julián Hernández', *BHR,* 22 (1960), pp. 9of.

[15] For Alfonso & Juan de Valdés see *Bib. Wif.* I, 66-77; J. C. Nieto, *Juan de Valdés;* J. N. Bakhuizen v.d.Brink, 'Juan de Valdés, Reformator in Spanje en Italië 1529-1541', *Mededeligen der Koninklijke Nederlandse Akademie van Wetenschappen.* Nieuwe Reeks, 25 (1962), 167-212, (reprinted in French, Geneva, 1969); Fray Domingo de Santa Teresa, 'Juan de Valdés 1498?-1541. Su pensamiento religioso y las corrientes espirituales de su tiempo', *Analecta Gregoriana,* 85, section B; P. Pourrat, *La Spiritualité Chrétienne* (Paris, 1925), III, 130, calls Juan 'the theologian of illuminism'.

[16] Alfonso de Valdés, *Diálogo de Mercurio y Carón,* edited by José F. Montesinos, (Madrid, Clásicos Castellanos, 1947), pp. vii ff.

[17] J. C. Longhurst, *Erasmus and the Spanish Inquisition* (Albuquerque, 1950) pp. 35, 47.

began to feel himself unsafe in Spain, and he left in 1530 for Naples, a place as yet unaffected by the Spanish Inquisition. He was accompanied by Mateo Pascual, the rector of the University of Alcalá de Henares.[18] In Italy Juan de Valdés exercised a great influence on the reform movement, and wrote several evangelical works; he also translated parts of the Bible into Spanish, but these seem to have remained unpublished during his lifetime. At his death in 1541 he was still officially a member of the Roman Catholic Church.

It is a commonplace to say that Erasmus prepared the way for Luther in Europe – and this is no less true for Spain than for the rest of the continent. Luther went well beyond the elimination of scandals, the criticism of purely external religious observances, and the tightening-up of morals to which Erasmus confined himself. He was tortured by a search for holiness that went deeper than Erasmus's desire for wisdom. We have some evidence that Luther's works in Latin were already in Spain as early as 1519.[19] The writings of German and Swiss Reformers became known first in Spain presumably through Flemings and Germans at the court of Charles V and the experience of Northern countries by those Spaniards who accompanied Charles on his travels.[20] Not all the Spaniards at the Diet of Worms were unsympathetic to Luther's cause.[21] The *marrano* merchants of the Low Countries sympathized with him because they saw in him the enemy of the Inquisition, and they began to make sure that his works found their way into Spain.[22] Luther's *Commentary on Galatians* was translated into Spanish in 1520, and was soon followed by other works.[23] As early as 1521, Pope Leo X issued briefs to the Constable and the Admiral of Castille, requiring them to adopt measures to prevent the introduction into Spain of Luther's writings and those of his sympathizers.[24] In one way and another, however, the ideas of a more radical religious reformation began to gain currency in Spain. Indeed, Gonzalo de Illescas, writing in 1578, felt they might well have gained the day, given a little more time, and, had it not been for the intervention of the Inquisition, which was formed for quite other reasons; but the machinery of the Holy Office could now be brought to bear on this new situation – not against New Christians who apostatized, but against both Old and New Christians whose ideas became too radical.[25] By 1525 oppo-

---

[18] Longhurst, *Erasmus and the Spanish Inquisition*, pp. 54f; Longhurst, 'Alumbrados of Toledo', p. 243.

[19] L. Pfandl, 'Spanische Lutherbild des 16. Jahrhunderts', *Historisches Jahrbuch der Görresgesellschaft*, 50 (Munich, 1930), 464, quoting a letter from the Basle printer, Johann Frobenius, to Luther, dated 14 February 1519, from *Luthers Briefwechsel*, I, 420.

[20] Bataillon, p. 110; G. de Illescas, *Historia Pontifical y Catholica*, (Burgos, 1578), II, 449; Selke de Sánchez, 'Algunos datos nuevos', p. 130.

[21] T. McCrie, *History of the Progress & Suppression of the Reformation in Spain* (London/Edinburgh, 1856), p. 61, states that when Francisco de Angeli, the provincial of the Order of Angeli, was at the Coronation of Charles V, he called at Basle on the way home from the Diet of Worms to have converse with Conrad Pellican about Luther, and professed to agree on most points.

[22] Bataillon, p. 111; P. Kalkoff, 'Die Anfänge der Gegenreformation in den Niederlanden', *Verein für Reformationsgeschichte*, 79 (Halle, 1903), 43; J. J. I. v. Döllinger, *Beiträge zur politischen, kirchlichen und Culturgeschichte* (Vienna, 1882), III, 280.

[23] J. Stoughton, *The Spanish Reformers* (London, 1883), p. 36.

[24] McCrie, *Reformation in Spain*, p. 61.

[25] G. de Illescas, II, 451; M. Geddes, *Miscellaneous Tracts* (London, 1702), I, 453.

sition was already hardening : on 2 April of that year the Inquisition banned the reading of all Lutheran books throughout Spain, and on 23 September 1525 quasi-Lutheranism was detected in the *alumbrados'* teaching.[26]

For a time, then, Lutheran ideas gained ground, especially in Seville and Valladolid, but to a lesser extent also in Toledo and in other centres. The writings of other Reformers also entered Spain, often by being deliberately ordered from booksellers abroad. In this way, Œcolampadius, Melanchthon, Bugenhagen, and others became known.[27] The writings of Erasmus and the Reformers found an echo in the hearts of the *alumbrados,* and before long the Inquisitors confused all three under the general title and condemnation of 'luteranos'. There is no doubt that this confusion has led to the Reformers' influence in Spain being over-estimated by Protestants – there is also no doubt that, after the Inquisition had done its grisly work, their real and potential influence has been underestimated by Spanish scholars and historians.

We shall turn our attention now in more detail to the situation and events in Seville in the years between 1528 and 1558. Situated in Andalusia, where the admixture of races is strongest, this opulent city, the main port for the Indies, was at the height of its grandeur, and open to many influences, as are all large ports. The very volume of the trade pouring in made the entry of books a relatively easy matter – till the Inquisition, being warned, became too vigilant.[28] It is hardly surprising that this was one place where the Reformers' ideas took the strongest root – even though the flower was by force of circumstances produced abroad. Eventually, only such adepts as were fortunate enough to flee the country were able to develop their evangelical spirituality – the rest had to recant or were crushed. Already Seville had its group of Erasmians, with some of whom the master himself had corresponded.[29] Just as important as this contact was the communication with the new University of Alcalá. The new evangelical ideas were spread as much by sermons as by books. The pulpit had been enlivened by Erasmian ideas, and most of the significant and influential preachers of Seville had come from Alcalá.

Three men, all of whom had studied together at Alcalá, had a great influence in Seville. They were Francisco de Vargas, Juan Gil (often known as Dr Egidio), and Constantino Ponce de la Fuente. According to Gonsalvius Montanus, the author of *Sanctæ Inquisitionis hispanicæ artes detectæ* (Heidelberg, 1567), Vargas had lectured on Scripture in the University, and had died in 1550, before the Inquisition had concerned itself with the other two. Schäfer, however, discerns his influence on them.[30] Egidio was for twenty years from 1537 the *canónigo magistral* – i.e. the official cathedral preacher. Reina's fellow-exile, Cipriano de Valera, writing in *Dos tratados* (London, 1588), says that Egidio was influenced greatly by an Andalusian gentleman, Don Rodrigo de Valer, who brought him to a profound knowledge of the Gospel, which made him bitterly

[26] H. Kamen, *Spanish Inquisition,* p. 71; Selke de Sánchez, 'Algunos datos nuevos', p. 129.
[27] Bataillon, pp. 438f.
[28] *Col. doc. inéd.,* V, 399, 529-32.
[29] Bataillon, pp. 84f.
[30] Bataillon, p. 524; Montanus, p. 281; *S. & V.* p. 9; Schäfer, I, 349, II, 372.

regret the time he had 'lost' in the study of scholastic theology at Alcalá.[31] Bataillon finds this hard to accept, but anyone who has a knowledge of evangelical circles will easily recognize the recurrent phenomenon – repeated, for example, by John Wesley – of the scholar who finds his spiritual resources released by a deep religious experience and henceforth tends to condemn what went before because it had not brought him to this experience. Valer was very much in the tradition of the *alumbrados*. From a pleasure-loving youth he was converted in about 1540 to a life of spiritual intensity by reading a Latin Bible, which he got to know almost by heart. He then saw it as his duty to proclaim the truth he found therein against the errors of the Church. The knowledge which he had reached by no human help or ministry he felt he had to share. Called before the Inquisition, he was released after a heavy fine, because they thought him mad. He continued to preach in and out of season, and was in 1545 once more condemned and imprisoned. Even then he would interrupt a sermon when taken to church, till, finally, he was confined in the monastery of Nuestra Señora de Barrameda in Sanlúcar, where he died.[32]

The ground had been prepared in Seville for the Erasmians – and for the Lutherans – by the *alumbrados*. In fifteen years of inspired Biblical preaching, Egidio made a great name for himself.[33] Constantino, who came about that time to Seville, supplied him with Lutheran books, and he introduced the new doctrines into his preaching, both in public and in conventicles.[34] In 1549, Charles V proposed Egidio as Bishop of Tolosa, but the Inquisition had already begun proceedings against him. He was required to abjure certain propositions, central to which was justification by faith, and all of which shewed that he was an Erasmian rather than a Lutheran. As Bataillon says, he was an Erasmian up to and including his dislike of martyrdom, for he abjured on 21 August 1552 those opinions listed by the Council of Trent as suspect of Lutheranism and in part condemned.[35] This leads one to suppose that the so-called Lutheranism of Seville at that time might have owed very little to Luther. Egidio was sentenced to one year in prison, later commuted to retirement to the Charterhouse of Jerez, and on his release he continued to be *canónigo magistral* till his death in 1555, although his sentence included a prohibition from preaching for ten years. Later, when the outbreak of anti-Lutheran persecution came along, his bones were disinterred, his goods confiscated, and his effigy was burnt at the auto de fe of 1560.[36]

It is surprising that no general inquiry into other persons in Seville followed at this stage, especially as the followers of Egidio considered themselves as a church within the Church, although not in breach with it. Only three people seem to have been attainted with suspicion by the Inquisition : Luis Hernández del Castillo in Paris, Diego de la Cruz in Flanders, and Gaspar Zapata in the

---

[31] *S. & V.* p. 8; Montanus, pp. 256-274; Valera, p. 204.

[32] M. F. v. Lennep, *De Hervorming in Spanje* (Haarlem, 1901), p. 201; Montanus, pp. 259-63; Valera, pp. 200-4, 246.

[33] Bataillon, pp. 524f; Montanus, p. 279; *S. & V.*, p. 8.

[34] *Heterodoxos*, V, 86.

[35] Bataillon, p. 526.

[36] *Heterodoxos*, V, 89.

service of a nobleman at the court of Flanders.[37] All of these latter lived to fight another day, and we shall meet two of them again. Such gentle treatment was possibly due to the favour in which Egidio was held by one of Seville's inquisitors, Corro.[38] As events were to shew, their successors were to receive more ferocious treatment! Nevertheless, it seems that Juan Pérez took the opportunity to leave Seville at this time. Although we cannot say so with certainty, he may well have been one of the seven people reported by Cipriano de Valera as leaving the city for Geneva in 1555.[39]

Constantino Ponce de la Fuente had accompanied the future Philip II to the Netherlands in 1548, and from 1549 onwards he was confessor and chaplain to Charles V. He returned to Seville in 1553, and preached with success in the cathedral and elsewhere. He was unanimously elected to succeed Egidio as *canónigo magistral* in spite of opposition by the Inquisitor-General, who objected to his Jewish blood, and he was sworn in officially on 12 June 1557.[40] Various writings of Constantino have survived, and so we can examine his views at first hand. His *Exposicion del primer Psalmo* (1546) puts forward the doctrines of justification by faith and of Christian perfection.[41] His *Suma de doctrina christiana* (1543) presents a remarkable affinity with Luther's teachings.[42] It went through five editions by 1551, and was the means of reinforcing Constantino's teaching and spreading it. It taught that faith in Christ was opposed to faith in works; that works and faith necessarily supported each other in the Christian life; that confession directly to God is preferable to auricular confession; that the eucharist is a memorial and should be taken more often than the once a year that was common at the time; that the Gospels and Epistles should be read, if possible, in Spanish; and that routine religion without a spiritual conversion is a dead thing.[43]

The manner of Constantino's preaching can be discerned in the *Exposicion del primer Psalmo*. He addressed himself to the man in the street, trying to bring him to consider seriously the question of how God's law should be obeyed, and to kindle in him the spark of sanctifying faith. Such preaching, begun by Egidio, continued by Constantino, brought about a movement of reform in Seville.[44] Bataillon states that,

> España se nos muestra, en Sevilla y en otras partes sin duda, agitada por una predicación que se podría llamar implícitamente protestante, que deriva claramente del iluminismo erasmiano, y que, entre 1535 y 1555, se adhiere a la

[37] *Heterodoxos*, V, 116.
[38] A. del Corro, *Lettre envoyée a la Maiesté du Roy des Espaignes* (Antwerp, 1567), fol. Av verso.
[39] Valera, p. 205.
[40] *Bib. Wif.*, II, 10f; Bataillon, pp. 527f; *S. & V.*, pp. 6f.
[41] *Exposicion del primer Psalmo de David, cuyo principio es Beatus vir, dividida en seis sermones, por el Doctor Constantino, con privilegio, Sevilla, 1546.* Second edition 1556.
[42] *Suma de doctrina christiana en que se contiene todo lo principal y necessario, que el hombre christiano debe de saber y obrar, Sevilla, 1544.*
[43] Bataillon, pp. 535-39.
[44] *Heterodoxos*, V, 92 (quoting from Alfonso García Matamoros, *Opera Omnia* (Alcalá, 1553), fol. 50f, a passage which was suppressed in later editions).

justificación por la fe sin deducir de ella conclusiones fatales para los dogmas católicos.[45]

At the same time, in the monasteries affected by Cisneros's reforms and in the young Society of Jesus, an entirely different type of spirituality was being fostered, which Montanus depicts as requiring fasting, mortification, repetition of masses and ceremonies, confessions, and the like.[46] The dividing factor between the two types of spirituality seems to have been Erasmus, in that the Jesuits dissuaded people from reading his works, whilst the followers of Constantino nourished their spiritual life from them.[47]

Constantino preached the same doctrines as Valer and Egidio, in spite of the treatment they had received. He became a leader in the opposition to the influence of the Jesuits, openly criticizing them in his preaching. The Inquisition called him for questioning, but could at first prove nothing. Eventually, the discovery of a large number of openly Lutheran documents written by him, and hidden in the house of one of his followers, Isabel Martínez, who had been imprisoned for heresy, gave the Inquisition its opportunity.[48] Constantino was imprisoned towards the end of 1558, and died in prison two years later, possibly by suicide. His bones were disinterred and his effigy burnt at the same auto de fe as Egidio's in 1560.[49]

The *Index* of 1551 of the Spanish Inquisition prohibited explicitly 'La Biblia en romance castellano o otra cualquier vulgar lengua', although it said nothing about partial translations, and the energies of the Inquisition seem to have been directed against only those Latin editions that were published abroad.[50] A *Censura de Biblias* undertaken in Seville, and published by the Inquisition in 1554, reveals the presence of large numbers of Bibles in the city and in the surrounding districts as far away as Osuna, Jerez de la Frontera, and Arcos. The owners were mostly clerics, but others are recorded. Two booksellers and two monasteries (St Paul & St Thomas) had more than ten each. The provenance of these Bibles was mostly Lyons (318 copies), Paris (68 copies), and Antwerp (36 copies). Various books by Erasmus were also noted in this *censura*.[51]

[45] Bataillon, p. 545.

[46] Of interest, as illustrating the attitude to Luther of this party, is a poem, consisting of thirty-six pages of sustained invective, Fr. Christobal Mansilla, *Inuectiua contra el heresiarcha Luthero* (Burgos, 1552), published in facsimile by A. Pérez y Gómez, *El ayre de la almena*, 4 (Cieza, 1961). I am indebted to Professor E. M. Wilson for this reference.

[47] Bataillon, pp. 545-48; X. le Bachelet, 'La Théologie dans l'ordre des Jésuites', *Dict. de Théol. Catholique*, (Paris, 1947), VIII (i), cols. 1011-14; A. Astrain, *Historia de la Compañia de Jesús en la asistencia de España*, 2nd edition, (Madrid, 1912), pp. i, lvii-lxi, 432-38. The Jesuits were established in Seville by 1554. Dr. T. O'Reilly has drawn my attention to the very strong similarity between the early background of John of Ávila and that of Francisco de Vargas, Juan Gil, and Constantino Ponce de la Fuente, divergent as their later lives were.

[48] Montanus, pp. 289f, gives these titles: De statu Ecclesiæ; De vera Ecclesia & de Ecclesia Papæ quem appelabat antichristiana; De Eucharistiæ sacramento, & de Missæ; De Iustificatione hominis; De Bullis & Indulgentjjs Papanis; De meritis hominum; De Confessione.

[49] *Heterodoxos,* V, 107-112; Montanus, pp. 290f.

[50] Bataillon, p. 552.

[51] J. I. Tellechea Idígoras, 'Biblias . . . secuestradas por la Inquisición de Sevilla', *BH*, 64 (1962), 236-43.

A large number of people in Seville began to gather themselves into a conventicle, or series of conventicles, that were in effect a Protestant Church in embryo.[52] Valera puts their number at eight hundred.[53] Both the latter in *Dos tratados* and Montanus in *Sacræ Inquisitionis hispanicæ artes* tell of their progress and downfall. The conventicles had appointed for themselves at least one preacher, Cristóbal de Losada, a physician who had been one of Egidio's pupils. He is also called the superintendent of the church.[54] Menéndez Pelayo puts the life of these conventicles at twelve years at the most. They met in the homes of Isabel de Baena, Luis de Ábrego, and María de Conejo.[55] At least one nobleman, Juan Ponce de León, the second son of the Count of Bailén, was one of their number and had at one time offered to buy them a house for their meetings. A preacher of Moorish extraction, Juan González (with his two sisters) was a strong influence in the group. Outstanding female members were María Bohórquez, an educated noblewoman, well-versed in Latin, and her sister, Juana, wife of Francisco de Vargas, María de Virués, and the Franciscan nun, Francisca Chaves, of the convent of Santa Isabel.[56] Two other influential supporters of the teaching were Escobar and Fernando de San Juan, the directors of the orphanage known as the Colegio de los Niños de la Doctrina.[57] All levels of society were affected, although Menéndez Pelayo would have us think otherwise.[58] In the lists of the Inquisition's punishments published by Schäfer, this can be clearly seen. The membership was drawn from well beyond the immediate area of Seville.[59]

Several monasteries and convents were affected, but none as much as the monastery of San Isidro del Campo of the Order of Observantine Hieronymites, which was in Sevilla la Vieja, nowadays called Santiponce, just outside the city boundary and near the ruins of the Roman city of Itálica.[60]

The Order of Spanish Hieronymites was established c.1370 and confirmed by Pope Gregory XI in 1374. Their emphasis was on the emotional rather than the intellectual side of the religious life. They exalted manual labour and tried to live the austere life of the Christian hermit. In fact, they took the name of Jerome, not from their founder, but from the translator of the Vulgate, the fourth-century hermit, whom they wished to emulate. They were sympathetic to the New Christians, many of whom joined the Order. As in all religious orders, a tendency to slacken off was observed after the first flush of enthusiasm for the ideal. When Lope de Olmedo was elected General of the Order in 1422,

---

[52] *Heterodoxos,* V, 116.

[53] Valera, p. 207.

[54] Montanus, pp. 232f; Valera, pp. 207f; J. A. Llorente, *Histoire critique de l'Inquisition d'Espagne* (Paris, 1817), II, 265. Schäfer, I, 371, doubts whether Losada was a pastor.

[55] Montanus, pp. 210-13; MacFadden, p. 62; Valera, p. 209.

[56] Montanus, pp. 200-13; *S. & V.*, p. 12.

[57] *Heterodoxos,* V, 120f.

[58] *S. & V.*, p. 14; *Heterodoxos,* IV, 41.

[59] Montanus, pp. 248f; Schäfer, I, 120f.

[60] Montanus, pp. 243f, mentions, besides San Isidro, its daughter-house, Nuestra Señora del Valle in Écija, the Dominican monastery of San Pablo, the Hieronymitesses' convent of Santa Paula, and the Franciscan nunnery of Santa Isabel.

he insisted on a strict observance of the rules, and tried to remove what he saw to be abuses that had crept in. When, as was to be expected, his insistence met with resistance, he withdrew to a Charterhouse to observe the Carthusian religious exercises and base upon them his reforms for the Hieronymites. In 1424 Olmedo went to Rome and informed Pope Martin V of his plans. The Pope called representatives of the Order to Rome, and, after discussion, promised that nothing would be changed, but gave Olmedo permission to set up a new order in the diocese of Seville named the Hermits of St Jerome, who came to be known as the Observantine Hieronymites. Their rule was basically that of Augustine, but modified by the Carthusian rule : e.g. study was not allowed in the convent, nor was any monk permitted to attend university courses (of course, it was possible to join the Order after graduation); no women were allowed within the monastery walls or into its churches; no meat was eaten and no linen worn; a fast was observed from the feast of St Jerome till Easter. Members were not, however, forbidden to go outside the convent, and they probably made considerable use of this freedom during the period 1553-1557. A community consisted of professed monks and lay-brothers. Their habit was the same as that of the Hieronymites, viz., white with a dark brown scapular and cape, the only difference being that for the Observantines the scapular was of a different shape and the belt was of white leather.

Olmedo returned to Spain in 1429 with the task of administering the Archbishopric of Seville. Soon afterwards, in 1431, he obtained for his new order the monastery of San Isidro del Campo. At first it was Cistercian, and was renowned as the original burial-place of the saintly Isidoro, the Bishop of Seville in the seventh century. It was built by the Guzmán family, who had provided accommodation for forty monks, and had endowed it richly. The current patron, Enrique de Guzmán, was dissatisfied with the perfunctory way in which the Cistercians were carrying out their duties, and obtained a papal brief to dislodge them, transferring the buildings to Olmedo, who lived there with the brethren.[61] It became the principal house of the Observantines, who had, at the time of our concern, six other smaller houses, one of which, Nuestra Señora del Valle at Écija, not far from Seville, with fifteen monks, was also affected by the movement.[62]

Some time before 1557, the prior of San Isidro was García Arias, a New Christian from Baeza, also known as 'El Maestro Blanco', because he was an albino. He had been one of Egidio's disciples and had a reputation for Biblical knowledge. He seems to have wavered between the Erasmian-Lutheran and the Jesuit opinions. Montanus praised him for introducing the light of true religion into the monastery. He worked on the monks, who were already prepared for a more evangelical outlook as against the mechanical devotion of the rule by reading Savonarola and Erasmus, and he awoke in them the desire for a

---

[61] MacFadden, pp. 20-26; Castro, *Aspectos del vivir hispánico*, p. 105; J. de Sigüenza, *Historia de la Orden de San Jerónimo* (Madrid, 1907), pp. xii, 165f; *Heterodoxos*, V, 117; Valera, p. 205.

[62] The others were: Santa Ana near Tendilla in the Kingdom of Toledo; Nuestra Señora de Gracia in Carmona; San Miguel de los Ángeles near Pechín in the Seville area; Santa María de Barrameda in Medina Sidonia; and Santa Quiteria near Jaén.

better form of Christianity based on a strong attachment to the Scriptures.[63] It is possible that the Jewish and Moslem origin of many of the monks helped in this process, since, as stated earlier, both religions have strong attachments to a holy book.

Then suddenly, some time about 1553, García Arias underwent a complete *volte-face*. This may have been connected with the fate of Egidio – but there has been a suggestion that he was not really sincere in his emulation of Egidio and Constantino, and that it arose out of envy of their success. In any case, he was apprehensive when the situation got out of hand, and tried to reverse the process. He banned all books from the cells, and attempted to return to the strict policy of the founder.[64] The excess of mortification thus occasioned even led to the departure of some monks. Most of them, however, did not accept this sudden change and continued their association with the evangelicals in the city. They soon reached the conclusion that they needed books of 'Lutheran' theology to attain complete knowledge.[65]

The story is taken up by one of the ex-monks of San Isidro, Antonio del Corro, writing, it is true, more than ten years after the event, so that one must perhaps make some allowance for the entrenched Protestant position he had taken up by that time. His *Lettre envoyée au Roy* (Antwerp, 1567) is an apologia for his leaving the old religion. Corro explains that, when Egidio was sentenced in 1550, he was puzzled and asked to see the documents of the Inquisition. When he saw them, he was amazed to find that, far from agreeing with the accusers, he concurred with Egidio's teaching, which seemed to him to be a continual praise of Christ, of the benefits of His death, and of justification by faith over against the 'works of hypocrisy and superstition'.

When Egidio returned from his period of punishment in 1553, Corro made a point of speaking with him. He states that he got to know Constantino, Escobar, and Juan González at about the same time. As Montanus and Corro agree here, we must suppose that the monks of San Isidro began in 1553 to go out of their monastery in search of what seemed to them purer and more solid teaching. Corro tells us he went further, and wanted books by Luther and other German Reformers, and that he obtained them from the Inquisition by bribery. This statement he repeats in a letter to Bullinger, dated 7 July 1574.[66]

At this point we must note with Bataillon that at this period a great transformation was taking place in Spain, closely linked with the events in the vast European network of which Geneva was the centre. Genevan presses were beginning to turn out evangelical propaganda intended for Spain. The Protestant Churches of Europe were becoming more self-confident and were moving in to the attack. In this those Spaniards were helping who had either remained away from Spain or who had fled thence because of evangelical views. A

---

[63] Montanus, pp. 237f, 244, 255; MacFadden, pp. 34f.

[64] McCrie, *Reformation in Spain*, p. 106; Montanus, pp. 245f; MacFadden, p. 28; *Heterodoxos*, V, 118; Lennep, *Hervorming*, p. 201. Later on, García Arias was to return to the evangelical point of view, and hold onto it with constancy when held by the Inquisition. He perished in the fires of the auto de fe of 28 October 1562 (Schäfer, II, 319).

[65] Montanus, pp. 247f.

[66] Corro, *Lettre envoyée*, fol. A vii ff; *Zurich Letters*, 2nd series, p. 156.

Spanish evangelical catechism had already been printed in Geneva as early as 1550, and had been sent in sealed envelopes to many important Spaniards in 1551.[67] *Marrano* merchants in Antwerp, Frankfurt am Main, and elsewhere were also engaged in similar ventures, providing Protestant literature for Spain, possibly for reasons of both conviction and profit. Indeed, in Antwerp at least nineteen Erasmian and Protestant works were printed in Spanish in the years between 1540 and 1560 (including three editions of Constantino Ponce de la Fuente's *Doctrina Christiana* (1549, 1555 & 1556) and Francisco de Enzinas's translation of the New Testament (1543)). All of these were hardly intended to remain in Belgium![68]

In this work Juan Pérez became deeply involved. Arriving in Geneva in the early 1550s, he became well-known for his piety and good character. He collaborated with Calvin, and Beza wrote well of him in his *Icones*.[69] By 1556, he had prepared his translation of the New Testament for the press.[70] It seems very likely that he had done much of the work before he arrived in Geneva, and that he had doubtless brought a considerable portion of it with him from Spain.[71]

Besides preparing his Spanish New Testament, Pérez was working on other Spanish books, helped by a countryman, Julián Hernández, otherwise known as Julianillo, who, before going to Geneva, had apparently worked as a proof-reader for Spanish Protestant works in both Antwerp and Frankfurt. When Pérez went on a mission to Frankfurt with Calvin and other notables, Julián was responsible for seeing at least five Spanish publications through the press. These were: a catechism entitled *Sumario breve de la doctrina Christiana* (1556), which has a preface by Pérez; an edition of Juan de Valdés's *Comentario sobre la Epistola a los Romanos* (1556), previously existing in manuscript only, and for which Pérez again wrote a preface; a similar edition of Valdés's *Comentario sobre la primera Epistola a los Corinthios* (1557), with a preface and a dedicatory epistle by Pérez; Pérez's own translation of the *Psalmos de David* (1557), with his dedicatory epistle to Maria of Austria; and a translation of Bernardino Ochino's anti-papal tract, *Imagen del Antechristo* (1557). As he worked, Julián seems to have conceived the idea of himself taking a consignment of the books to Spain. From the records of his trial by the Inquisition we know that he arrived in Seville in July 1557 with books concealed in casks and with letters to Protestants in Spain from Germany and the Low Countries. Copies of all five books mentioned above are reported in the prohibitory edict of 17 August 1559, and it was the *Imagen* that brought about Julián's down-

---

[67] Bataillon, pp. 704f.

[68] J. Peeters-Fontainas, *Bibliographie des Impressions Espagnoles des Pays-Bas 1520-1799*, 2nd edition, (Nieuwkoop, 1965); *Col. doc. inéd.*, V, 399f; MacFadden, p. 42.

[69] T. Beza, *Icones, id est, Veræ Imagines virorum doctrina simul et pietate illustrium* (Geneva, 1580), fol. I, i, iii.

[70] EL TESTAMEN | TO NVEVO DE NVES | TRO SENOR Y SALVA- | dor Iesu Christo. | Neua y fielmente traduzido del original Grie | go en romance Castellano. | (Device) | EN VENECIA, EN CASA DE | Iuan Philadelpho. | M.D.LVI.

[71] E. Droz, 'Note sur les impressions genevoises transportées par Hernández', *BHR*, 22 (1960), pp. 119-32.

fall. A copy of this book was delivered in error to a cleric who had the same name as the one to whom it should have gone. This cleric gave the alarm, and Julián was captured on 7 October 1557. It was the beginning of a trail leading the Inquisitors to, amongst others, the monks of San Isidro and Nuestra Señora del Valle. During three years in prison, Julián still refused to abjure his evangelical beliefs, although he seems to have revealed to his tormentors something of the situation amongst Reformed Christians in Antwerp. He was judged guilty of heresy and burnt at the stake in an auto de fe celebrated in Seville on 22 December 1560. On the same occasion thirteen others were slaughtered, there were thirteen *penetenciados,* and the effigies of three other men were burnt. Two of the latter were already dead : Egidio and Constantino Ponce de la Fuente; the third was Juan Pérez, safe in Geneva.[72]

Pérez stayed approximately two years in Frankfurt, during which time he set up a fund for the printing of an edition of the whole Bible in Spanish. This fund was held by a leading member of the French refugee Church, the merchant Augustin Legrand, who was also its chief trustee. After Pérez's death, Antonio del Corro was involved in a lengthy wrangle about this money, which by then amounted to some 1,000 crowns.[73] In 1569, Casiodoro de Reina obtained at least some of it to finance the printing of his Bible.

Pérez remained in Geneva till 1561, becoming a 'habitant' in 1558, and publishing several other Spanish works. These were : *Carta embiada a D. Philippe rey de España* (1558), a strongly-worded argument against the papacy, attempting to persuade the King not to support it; the translation of a work by Jan Philippson (Sleidanus), *Dos informaciones muy utiles* (1559), to which Juan added a preface entitled *Suplicacion a la Magestad del Rey* (1559); a translation of Calvin's *Catechisme* of 1549, *Catecismo* (1559), different from the anonymous *Catechismo* of 1550, and containing more material in the form of prayers and orders of public worship; *Breve tratado de la doctrina* (1560), a translation and expanded revision of Urbanus Regius's work, *Novæ doctrinæ ad veterem collatio* (1526); and finally *Epistola consolatoria* (1560), clearly written to encourage the Seville Protestants in their sufferings, and particularly prompted, one must suppose, by the plight of Julián Hernández. Pérez found time to be minister to a small congregation of refugee Spaniards till an illness in 1561, after which he responded to a call from France for pastoral help, and in 1563 he appears in Blois as a minister. By early 1565 he was in Montargis as domestic chaplain along with Antonio del Corro to Renée de France, (and briefly, therefore, as we shall see, in the company of Casiodoro de Reina). There he worked at the project which was dear to his heart, the translation of the whole

---

[72] Droz, as note 71; G. Bonnant, 'Note sur les ouvrages en langue espagnole imprimés à Genève par Jean Crespin', *BHR,* 24 (1962), pp. 50-57; G. Bonnant, 'Nouvelle note sur des imprimés genevois en langue espagnole dus aux presses de Jean Crespin', *BHR,* 26 (1965), pp. 318-21; J. E. Longhurst, 'Julián Hernández, Protestant Martyr', *BHR, Travaux et Documents,* 22 (1960), pp. 90-118; *Bib. Wif.* II, 77; J. Crespin, *Histoire des vrays Tesmoins* (Geneva, 1570), fol. 543; Schäfer, II, 291; A. G. Kinder & E. M. Wilson, 'The Cambridge Copy of the *Imagen del Antechristo', Transactions of the Cambridge Bibliographical Society,* 7 (1974), pp. 52-8.

[73] MacFadden, p. 241; Shickler, III, 74-77.

Bible into Spanish. At his death, in October 1568, he was supervising the printing in Paris of a Spanish New Testament and of several pamphlets.[74]

Returning to the monks of San Isidro, we see that before long they were much better supplied with evangelical literature than their early mentors had been. Corro tells us he had read at least Luther, Melanchthon, and Bullinger. In 1561-62, when the Inquisition published lists of forbidden books collected in the preceding five years, these included works of more than eighty authors, amongst them Luther, Calvin, Zwingli, œcolampadius, Melanchthon, Bucer, Servetus, Castellio, and Osiander. The list is very full, and the books must have had a very strong influence in such a small community.[75] In fact, it was not long, we are told, before the canonical hours were replaced by readings from Scripture, and many of the more rigorous exercises were abandoned.[76] Eventually, of San Isidro's forty residents, twenty-two were to flee or be condemned for heresy, including the Prior, the Vicar, and the Procurator. At Écija the Prior fled and the Vicar was executed.

Up to this point their views were not essentially different from those of the *alumbrados* and the Erasmians (reading and meditation on the Scriptures in the vulgar tongue; goodwill of God towards men; a living faith which issues in charity), even when their views went so far as to condemn images. But the advent of German and Swiss Protestant theological works opened their eyes to abuses not noticed before. Corro states that they condemned the papacy; auricular confession; the Inquisition; attrition; purgatory; asceticism; baptismal regeneration; the use of Latin; the idea of sacrifice in the mass; the monastic life in general; the idea of seven sacraments instead of the two instituted by Christ. This is plainly Protestant, and, even when due allowance is made for Corro's ten intervening years of experience, we are left with the picture of a body of thought in Spain which was clearly Protestant.[77] And if Corro was so affected, it is hardly likely that those of his companions who took flight with him, and passed into Protestant communities abroad, were less affected.

Suspicion was growing amongst the monks that the Inquisition was becoming interested in their activities. A decision was taken to escape abroad, but a dilemma immediately presented itself. If they went in a body, they would arouse too much interest, and suspicion would fall on them. If they went singly, there was a strong chance that the later ones might not be fortunate enough to escape, and might fall into the hands of the Inquisition. In the event, the latter plan was the only feasible one, despite the risk.[78] It was a great feat for twelve of them to escape in a single month and proceed to Geneva by various unrecorded routes, as they had previously arranged.[79] Geneva seems to have been

[74] For a fuller treatment of Juan Pérez, see *Bib. Wif.* II, 57-99 and my unpublished Ph.D. thesis (Sheffield University, 1971), pp. 34-61, 199-279.

[75] The list is given by Schäfer, II, 392-400; for a similar list of books taken in Valladolid, see Schäfer, III, 101f.

[76] Montanus, pp. 247f; Llorente, *Histoire critique,* IV, 243; McCrie, *Reformation in Spain,* pp. 106f.

[77] Corro, *Lettre envoyée,* fol. A viijv-G ijr.

[78] MacFadden, p. 56.

[79] Valera, pp. 205f; Montanus, pp. 249f.

chosen because other Spaniards, as we have seen, were already there, though the city was strategically in a weak position, that is, if the Emperor should decide to attack, whilst at the same time the theological climate was hardly congenial to such independent thinkers as Corro and Reina. Neither of these disadvantages need have been obvious from the distance of Seville.

Reports vary as to whether eleven or twelve monks fled from San Isidro some time during the late summer of 1557 : the Prior, Francisco Farías; the Vicar, Juan de Molina; the Procurator, Pedro Pablo; and the monks, Antonio del Corro, Peregrino de Paz, Casiodoro de Reina, Alonso Baptista, Miguel [sic], Cipriano de Valera, Lope Cortés, Hernando de León, and Francisco de la Puerta are named. Valera adds the information that the Prior of Écija fled at the same time, but he does not name him. The lay-brother, Juan de León, also escaped. Several lay-people, including Luis de Sosa, a man from the Canaries, and Francisco de Cárdenas, a Seville merchant, also took the opportunity to flee. Of course, no effort was spared to apprehend those who had fled abroad, in particular those from San Isidro, but, with the exception of Juan de León and Luis de Sosa, all appear to have managed to remain at liberty.[80]

They were correct in their decision to flee, but the tragedy is that it was not made quite soon enough, for the arrival of Julián Hernández with the books smuggled from Geneva, intended for the conventicle, in July 1557, was the eventual cause of the full fury of the Inquisition being loosed. The trail whose first clue was Julián led to numbers of others. Before long the leaders of the movement who remained in Seville were all captured; Juan Ponce de León had fled to Écija and was taken on 4 October, before Julián himself, and Juan González was arrested on 9 October. Before the end of the year, monks from San Isidro were imprisoned with them in the Inquisition's headquarters in the Castle of St George, in Triana, just across the river from the city. Cristóbal de Losada and Juan de Castillana were arrested on New Year's Day; Constantino Ponce de la Fuente remained at liberty till August of 1558, and in the same month García Arias, who had finally firmly embraced the evangelical cause, was also taken. Eventually, besides Arias, from amongst the monks of San Isidro, Juan Crisóstomo, Juan Sastre, Diego López, Bernardino Valdés, Domingo Churruca, Gaspar de Porres, Bernardo de San Jerónimo, Miguel Carpintero, Francisco Morzillo, Benito [sic], and Andrés de Málaga were all in custody, together with Cristóbal de Arellano of Écija. The total of those taken came to about one hundred, of whom about forty were burnt at the stake in the autos de fe of 24 September 1559, 22 December 1560, and 26 April and 28 October 1562, whilst the rest were condemned to various terms of imprisonment and/or degradation. Those who for reasons of prior death or absence in the safety of some Protestant land could not be arraigned were condemned *in absentia* and consigned to the flames in effigy. Isabel de Baena's house, which had been their principal meeting-place in Seville, was razed to the ground, the site was sown with salt, and a marble column bearing an inscription recording the event was erected on 'the spot. Montanus claimed them all as Protestant martyrs, but, as MacFadden points out in his study of Antonio del Corro, they had neither

[80]Valera, p. 206; Schäfer, II, 282; M. de la Pinta Llorente, *La Inquisición española y los problemas de la cultura y de la intolerancia* (Madrid, 1948-58), I, 249.

liturgy, nor church buildings, nor ordained ministry, and so formed only the first stage of a nascent church, which might well have developed into an indigenous Protestant Church, if the Inquisition had not intervened so savagely. Nevertheless, both Montanus and Valera give the movement the name of church.[81]

---

[81] Montanus, pp. 218, 234f; Valera, pp. 207, 209, 269; Schäfer, I, 377f, II, 356, 386; MacFadden, p. 61; F. de Texeda, *Scrutamini Scripturas* (London, 1624), fol. b iᵛf.

# II

# From San Isidro to his Flight from England

The place and date of birth of Casiodoro de Reina are known only by deduction, if not conjecture. He consistently signed himself 'Hispalensis', which would indicate Seville as his birthplace, but, since it appears to have been a custom of the Observantine Hieronymites to use the place of origin as part of the professed name, thus obscuring the family name, it can be credibly argued that he came from a place called Reina, although the records of the Inquisition give Montemolín as his birthplace. The latter is sufficiently near Seville to justify his use of 'Hispalensis'; but so would the fact that he had studied in that city and lived in a convent there.[1] Menéndez Pelayo took delight in reporting him to be a 'morisco granadino' on the strength of a letter written about Reina by the Ambassador's secretary, from England on 5 October 1563. This seems to have been an attempt to discredit Reina, but, if it were true, it hardly matters to any but the Spaniards of the sixteenth century, bothered as they were by *limpieza de sangre*.[2] Nicolás Antonio says that he was from Reina in Extremadura, and that he was certainly Christian and not Jewish.[3]

The date of Reina's birth must have been about 1520, or soon thereafter. This date is obtained by arguing back from 1573, when he described himself as 'senectutem præsertim jamdudum ingresso',[4] and from the fact that we consider him to have been somewhat older than Cipriano de Valera (born ?1530) and the contemporary of Antonio del Corro (born 1527).

In short, nothing very definite at all is known of Casiodoro till he was a student at the University of Seville – and even this we know from later reference to it by himself. His graduation we assume because he was allowed to matriculate at the University of Basle in 1567, from his description of himself as 'homo in literas educatus', from the evidence of his erudition provided by his work, and by the universal testimony of his contemporaries, together with his friendship with many erudite men.[5] That he was ordained priest appears

---

[1] *Bib. Wif.*, II, 177, 298, 300; Schäfer, II, 312f; L. J. Hutton, 'The Spanish Heretic', *Church History*, 27 (1958), p. 24; J. A. Pellicer y Saforcada, *Ensayo de una bibliotheca de traductores españoles* (Madrid, 1778), p. 31.

[2] *Heterodoxos*, V, 151; this description would seem to be appropriate for a heretic, no doubt. It is repeated ad loc. by the *Enciclopedia Universal Ilustrada* (1933), where Reina is also identified with Cipriano de Valera!

[3] N. Antonio, *Bibliotheca Hispana Nova*, 2nd edition (Madrid, 1783), pp. 234f.

[4] C. de Reina, *Evangelium Ioannis* (Frankfurt, 1573), fol. a. 2 recto; A. Dietz, 'Cassiodorus Reinius', *Frankfurter evg.-Luth. Kirchen-kalender* (1894), p. 16.

[5] Letter to the Scholarchs, Strassburg AST 48/29; *Heterodoxos*, V, 150. *Bib. Wif.*, II, 177, gives the University of Basle Matriculation Book entry in 1567 (no date specified).

from his later statement that he had said masses in Spain which had had more effect than his sermons in London.[6]

After graduation he became a member of the Order of Observantine Hieronymites and lived in the monastery of San Isidro del Campo. It is during his time there that we begin to have some definite evidence about him. Casiodoro seems to have been one of the prime movers in the development of a cell of Protestant belief in Seville in general, and in San Isidro in particular. We are told that he made such progress in the teaching of García Arias that he managed to get almost all the monks of his convent to embrace it. During the trial of María de Bohórques, natural daughter of Pedro García de Xeres, reference was made to her mentor, Fray Casiodoro, whom Schäfer definitely identified as Reina. It is puzzling that we are told of the death at the stake of this Fray Casiodoro. One wonders, but it is hard to believe, whether there were two monks with this unusual Christian name active in the movement in Seville at the same time. What is certain is that Casiodoro's effigy was burnt in an auto de fe on the Sunday called Cantate, 26 April 1562, on the Plaza San Francisco in Seville, along with the effigies of Valera, Corro and others. There may be some confusion here in the minds of reporters between actual death at the stake and being burnt in effigy.[7]

Of course, as has already been reported, Reina had fled with the San Isidro exodus at a date prior to Julián Hernández's capture in the summer of 1557.[8] We have no record of the route he took to reach safety, but he turned up eventually in Geneva, as Pérez and others had done before him. With him came his parents.[9]

There appear to be no references in the City records to his presence in Geneva – no doubt because he considered his stay there as very temporary. Later, however, in various sources, there is reference back to his stay in that city. These are found mainly in a series of depositions in the archives of the French Refugee Church of Frankfurt am Main.[10] It is stated there that every time he passed the place where Servetus had been burnt at the stake 'tears came to his eyes'. Reina's opinions on Calvin and Servetus's execution are divulged at length, and the Sardinian, Angel Victor, reported seeing a fellow Spanish exile, Cortés, carrying a letter from Reina in Geneva to Sebastian Castellio in Lausanne.[11] From such references we can be certain that Reina was in Geneva, and that he was known to other members of the Spanish community there. The refugees from San Isidro, however, arrived in Geneva during Juan Pérez's absence in Frankfurt, and therefore before the formation of the Span-

[6] Frankfurt docts., fol. 592.

[7] Llorente, *Histoire critique,* II, 262-4; Schäfer, II, 274, 283; *S. & V.,* pp. 12, 51f.

[8] The letter to the Scholarchs (note 5), written in early 1565, says, 'Quum iam per nouennium propter Euangelium Christi ex Hispania exulem'. This would mean that he left Spain in mid-1556.

[9] T. Schott, 'Frankfurt als Herberge', *Verein für Reformationsgeschichte,* 3 (1886), p. 32.

[10] The origin of these documents is discussed below. Although noted by Tollin, Van Schelven, and Boehmer, they have never been published. My article, 'Two Unpublished Letters of Jean Cousin', *HSP,* 22 (1971), pp. 51-9, gives an account of them without reproducing them. The main documents are therefore given in Appendix III.

[11] Frankfurt docts., fol. 591, 593.

ish congregation in the Temple of St Germain under Pérez's leadership. Reina, Corro, and Valera all became members of the Italian congregation, to which Reina later expressed his gratitude for help received at this period.[12] By the time of Pérez's return, all three were ready to move on, since they seem to have found uncongenial the rigid system of Geneva. From the tone of later correspondence between them, we know that Reina and Beza had met, but we cannot be sure whether it was in Geneva or later in Poissy. It is said that Reina exercised an unsettling influence on the Spaniards in Geneva, provoking even the saintly Juan Pérez to disputation, and earning for himself the sobriquet of 'Moses of the Spaniards'.[13]

One of Reina's San Isidro companions, Juan de León, was captured by the officers of the Inquisition at Strassburg on the journey from Geneva to England and taken back to be burnt in an auto de fe in Seville.[14] Journeying between various Protestant centres was a perilous business. The King of Spain's agents were everywhere, and his authority stretched over much of Europe. A particularly close watch was kept on the ports of the Low Countries for people trying to embark for England, where a haven for persecuted continental Protestants had been created by the accession of Queen Elizabeth in 1558.[15] Once again, after the Marian interlude, people from many nations were arriving to claim religious asylum, particularly in London. Amongst them came Spaniards. Casiodoro did not, however, proceed directly to England from Geneva, but went first to Frankfurt for a brief visit. He arrived in London soon after Elizabeth's accession, nevertheless, and with him his parents. Tollin tries to argue that he had been in England before Queen Elizabeth came to the throne, but his argument is not convincing.[16]

The most numerous refugees, naturally, were those from the nearest countries, and strong, well-organized and enduring congregations of French and Flemings were quickly re-established in the City of London. The main French congregation met in the old church of St Anthony in Threadneedle Street and the Flemings in Austin Friars. The Italians, too, for a short period, had a separate existence. All these congregations were strongly Calvinist in theology and church discipline – although, according to the quaint English custom of compromise, they came legally under the jurisdiction of the Bishop of London, who was at that time Edmund Grindal, whose years in exile in a similar position would render him sympathetic to their plight. They were left fairly free to

---

[12] Geneva MS fr. 407, fol. 16; *Bib. Wif.*, II, 210: 'Ecclesiæ Italorum cui omnia debeo, tum quod, dum Genevæ vixi, fui ei adjunctus.'

[13] Frankfurt docts., fol. 601.

[14] Tollin, p. 387.

[15] *Collection de Chroniques Belges* (Brussels, 1882), I, 478:
Aqui han venido tres o quatro Españoles de Geneva llenos de santa doctrina. Seria bien hacer alguna prevencion en los lugares de la marina desos estados para que no dexasen pasar tan mala canalla, como la que aqui viene, a lo menos Españoles, que es cosa de que los ereges se honran mucho.

[16] Tollin, p. 388. His argument is based on a misunderstanding of the English dating of the period, viz., the fact that at the time concerned England still observed New Year's Day on 25 March, and therefore for three months each year the number of the year was different from that in use in Roman Catholic Europe.

organize themselves after the Presbyterian manner, and the bishop did not inter-
fere unless called in to arbitrate in a dispute, or when his help was needed in
the matter of a petition to the Queen. Their church councils, called consistories, held very frequent meetings, and once a month a joint meeting of the three
consistories, called the Coetus, met to discuss matters of common interest and
concern. There was a certain coming and going of members between the various congregations. In this situation the Spaniards found no obvious home. Some
attended worship with the French, others attached themselves to the Italian
Church.

With this Casiodoro was not satisfied, and during 1559 he collected round
himself a group of his countrymen, for whom he held services in a private house
thrice weekly and to whom he preached in their own language. By 4 January
1559/60 they had written a Confession of Faith to justify their presence in London. This *Confessio Hispanica* was considered to have been largely, if not entirely, Reina's work, and was to play an important part in his subsequent difficulties in several cities, as will be seen. There is some suggestion that Cipriano
de Valera helped in its compilation. It was carefully enough worded.[17]

The Confession is in twenty-one chapters, and is clearly the work of an independent mind that will not be bound by the rigid doctrinal preconceptions
of denominationalism. It feels free to point out, daringly for its generation,
that infant baptism is nowhere mentioned in Scripture. This must be the reason
why the French Church took exception to the section on baptism. In the com-
bative situation of the period, such observations were best left unvoiced if one
wished to be considered orthodox. The first chapter (on God) gives a highly
orthodox statement on the Trinity, and certainly does not prepare us for the
loud accusations of anti-Trinitarianism that were soon to be flung at Reina.
Chapter 11 (on the Sacraments of the Christian Church) reduces the sacraments
to two and takes a broadly Calvinist view of the eucharist as a memorial. Chapter 13 (on the Lord's Supper), however, takes a fairly Lutheran, consubstantiationist, standpoint, thus foreshadowing Reina's conversion to Lutheranism in
later years. Lessing sees the Confession as a reconciliation of the Confession of
Augsburg with the 42 articles of Ridley and Cranmer,[18] whilst Reina's opponents were able to detect Servetism in it. Reina himself was later to use it both
to justify his Calvinist orthodoxy and to justify himself as a Lutheran minister!
The main point was that it satisfied Bishop Grindal, whose goodwill was vital.

By 1560 this small Spanish congregation must have felt securely enough established to wish for recognition as an independent foreign congregation after
the manner of the French, the Flemings and the Italians. Accordingly, Reina
·addressed a petition to this end to Secretary Cecil and the Bishop of London.

---

[17] *Bib. Wif.*, II, 165; P. J. Hauben, *Three Spanish Heretics* (Geneva, 1967), p. 86. It
seems that this Confession existed only in manuscript form till Reina published it in
Frankfurt in 1577. The one copy noted by Boehmer in Frankfurt University Library (*Bib.
Wif.*, II, 232) was reported lost in 1968. A second edition was published in Cassel in
1601, with a parallel German translation. The German version alone was published in
Amberg in 1611.

[18] *Bib. Wif.*, II, 166, note 12, gives the extract from Lessing, *Analecta,* II, 631-9, but the
reference to W. Nicholls makes no sense at all.

This petition in Reina's own handwriting is still extant in the British Museum.[19] He asks for a church to be allowed to them and gives various reasons : many people, he said, were afraid to meet in a private house, because Spanish spies were more active there than they would be in a public place; people were afraid for their affairs in Spain; whilst meetings continued in private it was easier for their enemies to fabricate charges of doctrinal extravagance, which were believed by both opponents and friends alike; in a public place their beliefs would be open to view; they did not think it would cause greater difficulties with the King of Spain than were already experienced, but if it did, they were willing to leave England rather than cause quarrels between monarchs. We have evidence that the Spanish Ambassador, Don Álvaro de la Quadra, Bishop of Ávila, was trying unsuccessfully to entice evangelical Spaniards into the embassy in order to be able to spirit them out of England.[20]

This request was granted, and a church which had been in use as a warehouse, St Mary Axe, was allocated for their worship, together with a royal pension of £60 for Casiodoro.[21] Secure as this made him for the moment, Reina apparently would have preferred Corro to come and replace him, as is revealed by a statement made later by Angel Victor.[22]

On Friday, 22 October 1560, Casiodoro appeared before the French consistory on behalf of the Spanish brethren asking permission for them to make a public confession of faith before the whole congregation, because they had been suspected of holding Servetan views on the Trinity. He was unwilling to say who had made this accusation.[23] In view of Reina's unconcealed opinions about

[19] Lansdowne MSS 4 (Burghley Papers), art. 46; *Bib. Wif.*, II, 190f. The complete text is given in Appendix I.

[20] M. Fernández Álvarez, *Tres embajadores* (Madrid, 1951), p. 210.

[21] *Bib. Wif.*, II, 170; *Heterodoxos*, V, 137; *HSP*, 38 (1937), p. xx. A map in B. E. Ekwall, *Street Names of London* (Oxford, 1954), shews that this church was situated in the street which now bears its name. All trace of it is now completely obliterated, and not even a plaque marks its site.

[22] Frankfurt docts., fol. 601.

[23] Archives of the Église Réformée Française de Soho Square, Actes du Consistoire de l'Église de Threadneedle Street 1560-65, fol. 23 :

Mardy 22 Doctobre 1560 ung nomme Casiadore espagnol comparut deuant nostre consistoire Requerant au nom des aultres freres espagnol qui sont ycy en la ville De leur permettre de faire leur confession de foy publiquement Deuant toute leglise, pour cause, se dissoit il que il ont este suspesonne de tenire quelque erreurs de seruetus, & A quoy il luy fut dit et demande sy cestoit generalment que on ne luy tell suspeçon de eulx ou sy cestoit quelqung particulier a quoy il nous dit que luy estant a Frangfort on luy rescrivoit letre de cest ville, et de Geneve. Lequel toutfois ne nous volut dire ceulx qui cestoit qui avoient escript, mais on nous dit quil avoit entendut que tell suspetion estoit venu a cause dung de leur frere qui avoit dit que quant au mot de Trinite que on ne trouve point tel mot en la Sainte Escripture, requerant que on ne le requerit point de dire son nom, car il ne le dira point veu que la chose est passe et tenu pour morte et assoupie, et que la confession quil feront pourra satisfaire quant a cela. Dont, apres avant tout ouy ses susdits alegations luy fut respondu que long desiroit bien scavoir celuy quy a dit ce mot touchant de la Trinite, et puis celuy quy a eut suspecon de eulx et que quant a faire leur confession que on ne leur volloit refuser. Sur quoy nous dit que il savisera avec ses freres.

Schickler, I, 123; *HSP*, 38 (1937), p. 13; P. Denis, 'Les Églises d'étrangers à Londres' (unpublished mémoire de licence, University of Liége, 1974), Chapter III, p. 4, suggests that only Reina could be the 'ung de leur frere' concerned.

Servetus, his doctrines and the manner of his death, and later accusations against Reina, these suspicions were not unexpected, although probably groundless. But it is also a fact that the two best-known holders of Unitarian views, Servetus and Socinus, were Spanish and Italian respectively, and this tended to make all Spaniards and Italians automatically suspect of similar views. Reina did himself no good by befriending people whose doctrines were regarded with suspicion. The practice has, of course, plenty of precedent in the Gospels, and Reina was doubtless able to distinguish between a man and his beliefs. He was called to task for his friendship with Adriaan Haemstede,[24] and he was criticized not only for allowing the Italian, Acontius, to attend his church, but also for appointing him to office within it.[25]

On 21 January 1560/61 the Spaniards carried their Confession of Faith to the French Consistory and asked for it to be approved formally by signature. They were asked to go into more detail on the subject of infant baptism and secular authority.[26] Although Reina's Confession of Faith did not win complete acceptance, the little Spanish congregation began its separate existence with eventual reluctant approval from the French Consistory. Gathering members, as it had to, from the other three foreign congregations, it was not looked on with too much favour and seems never to have had its consistory fully accepted as a constituent member of the Coetus. In March 1560/61 some discontent is evident, in that the Flemings proposed to the French that they should call the Spanish minister before them to shew them the Confession, because many former members of the two congregations were meeting with the Spaniards.[27] The latter were not very cooperative about the matter, since doubtless they considered themselves an independent church, equal in standing to those of the French and the Flemings. Even so, as late as April 1563 they were still trying to gain recognition of their equality through being permitted to celebrate their own

[24] A. A. van Schelven, *Kerkeraads-Protocollen der Nederduitsche Vluchtelingen-Kerk te Londen 1560-1563* (Amsterdam, 1921), p. 131; *HSP*, 38 (1937), p. xix. Adriaan Cornelisz Haemstede (1525?-1562?), the minister of the Flemish Refugee Church, was excommunicated in November 1560 for sympathizing with Anabaptists. Reina had defended him strongly, and had maintained a correspondence with him after he had returned to live in Holland (Frankfurt docts., fol. 591-3).

[25] Van Schelven, *Kerkeraads-Protocollen*, p. 137; Frankfurt docts., fol. 601; MacFadden, p. 190. Giacomo Concio (Acontius) was an Italian military engineer who had been in London since 1559. He was censured for advocating tolerance to Anabaptists, and for denying the virgin birth. A friend and correspondent of Haemstede, he wished to reduce creeds to an essential minimum.

[26] Schickler, I, 123; Actes, fol. 57:
Sur quoy fut trouve bon quil pourroient bien ung peu plus esclarcire larticle touchant du baptesme des petitz enfans et du magistrat.

[27] Actes, Fol. 76; *HSP*, 38 (1937), p. 35:
Item les flamens nous proposirent scavoir sil ne seroit pas bon dapeller a ladyt assemble Le ministre des Espagnol, et desiroient aussy de voire leur Confession de foy quil ont mis par Escript a cause que ceux qui se Retirent des deux Eglises sont receu auec eulx, qui est chosse a Considerer Et mesmes quant ils ont presente audyt ministre espaignol les articles et affaires quil ont eut a lencontre de maistre adrian hastedius, il ne les a point voulu voire dissant quil auoit des aultres affaires asses pour socuper pour lors fut aReste que dedans 15 jours lon se Retrouueroit encore ensemble pour ladyt affaire.

communion services and by the right to a seat on the Coetus for their minister. The matter was deferred and seems never to have been resolved.[28]

It is not to be expected that the representatives of the Spanish government and the spies of the Inquisition in London would leave unnoticed this group of Spaniards and their leader. We have seen some hint of this already in the petition for a church. Several references to Reina and his flock were made in notes that passed between the Spanish Embassy and the King of Spain. The ambassador had a conversation with the Lord Chancellor and Dr Wootton concerning charges made against the ambassador. He had reported that the Queen and Cecil greatly favoured the Spanish heretics. The ambassador replied that he had in fact written that the Spaniards had been given a large house belonging to the Bishop of London where they preached three times a week, and as evidence of the favour he pointed out that Casiodoro was given a considerable sum of money to attend the Colloquy of Poissy. He had been aided financially by Throgmorton and the Earl of Bedford, and his father and mother and the rest of them here were well provided for.[29]

The Colloquy of Poissy was a meeting between representatives of the Protestants and the Roman Catholics called together to attempt to find a way to reconcile the two opposing viewpoints and bring about religious unity in France. It was held from the end of August 1561 onwards. The Protestant representatives were headed by Beza, later aided by Peter Martyr. Amongst the twelve ministers and twenty laymen who officially represented this side was the minister of the French Church in London, Nicolas des Gallars, Sieur de Saules, whose attendance had been specially requested by Admiral Coligny.[30] It may be that Casiodoro came as an observer in des Gallars's company. The only reference to his presence there is in the above-mentioned correspondence of the Spanish Ambassador to England, from whom we also learn that Reina fell ill whilst there and was aided in his distress by the English Ambassador to France, Throgmorton.[31] An imposing array of six cardinals, forty archbishops, twelve doctors of the Sorbonne and twelve experts in canon law, represented the Roman Catholic side. The King of France, the Queen Mother, princes of the blood royal and the Council of State completed the august assemblage, which

---

[28] Van Schelven, *Kerkeraads-Protocollen,* p. 395.

[6 April 1563] De ecclesia hispanica, quæ cupit usum sacramentorum, quatenus id consultum. Differtur in aliud tempus. Item an consultum ut dominus Cassiodorus adsit menstruis coetibus.

[29] A. García Hernández, *España y el Vizconde Palmerston* (Madrid, 1848), p. 235, quoting Arch. gen. de Simancas, Inglaterra, Leg. 815, fol. 193:

Cargo 4º Que yo he escrito a S.M. que la Reina ha dado en Londres una Iglesia a los hereges de España los cuales he dicho que son aqui sostenidos y favorecidos della y de su consejo. Contestacion. Yo he escrito que a los Españoles hereges que aqui estan se les ha dado una casa del Obispo de Londres muy grande en que predican tres dias de la semana como es verdad y que a Cassiodoro que fue a la Junta de Poysy le fueron dados dineros en notable suma para el camino, y que en Poysy donde enfermo le dio dineros el Embajador Fragmarten [sic], y el conde de Batfort se los ha dado aqui ael y a su padre y madre que aqui estan y a todos los otros se les dan entretenimientos.

[30] *Actes,* fol. 118; *HSP,* 38 (1937), p. 54.

[31] Throgmorton's despatches from this colloquy, however, make no mention of Reina's presence there.

in the end achieved nothing.[32] This may be the time from which we can date Reina's acquaintance with Beza, although, as has been stated, it is also possible that they had met earlier in Geneva. Beza's considerable extant correspondence written from Poissy makes no reference to Reina, although mention is made of des Gallars and of the English Ambassador.[33] If we are to believe the Spanish Ambassador, Reina would have been in their company and would thus have met Beza, for Beza's later exchange of letters with him makes it obvious that they had had previous acquaintance. Nicolas des Gallars returned to London from Poissy on 14 December 1561, and with him, presumably, Reina.[34]

On 24 April 1563 Bishop Quadra reported to his King that he had intercepted a letter to Casiodoro from a Spanish resident in Antwerp (small wonder that Corro's many letters failed to arrive!). This letter had been returned to the King's agent in Antwerp, Alonso de Canto, so that its author might be apprehended. On 26 June 1563 Quadra reported the arrival of the Andalusian Francisco Zapata from Genoa with his Saragossan wife. He was a 'great heretic' and was lodging with Casiodoro, who had recently married again. Zapata's purpose in coming was to help to revise the text of the Spanish translation of the Bible on which Casiodoro and others were engaged.[35]

Mention of Reina's remarriage raises the question of his first marriage. So far, no record of this has come to light. Of the second marriage, if second it was, we have a declaration made by his widow in 1595. She was Anna, daughter of Abraham Leon of Nivelles in Belgium, and widow of Dr Thomas Le Feure, and she declared that she had made her second marriage to Casiodoro de Reina, Spanish preacher in London, in 1561. The Ambassador further reported that Reina had lost his royal pension consequent upon his marriage.[36]

In distant Béarn, Reina's close friend and former collaborator in San Isidro, Antonio del Corro, was writing frequently to him, but without apparently receiving any replies. On 24 December 1563 he wrote in Spanish from Théobon, referring to a four-month silence on Reina's part, during which time he had sent many letters, hoping that he would by this means gain at least one reply. The intervening letter of Reina's he had received 'almost miraculously' during a period of extreme restlessness caused by the enforced separation from Reina,

---

[32] Hauben's statement (pp. 86, 101) that the Colloquy condemned the Spanish Confession of London as 'crypto-Lutheran' is not borne out by his sources.

[33] Beza, *Correspondence* (Geneva, 1963), III, 144-66.

[34] Beza, III, 239; Van Schelven, *Kerkeraads-Protocollen*, p. 272, says 9 December.

[35] *C.S.P. Eliz.*, I, 320, 339f; *Heterodoxos*, V, 137. Since it is reported that Zapata came via Genoa, it seems possible to identify him with the Sardinian listed by Schäfer, II, 215.

[36] Neither Anna nor Thomas is mentioned in the *Returns*, but then, nor is Casiodoro himself. W. K. Zülch, *Frankfurter Künstler* (Frankfurt, 1935), p. 457:

1595 läßt Anna Leon, Witwe des französischen Predigers Cassiodorus Reinius durch Zeugen gestellen, daß sie in erster Ehe mit dem Dr. med. Thomas le Feure verheiratet war, 1561 heiratete sie zum zweiten Male in London den dort als Prediger in Spanischer Sprache tätigen Cassiodorus Reinius mit dem sie nach Frankfurt zog. Ihr Bruder Franz Leon ist Zeuge.

*Col. doc. inéd.*, XXVI, 465:

A Casiodoro, morisco granadino, que ha sido fraile y predicaba a los pocos españoles hereges que en Londres residen, quito la Reina la iglesia que le habia dado y las sesenta libras de pension, el cual habia poco que se habia casado.

for whom several passages express inordinate affection. He referred to the Spanish Bible, for the printing of which he had made careful arrangements, including a supply of paper, a printer, and the use of a castle from the King of Navarre where the work might be carried out. Besides money, only a proofreader was lacking, and Corro urged Casiodoro to bring with him for this purpose Cipriano (de Valera?), whom they had both known in San Isidro. He gives careful instructions on how to travel from England to Navarre.[37]

Corro was not easily discouraged, for by March 1564 he had written twenty-one letters to Casiodoro since the last letter he had received from him the previous September. This is revealed in a letter written in French from Bergerac and dated 25 March 1564. That letter made reference to one of Reina's that Corro had never received, and Corro seemed to think it was hardly possible that Reina had not written others to him. In the September letter Reina had mentioned his plans concerning the Spanish Bible, which Corro approved whole-heartedly. He repeated that he had access to excellent facilities both for printing and for distribution within Spain. Thus it was imperative for Reina to travel to him. If, on the other hand, Reina had better to offer, then Corro would follow him to England. In any case they must compare notes. Again, detailed instructions follow for Reina's journey to Bergerac, and equally detailed instructions of how to send letters to him. Till he has a reply from Reina, all Corro's future letters will be but copies of this one.[38]

But, whereas the Bergerac letter merely asked in general terms for Casiodoro to bring or send him such small treatises as he thought fit, in the letter from Théobon Corro specified just what he would like, viz: Osiander's books on the justification of the Christian man.[39] He goes on to discuss fairly extensively Peter Martyr and the heterodox writers Caspar Schwenkfeld and Valentin Krautwald, asking for Reina's observations on their teachings and on other doctrinal points.[40] He also asks for Reina's opinion of Justus Velsius and Acontius.[41] These questions, he says, will enable Reina to understand what sort of books to send him, besides preparing him for the next time they can meet and discuss together.

[37] See full text in Appendix II. The letter was published by Corro in *Acta consistorii ecclesiæ Londinogallicæ* (London, 1571), an extremely rare work (copy in the Bodleian Library). Latin and Spanish texts of the letter are given; the Spanish text is fol. A4*-A5***, and is given in Appendix II.

[38] See full text in Appendix II; Hessels, III, 1, 32.

[39] Andreas Hosemann (Osiander) (1498-1552). He had played a leading part in the Reformation, particularly in the conferences of Marburg, Augsburg, and Schmalkald. His later religious opinions were unpopular, and he came under attack from Melanchthon and other Lutherans.

[40] Caspar Schwenkfeld (1489-1561) was at first an orthodox Lutheran, but deviated from this position in several ways. He had his own peculiar views on the eucharist, Christology, the indwelling of Christ in the believer, mystical piety, and figurative understanding of Scripture. Valentin Krautwald (Crotoaldus) was the most important and earliest of Schwenkfeld's followers.

[41] Justus Welse (Velsius) (1520?-1582?), doctor of medicine and botanist; lectured in philosophy in Cologne; came to London in 1563 and caused a great stir amongst the Refugee Churches with his heterodox views on the person of Christ and original ideas about 'double regeneration'. His ideas were condemned the same year. The details of the cases of Haemstede and Velsius take up a great deal of space in the last volume of Acta of the Consistory of the London-Dutch Church (Guildhall Library MS 7397/1).

The doctrinal points to which he gave closest attention are all concerned with the person of Christ; how He communicated Himself to the believer; whether the glorified Christ is a creature or not; whether or not to accept the doctrine of the ubiquity of Christ.[42] All of these are questions which hover around the teachings of Servetus like a moth round a candle flame.

It is necessary to deal with the Théobon letter in some detail, in view of its subsequent history and the effects it had on the later career of Reina. Of course, Corro was not to know that, by the time it would arrive in London, Reina would have fled the country. The letter was sent to Pierre du Perray for onward transmission to Reina. Perray sent it to Jacques Fichet, a French merchant in London and a member of the Threadneedle Street Church. It bore an endorsement in some such words as 'For matters of importance concerning the Church of God' – probably a device of Corro's to expedite its delivery. These words were the excuse for its being opened. Fichet had brought it to the Consistory of the French Church on 12 March 1564.[43] In 1563 Jean Cousin (Cognatus) had there replaced Nicolas des Gallars as minister, and had shewn himself to be a determined opponent of Reina. With the approval of the Consistory he decided to open the letter and read it. For him, despite the impropriety of opening private mail (justified by appeal to the endorsement), the letter certified Reina's guilt on doctrinal grounds, and Cousin was thereafter to seek continually to thwart Casiodoro's aspirations when and wherever he could.

Later, Corro was to be accused of Servetism on the strength *inter alia* of this letter. It is perhaps not surprising that minds already prejudiced against the Spaniards for establishing a new congregation with members taken from theirs, and that minds already suspicious of Spaniards, and ready anyway to smell out heterodoxy, should find in the letter confirmation of their apprehensions in Reina's case. One wonders how ministers were expected to combat heresies of which they had no knowledge. It seems to be necessary to take cognizance of a doctrine before it can be refuted or rejected. But those were days of bitter partisan struggle within the Church, and such calm reflections and sane counsels were hardly likely to prevail.

Aware of his presence and conscious that a group of Spanish Protestants had an importance far exceeding their numerical strength, Spanish agents were actively sowing trouble for Reina. Strike the head and the members are immediately affected. Their aim was, of course, to engineer his departure to some land where the Inquisition would be able to lay hands on him, as it had done to his companion Juan de León in Strassburg. In some way, suspicions regarding his doctrinal soundness were fanned into flame once more. (This was before the arrival of the letters from Théobon and Bergerac.) Reina himself later said that he was accused on five or six charges, including Servetism and sodomy.[44]

In fact, the charges against him can be pieced together from various sources,

---

[42] The ubiquity of Christ is the doctrine around which strife between Lutherans and Zwinglians raged. Luther held that because of ubiquity Christ's body and blood were really present in the bread and wine. He understood the phrase, 'Hoc est corpus meum' to be taken literally est=est. Zwingli understood 'est' to mean 'significat', which was more or less the Calvinist position.

[43] Hessels, II, 272; III, 1, 67.

[44] *Bib. Wif.*, II, 193, 199; MacFadden, p. 194. See note 52 below.

but they contain so many contradictory statements that it remains extremely difficult to make coherent sense of them. These sources are the minutes of the French and Flemish Consistories, other items from the archives of the two churches, and a series of documents collected at Frankfurt in 1571, when Reina wished to become a member of the French Refugee Church there.[45] These last consist of a careful transcript made by Reina himself of the evidence collected against him and deposed at the examination of the case, together with several letters about it, of which two, written by Jean Cousin, are particularly detailed and informative as to the time-table of what happened.[46] Taken together, these documents provide accusations and hints of an amazing and unlikely combination of offences : dishonesty, embezzlement, immoral, or, at least, indiscreet, conduct with certain female members of his congregation, sodomy with a seventeen-year-old youth (the son of one of the women concerned!), and a number of points of doctrine and ecclesiastical practice which differed from the strict Calvinism of the refugee churches, amongst all of which were also listed friendship with persons suspected of heterodoxy, and secrecy concerning the translation of the Bible on which he was engaged.

On Tuesday, 31 August 1563, Casiodoro came to the French Consistory to announce that he had been accused of deceit, heresy, adultery and sodomy, and that the matter was being publicized. The prime mover in the affair seemed to be Balthasar Sánchez, who accused Reina of embezzling £200, of indiscreet relations with the wife of one of the church members, and of sodomy with Jean de Bayonne.[47] Before his marriage, Reina had had an appartment in the Bayonne house in Shoe Lane, as also had the French minister, des Gallars.[48] The youth had been Reina's servant, with whom he had shared a bed for some time, since Reina claimed not to be able to afford another. When defending himself against this latter charge, Reina claimed to have been embarrassed by the proximity and to have had four or five 'pollutions' in his sleep. The youth appeared to have been embarrassed too, and Casiodoro had bought another bed so that they could sleep separately. The youth's version was that he had been sexually assaulted at least six or seven times, being held so tightly that he could not escape. Somehow this came to the ears of Sánchez. Casiodoro's story was that a young visitor from Flanders was enticed away from his house by Sánchez, and that it was from him that Sánchez had his information. This visitor would seem to have been Francisco de Ábrego, from whom were gleaned the beginnings of the leak of information, and this takes us back to the time before Reina's marriage, at least seventeen months earlier, when the young de

[45] Stadtarchiv, Frankfurt am Main, Kirchendokumente B.Fr.-ref. Kirche 195, fols. 585ʳ-634ʳ. Since the depositions recorded in these documents remain unpublished, they are reproduced here in Appendix III. As these are given in full, the ensuing account will not indicate references to facts derived from them, or from the two letters mentioned in note 46.

[46] These letters are also unpublished and are given in Appendix IV. They are fols. 627ʳ-634ʳ of the documents mentioned in the previous note. See also my article, 'Two unpublished letters of Jean Cousin', HSP, 22 (1971), pp. 51-9.

[47] Sánchez is mentioned many times in the Returns. He was a 'spicer' and a comparatively rich man who contributed to English government funds and became comfitmaker to the Queen's household.

[48] Returns, 10, I, 281, 291 ; Jean de Bayonne was a boot- and shoemaker.

Bayonne might have been as young as fifteen and a half.[49] This introduces a time-lag into the affair which it is hard to justify in terms of anything other than a conspiracy. Ábrego said that he was sharing a bed with Jean de Bayonne Jr shortly before Casiodoro's wedding, and that Jean began to ask questions about Reina's wife-to-be, and then made indiscreet hints about how sexually potent Reina was. Ábrego's curiosity was aroused, and he ferreted till Jean was prompted to accuse Casiodoro of sexual assault and anal penetration on several occasions. It appears that Ábrego informed Sánchez on the latter's return from Cambridge, Sánchez confided the matter to Angel Victor,[50] and together they decided to tell Gaspar Zapata and two other brethren.[51] Ábrego seems to have had a very poor opinion of Casiodoro's ability to acknowledge his faults. A feature of this case is that whoever heard the accusation was at first most reluctant to believe it. Cousin later wrote that all concerned were very much Reina's friends and had no reason to invent such accusations, but, when one reads Sánchez's depositions, one is bound to feel that at least one man was very willing to believe the worst, and very quickly too. Certainly Zapata (called 'a nobleman and former secretary to the Viceroy of Naples') very properly refused to consider the matter till he had spoken to the youth. Accordingly, the next day Zapata, Ábrego and Jean de Bayonne Jr met at St Paul's, and the youth repeated what he had told Ábrego. On this occasion he stated that Reina did not hurt him at all. Zapata and Ábrego returned to consult Sánchez and Angel Victor, and together all went to tell the youth's father (also named Jean de Bayonne), whose immediate reaction seems to have been rather theatrical. He referred to this as a 'second' outrage of Reina against him. Thereafter, a meeting was arranged at which Casiodoro and Jean de Bayonne Jr could confront each other in the presence of Zapata, Sánchez, Angel Victor and Ábrego. The two last-named, by now apparently convinced of his guilt, urged Reina to confess. Reina stuck to his story, and insisted that what a man does in his sleep he cannot be guilty of. Nevertheless, it appears that on the following Sunday he suspended himself from the ministry, pending an enquiry, being, as he put it, unwilling to continue his ministry till he was cleared of the charges. As he later said, he had a far more pressing task in hand translating the Bible, and he preferred to devote his time to that, undistracted by backbiting.[52] His accusers, however, put it out that he had been suspended for here-

---

[49] There is no mention of Ábrego in the *Returns*.

[50] *Returns*, 10, I, 392; Angel Victor was a schoolmaster from Sardinia, often referred to as Angelus Victorius Sardius. He and his wife seem to have been extremely fractious characters (*HSP*, 48 (1969), pp. 92, 97, 120, 133). He is confused with Michaelangelo Florio in the Index of *HSP*, 48, and in Hessels, III, 1, 45, note 2.

[51] Gaspar Zapata is not to be confused with Francisco Zapata referred to above. Neither is mentioned in the *Returns*. Gaspar appears to have been a Seville printer who escaped from Spain, but whose wife was captured en route for liberty. He was burnt in effigy on 28 October 1562 (Schäfer, I, 357, 376, 393; II, 320, 365), and finally returned to the fold of Roman Catholic Spain in early 1565 (*Col. doc. inéd.*, XXVI, 540).

[52] Geneva, Bibliothèque publique et universitaire, Correspondence ecclésiastique, MS fr. 407, fol. 10ᵛ; *Bib. Wif.*, II, 199f:
Certifiant devant le Seigneur que j'avois esté blasmé et calomnié à tort de cinq ou six calomnies, que la moindre d'icelles, estant vraies, meritoit bien la corde; dont l'une estoit des herésies de Servetus, et que me voyant aussi pressé de nécessité de perdre

sies and crimes. Casiodoro was called before the Consistory, where he put forward his case, stating particularly that he had no need to defend his doctrine (they had the Spanish Confession of Faith and he had been preaching openly) and that he wished the matter of sodomy to go before the magistrate. The Consistory declared that it would give its answer at its next meeting on the following Thursday, when the advice it duly gave was that he should put his case before the Bishop of London rather than a magistrate. Reina agreed to follow their advice, and then he asked whether he would be admitted to communion the following Sunday, since he felt the need of spiritual strengthening. The Consistory did not wish to deny him this privilege, especially as his case had not been examined.

On the following Tuesday, 7 September 1563, Casiodoro again appeared at the Consistory, saying that the Bishop had heard his complaint and had given him the right to choose certain men to examine the matter. He had decided to call on Messrs. 'Couverdale, Witinguen and Withemme', and to ask the Consistory to appoint one of their number in addition.[53] The Consistory pointed out that he knew all of them, and that in any case he had the right to choose.

On Wednesday, 8 September 1563, the Bishop sent out a letter to six men, appointing them his commissioners to examine the case on his behalf, since Casiodoro had presented him with a long remonstrance in Latin. These men were : Jean Cousin, minister of the French Refugee Church; Johannes Utenhovius, minister of the Flemish Church; the Rev. Robert Crowley of St Peter's; the Rev. James Young of St Bartholomew's; Antoine Cappelle and Jean Hettié, elders of the French Church.[54] It seems probable that these six met together with those chosen by Reina as a commission of enquiry, since sodomy was an

---

mon temps en ma defense, j'ai esté d'advis de m'acquiter moi mesme de mon ministere, et pour enfuir les debats m'enfuir aussi de Londres pour vaquer es choses plus utiles à l'Eglise du Seigneur, que j'avois entre les mains.

[53] The famous Bible translator, Miles Coverdale (1488-1568), had been in exile during Mary's reign. On 3 March 1563 he accepted the living of St Magnus, near London Bridge. William Whittingham (1524-79) had been an exile in Geneva and Frankfurt. He was chaplain to Bedford, English ambassador to France 1560-61, and as such was at Poissy. In 1563 he was in London, and in the habit of attending the Refugee Churches. It has proved impossible to identify the third man named, unless he were one of the several men named Withers listed by C. H. Garrett, *The Marian Exiles*, 2nd ed. (London, 1966), pp. 340-3, whose name seemed to be interchangeable with Withen.

[54] Robert Crowley (1518?-88) was another Marian exile. He became Archdeacon of Hereford in 1559, and also held St Peter's le Poor, one of the nearest churches to the Refugee Churches. He was made a prebendary of St Paul's on 1 September 1563. There is no record of a James Young at any of the three St Bartholomews of the period, but a James Young was listed as one of the clergy of St Peter's le Poor in 1563. On the other hand, a church called St Bartholomew's was situated in Threadneedle St at the time, and 'monsieur Yong ministre englois' is mentioned several times as attending the French Church, and he appears to have had some special interest in the Refugee Churches, perhaps some oversight, and was clearly one of the clergy of the district (*HSP*, 38 (1937), pp. 48, 60, 82). Antoine Cappelle was a silk-weaver living in Norton Folgate Ward (*Returns*, 10, I, 260, 292; 10, III, 417). He had a disagreement with Jean Cousin in 1563 (*HSP*, 38 (1937), pp. 4, 66). Hettié must be identified with Jehan Hette (*HSP*, 38 (1937), p. 4 and *passim*).

ecclesiastical offence at the time. The depositions received by them remain the main source of our information on the matter.[55]

On Thursday, 9 September, the commissioners met in the French Church, and the Bishop's letter of authority was read, after which Casiodoro was asked to put his case. He repeated the gist of what he had written to the Bishop and named his accusers and calumniators. The commissioners then appointed Monday, 13 September, as the day on which they would hear those named. Accordingly, on that day Gaspar Zapata, Balthasar Sánchez, Angel Victor, Francisco de Ábrego and Jeremias Ackermann were called before the commission, and, on that occasion, were asked to comment only on Reina's doctrinal views.[56] All five wished to place on record that they did not appear as accusers, defamers or calumniators of Casiodoro, but that, if they were required to do so, they would submit certain points with which Reina could be confronted, and they hoped they would be shewn to be right. The commissioners insisted on their authority to require such information, and assigned Wednesday, 15 September, at 3.00 p.m., as the time at which they would receive depositions concerning Reina's doctrine. Having complied with this order, they were told to reappear before the comission on Friday, 17 September, at 2.00 p.m., to make their declarations about the accusation of sodomy, and they were then required to depose these in writing on Tuesday, 21 September. That same Tuesday one of the commissioners was asked to convoke Casiodoro to appear after dinner that same day to answer the charges, whereupon it was discovered that Casiodoro was not at home and nobody knew where he was. By Thursday, 23 September, it was known that on Tuesday the 21st Reina had fled London in the early hours of the morning to cross the Channel, being under the misapprehension that sodomy was a capital offence, and that the simple accusation of the youth would be sufficient evidence to convict.[57]

On Friday, 24 September, the commissioners decided to write and ask the Bishop for an appointment to report to him on the case. On the same day Reina's father appeared to excuse his son's absence. Reina's former superior in San Isidro, Francisco de Farías, also wished to lay before them certain letters from Reina concerning the case, and letters by others in defence of Reina. Farías was refused a hearing on the grounds that he had nothing to do with the case, which seems to indicate a certain bias on the part of the commissioners. Nevertheless, at the end of April 1564 Farías wrote to Grindal a letter in Jeanne Fouet's name, condemning the slanderous statements of Angel Victor and Zapata, and criticizing the French Consistory.[58] Cousin sent a counter-complaint to the Bishop, and his bias against Casiodoro is also clear in the two letters that Cousin wrote to the French Refugee Church at Frankfurt, and which are the

---

[55] The copies of these depositions that we have are written in Reina's own handwriting, with various passages underlined as if to comment on them or to draw out some hidden meaning. No doubt the key to the whole matter is to be found in these underlinings, if only they could be correctly interpreted. They are reproduced as italics in the transcripts given in Appendix III.

[56] *Returns*, 10, I, 275, 318, 386; Jeremias Ackerman was a locksmith.

[57] The affair of Casiodoro provides an interesting sidelight on the law concerning sodomy in England, which is treated at greater length in Appendix V.

[58] *HSP*, 38 (1937), pp. 59, 69f.

source of the dates given above. Although he makes a point of stressing the popularity of Reina before this matter arose, he makes it clear that he was fully persuaded of his guilt. He also tells us that the commission never managed to get Jean de Bayonne Jr to appear to give evidence, since the youth's father, also fearing capital punishment, shipped him overseas, in spite of assurances from the Bishop that there was nothing to fear in that direction.

Casiodoro left behind at least three letters. One to Farías we have already mentioned. Another was addressed to the Bishop of London, which we know from two transcripts of it made by Cousin.[59] A third went to the commissioners and contained a list of questions to be put to the youth. This last letter seems now to be lost, but we learn of it from a deposition made on 1 May 1564 by an Italian Protestant of Antwerp, G. Francesco Cando, and reading it makes one feel that Casiodoro was indeed shabbily treated by his co-religionaries in England.[60]

The youth was sent to Flanders, where, at least at first, he stayed in Bourbourg, a small town between Gravelines and Cassel, at the home of what may have been his maternal uncle. He was seen there on 30 October 1563 by Paschasius de la Motte and Christoffle Marschal (also known as Fabricius) and questioned by them about the affair.[61] On this occasion his memory was that he had been hurt, especially on two occasions.

Cando's deposition mentioned above states that in early February 1564 a certain G.C. had come to Antwerp with a letter in Casiodoro's handwriting, asking for Jean de Bayonne Jr to be examined about the accusations made against Reina. The examination took place at the home of one of the Bayonne's relatives in the presence of Cando and another Italian. G. C. took no notes, and after the examination wrote an account in French, which Cando refused to sign, because there were additions and omissions and it seemed altogether too partial. In Cando's opinion the youth should have been examined properly before 'M. & A^{ni}.' in London.[62] As this was in progress, letters about the matter

---

[59] One of them is given in his letter of 9 August 1572 in the Frankfurt documents (see above, note 46). The other is preserved amongst the papers of the Dutch Church of London (Hessels, III, 1, 36) as an endorsement to G. F. Cando's deposition (on which, see below, note 62).

[60] Hessels, III, 1, 35f; the man's name is given variously as Cando or Cardo.

[61] Paschasius de la Motte is not mentioned in the *Returns*. His deposition was made later, but forms part of the Frankfurt documents, which are reproduced below. Fabricius was a minister, also not mentioned in the *Returns*. His letter to Utenhovius, dated 10 April 1564, is also part of the Frankfurt documents (fol. 602), but it is not reproduced here, because it is given in full by A. A. van Schelven, 'Cassiodorus de Reyna, Christophorus Fabricius en Gaspar Olevianus', *Nederlandsch Archief voor Kerkgeschiedenis*, 8 (1911), pp. 322-32, and also because it repeats very closely what Paschasius wrote.

[62] Hessels, III, 1, 35:
Al principio de Febraro 1564 vene in Anuersa G.C. mostrandose afflito del caso del Cassiodoro auendo portato con lui vna istrucione di diuersi capitoli scritti de man propria de detto Cassiodoro come uoleua fusse seminato il garzone Gio di Baiona. dette G.C. condusse detto garzone in casa di vn suo compare partente di detto Gio di Baiona in presenza di me et d'vno altro italiano che erauamo quatro in tutto cosi al longo saminasemo detto garzone senza farne scritura. che dapoi dette G.C. et il suo compare sudetto nefece scritura tra essi; vero e che me la lesse in francese, et io gli disse, che non me piaceua per esserli agionto et sminuito et mi protestaj non uolere

32

from Casiodoro arrived for both G.C. and Cando, whereupon G.C. seemed to lose interest in it and begged Cando to send help to Reina, who was now in Frankfurt. At the time of writing Cando found it strange that some were claiming that the boy had signed a declaration about the matter on 6 February, which was not true.

We might have learnt more of the matter from the minutes of the French Church, but the relevant section was removed in 1578, when the affair was brought up again, and replaced, but has since vanished.[63] The corresponding section of the minutes of the Flemish Church is also missing.[64] After the gap in the French minutes there is a reference to a letter from the Regent of Flanders to the Bishop of London concerning Casiodoro and the son of Jean de Bayonne, who had been examined by the court at Brussels.[65] And elsewhere we are told that when questioned officially in Antwerp the youth said he had no idea what all the fuss was about, and that he supposed it was all trumped up out of hatred for Casiodoro.[66]

---

sotto scriuere ne inpaciarme inconto alcuno di questa cosa conosendo che detto **G.C.** era troppo parciale, et gli disse che se faceua gran torto alla parte uolere nui piliarse carico quasi de magistro seza notificar alla parte il bisogno a fine que detta parte auisati potesse ancor essi produre le lor ragione. dicendoli ancor che si doueua dar detto Gio di Baiona in mani di M. et A$^{ni}$ che essi lo saminasse et notificasse il tutto a Londra. in quel tempo medesimo uene de Londra certe Litere a detto G.C. et a me per questa causa medema del Cassiodoro; a tal che G.C. me disse che non era piu bisogno di nostre scriture et che tutto quello aueua fatto non era nulla et che arebe straciato il tutto, et che conoseua bene la cosa del Cassiodoro esere redutta a termine, che non poteua justificarse, pregandomi facesse opera trouar dinari per aiutare et suuenire detto Cassiodoro, per che subito gionto a Francfort, non lo uoleua tenir piu in casa sua, dolendosi fusse maritado, che lo arebe consigliato andarsene in Turchia et consimile parole se ne torno in Francfort.

Sotto breuita dico non esere vero che io ne laltro testimonio italiano se siamo trouati presente quando il garzone sotto scrisse la samina che certo per me non ne so nulla: parimente me marauiglio che in questa supplica mostratomi et letomi sotto scritta da otto testimonj sotto il 22 di marcio 1564 datta in Francfort nella quala si contene facendo fede detti otto testimoni che la samina fu sotto scritta del garzone sotto il di 6 Febraro presente li quatro testimoni replico non esere vero.

Hessels interprets 'G.C.' as 'Giovanni Cousin', and there seems every reason to agree, but he found it impossible to guess at the meaning of 'M et A$^{ni}$', which I suggest must mean 'the minister and the elders'.

[63] *HSP*, 38 (1937), p. 56; Actes du Consistoire, fol. 133; the note says it was there in 1605.

[64] These records have been deposited in the Guildhall Library, London, Acta of the Consistory of the London-Dutch Church, of which volume II (MS 7397/2 SR 83-5) ends on 5 September 1563 and volume III (MS 7397/3 SR 83-5) begins on 10 November 1569. The gap indicates a missing volume at just the vital dates.

[65] *HSP*, 38 (1937), p. 89; Actes du Consistoire, fol. 234:

[16 November 1564] Ledyt jour Monsieur Cousin nous declaire que leuesque de Londres auoit Receu des letres de Madame la Regente de flandres touchant Casiadore et le filz de Jehan de bayonne, lequel auoit este examine a lacour de bruselles et deliberoient de ne laisser Impugny vng telle subject.

[66] *Mémoires anonymes sur les troubles des Pays-Bas* (Brussels, 1869), V, 58f :

Le bruict couroit qu'il [Reina] s'estoit absenté dudict Angleterre pour estre chargé et accusé du péché de sodomiste dict vulgairement bougrerie, dont il en feist après sa justification par l'examen d'ung garçon en ladicte ville d'Anvers, sur la poursuyte de

Cousin's letters mention a further examination of the youth at Antwerp by Sieur Jacques de la Croix and others, and the reference could also be interpreted to mean that Casiodoro was also interrogated, for the questioners sent a letter to London, declaring Reina's innocence. This investigation could possibly be the same one as that mentioned in the previous paragraph.[67]

Casiodoro went to earth for a while in Antwerp, much to the chagrin of the officers of the Inquisition, who made repeated efforts to find him there. Disguised as a sailor, his wife crossed over via Flushing to join him.[68]

The letters left behind by Reina and the letter of Jacques de la Croix make nonsense of the claim that he made no attempt to defend himself before he met Nicolas des Gallars in Orleans.[69] Later, however, when these charges were again brought up in correspondence with Beza, Reina shifted his ground somewhat, and was to state categorically that he had slept near the boy, but had had no pollution on or near him.[70]

As so often in Western Europe, the mere hint of homosexuality was an infallible method of whipping up hysteria and creating suspicion. The mention of Servetus in orthodox Calvinist circles of the period had very much the same effect. Tongues were set wagging and the rumours grew. Cousin and Utenhovius shot letters off to various people to appraise them of the affair whilst it was still, after all, *sub judice*. This is only one aspect of the very strange behaviour of many people concerned with the affair. One cannot help feeling that the two ministers seized on this as an ideal opportunity to work off their distrust of Casiodoro because of his friendship with Velsius, Acontius and Haemstede, and their dislike of him engendered by his having drawn church members away from them, this notwithstanding the protestations of friendship contained in Cousin's letters.

Other strange factors in the case include the following : firstly, the strange and long silence of Ábrego. It was at least seventeen months before the matter came to Reina's ears, and presumably at least a year before it was made public. If the acts did in fact take place, it is fairly easy to suppose that Jean would not talk of them, as one who was principally involved, but it is inconceivable that Ábrego should be equally silent for so long, especially when we recall the glee with which he finally communicated the affair.

Secondly, Jean de Bayonne Sr's evident resentment against Reina's rumoured relationship with his wife might easily have resulted in some attempt at

---

certains députez dudict Angleterre ayant icelluy garçon declaire qu'il ne sçavoit que c'estoit dudict faict et qu'il n'en sçavoit a parler dudict Cassiodore, auquel se disoit avoir esté imposé ledict faict de sodomiste per une hayne et envye que ses malveullans luy portoient, disoit-il.

[67] Jacques de la Croix is evidently a gallicization of the Spanish name, Diego de la Cruz, since Jean Cousin refers to him as 'Jacques de la croix Espagnol' (below Appendix IV, letter of 8 August 1572). (See also Schäfer, I, 355; II, 357f).

[68] *Bib. Wif.*, II, 172 (quoting Brussels, Archives du Roy, Fardes d'Audience 273, 278): Au mois d'octobre 1563 un prisonnier français declare devant un magistrat que 'le nommé Cassiodore, prêcheur des hérétiques, a quitté l'Angleterre depuis cinq mois, et que l'on ne sait pas où il a passé'.

[69] MacFadden, p. 205; Hauben, p. 19.

[70] Geneva, Correspondence eccl., MS fr 407, fol. 20r.

revenge by inventing the charge and instructing his son what to say. Once launched, such a tale would make its way without much help. This supposition is further supported by the father's refusal to allow his son to testify in London, and by the speedy disappearance of the youth to Flanders, where his story, though kept up for a time, was soon changed to one more favourable to Reina.

Thirdly, Angel Victor emerges from the story as a scandalmonger, eager to keep adding to the tale till brought up short, then equally eager to retract and contradict what he has said.

Finally, the sinister shadow of the Inquisition cannot be ignored. Eager to engineer Reina's departure from England to a place more within its influence, it could well have set the whole story in motion. Gaspar Zapata's return to Spain in 1565 seems to be in some way connected with this; he was conceivably an agent-provocateur.

Set against the above, we must say that Grindal retained a favourable attitude to Reina throughout, and that Casiodoro's former prior, Farías, was his constant champion. Cipriano de Valera also was willing to speak for him years later.

Rumour grew once Casiodoro was accused, no doubt helped by his precipitate flight. The moral side of the accusations was exaggerated by the prurient gossip-mongers, as can be seen from the minutes of the French Church for 10 April 1564, when these rumours were investigated. Pierre Fouet complained that Angel Victor had said that Madame Fouet was of easy virtue. Jean Giblon testified that, when he was in the company of the Spaniards, Jean Simony and Jacques Cousturier [sic], he had heard Angel Victor say that Casiodoro had had his pleasure of Pierre Fouet's wife, and of Jean de Bayonne's wife, 'who was a whore'. On another occasion in the same company Angel had said that Casiodoro kept company with one woman for one week and with the other for the next and so on. Jacques Cousturier was willing to testify to the same statements, but when Angel Victor was questioned he denied the charges and claimed they were made from hatred. He bore witness to the respectable life Casiodoro led, and praised his Confession of Faith. The accusers were told to take more care of what they said and to be more careful of the reputation of others.[71]

---

[71] *HSP*, 38 (1937), p. 57; Actes du Consistoire, fol. 136f:
[10 April 1563] Ledit jour piere fouet et sa femme vindrent plaindre a lencontre de Angele Espagnol disant quil blasmoit sa femme de paillardise et de deshonneur et quil auoit proeuue pour le prouuer scauoir est jehan Giblon et vng Jaques cousturier espagnol.

Jehan Giblon dit quil auoit ouy dire a Angele Victor espagnol estant en sa maison entour 15 jours deuant la caresme estant en la compagnie de Jehan simony espagnol et Jaques cousturier espagnol, quil disoit telles parolles que Casiadore auoit eut a son plaisir la femme de piere fouet et de Jehan de baione et quelle estoit vne putaine.

Item vne autre fois estant a souper auec ledyt Angele et en ladyte compagnie dit de Rechief ledyt Angele que Casiadore tenoit vne sepmaine lune des dytes femmes et lautre vne sepmaine, etc.

Item Jaques le cousturier espagnol dit quassy semblable pourpos, mais il ne furent Receu pourtant quil nest point de leglise.

Angele estant apelle pour estre Interrogues en nostre presence dit que lesdytes pourpos sont faulx et alegue que lesdyts tesmoigns le disent par haine . . . ce que on a faict

The doctrinal side did not escape attention. About this time, as we have seen, there arrived Corro's Théobon letter, with its references to well-known heterodox theologians and questions about doctrinal disturbances amongst the refugee Protestants. In the circumstances, this could do Reina no good. The doubts regarding his soundness on the Trinity had never been completely allayed, and this brought them up in definite form. The minutes indicate this : on 9 June 1564, Utenhovius and Cousin were asked to examine what Casiodoro had written about the Bible; on 10 April Angel Victor had declared that Casiodoro's Confession of Faith was good, which presupposes that some questions had been asked about it. In minds only too ready to believe the worst, the Théobon letter merely confirmed suspicions of Reina's Servetism. These suspicions remained obstinately active in Calvinist minds for the rest of Reina's life.[72]

With the calmness and tolerance of a later age we can look at these charges with some detachment. To begin with, one is bound to acknowledge that, once a person was suspect, it was considered normal in the sixteenth century to accuse him of the worst crimes, for these were, after all, the logical outcome of the incipient errors that could be discerned. The charges of sodomy and atheism (which often meant merely erroneous views about God) were particularly beloved of the sixteenth-century polemicists. Hence, one takes the detail with a certain reserve. The fact that Reina was able to clear himself completely in 1579, to the satisfaction at least of Grindal, is itself indicative.

What meanwhile of the work that Reina saw as his overriding purpose in life? He had never ceased to work on the translation of a Spanish vernacular version of the Bible, the provision of which was a major concern of so many of the Spanish religious refugees. We have learnt that he had collaborators in this work, such as Francisco Zapata, and presumably Valera. We can deduce from Corro's two extant letters that the work had proceeded well in England, although it was not by any means finished. When the work was finally at an end, he inscribed in a copy of it which he presented to Grindal a dedication in which he expressed his thanks to him for saving the manuscript from his enemies.[73] It has been credibly suggested that the circumstances which put the manuscript into Grindal's hands would have been the occasion mentioned

---

contre casiadore est juste et que sa confession de foy quil a faict est bonne selon quil a veu. lesdyts tesmoigns furent avertys de Regarder ce quil disent et de nestre sy prest a Raporter mauvais pourpos, qui son de sy grande Importance pour lhomme et sa femme. Et a piere fouet fut dit et a sa femme De ne faire sy grand bruit, etc.

The names Jean Simony and Jaques Cousturier are clearly French in form, but it is usual in the minutes of the French Church to gallicize names.

[72] *HSP,* 38 (1937), p. 63; Actes du Consistoire, fol. 152 :

Item quant a laffaire de Casiadore il a este donne charge a monsieur Utenhove et a monsieur Cousin de visiter ce que ledyt casiadore a escript sur la Bible, et monsieur leuesque a delibere de faire la fin de toute le premier de Julet et que la chose luy soit Ramentu, etc.

[73] The dedication, in the Bible preserved in Queen's College, Oxford, reads :

Ampliss.Antistiti.ac Dno. Rmo. Edmundo Grindalo, Archiepiscopo Cantuariensi, et totius Angliæ. Primati digniss. ob erepta hujus Hispanicæ versionis sacrorum librorum scripta ex hostium manibus, C[us] R[us] eiusdem versionis author gratitudinis ergo et in perpetuæ observantiæ pignus. d.d.

above when Cousin and Utenhovius were asked to examine Reina's writings and report on them to the Bishop. By what means and exactly when the manuscript was restored to him we cannot say, but the Bishop's agents were in Frankfurt very soon after Reina's arrival there.

# III

# From his Flight from England to the Publication of his Bible

The question of where Casiodoro hid in Antwerp is intriguing. Spies were everywhere, and we have seen that there was correspondence between the King of Spain's agents in London and Antwerp and that a constant watch was kept on the latter port. Perhaps, like his wife, he went via Flushing or some other port and then travelled to Antwerp by land. In January 1564 a price was put on his head, and for some months he remained concealed, but before his whereabouts could be discovered he had fled to Frankfurt, where he arrived by the end of January 1564.[1]

Antwerp's history in the sixteenth century was extremely turbulent, and the fortunes of the evangelical Christians there fluctuated enormously. Despite the Spanish presence during the period 1563-64 the city was fairly safe for Protestants, unless they happened to be native-born Spaniards. Its situation made the city fruitful ground for the propagation of new ideas springing from the Reformation. Great numbers of foreign merchants, bankers and financiers who had embraced the new faith lived within its walls and it became a rallying-ground and a relatively safe refuge for those who came to be called 'les religionnaires'.[2] The *marrano* merchants were particularly affected by evangelical ideas, as they were in various other centres outside Spain. In the history of the Spanish Protestant movement the Jewish *converso* families played a significant part.

Because of these foreigners the laws against heresy were not strictly applied; otherwise the whole business life of the city would have been disrupted. As early as 1550 the magistrates had opposed the setting-up of the Inquisition, and the King and Governor had to agree repeatedly not to allow it. There were substantial numbers of Calvinists, Lutherans and Anabaptists in the town and evangelical literature was freely printed. By 1566 Protestants had begun to feel

---

[1] *Bib. Wif.*, II, 172; MacFadden, p. 202; Hessels, III, I, 35; A. Bernus, *Un Laïque du 16me siècle: Marc Pérez* (Lausanne, 1895), p. 15; A. A. van Schelven, 'Cassiodorus de Reyna', p. 324; C. Rahlenbeck, *L'Inquisition et la réforme en Belgique (Anvers)* (Brussels, 1857), p. 33 (quoting Brussels, Archives du Roy, Fardes de l'Audience 273):

Madame, j'entens que Sa Majesté a despendu de grandes sommes de deniers pour treuver et descouvrir le dict Cassiodoro, pour si dadventure il se retrevoit par les rues ou quelque aultre lieu, le descouvrir, promettant à celluy quelque somme dargent en cas quil le descouvriroit, comme jay faict à ceulx lesquelz en cest endroict jay entretenus (letter from the Margrave of Antwerp to Marguerite of Parma).

[2] L. van der Essen, 'Les Progrès du Luthéranisme et du Calvinisme dans le monde commercial d'Anvers', *Vierteljahrschrift für Sozial= u. Wirtschaftsgeschichte,* 12 (1914), 153.

sufficiently well-established to make demands, and Calvinists began even to invade Roman Catholic churches in an excess of iconoclastic zeal.[3]

One of the leading Calvinist laymen and a rich *marrano* financier was Marcos Pérez, a member of a widely-spread merchant family, established in many of the strategic trading centres of Europe. He was an extremely gifted man, speaking fluent Flemish, French, German, Spanish, Italian and Latin, besides being very influential amongst the commercial community of Antwerp, and wielding considerable political power.[4] He laboured indefatigably to ship evangelical literature to Spain in great quantities, and he sent via his agents Bibles, New Testaments and catechisms. Some idea of the amounts involved can be gained from the information that 30,000 copies of Calvin's *Institution* were sent.[5] He carried on correspondence on Protestant topics with many parts of Europe. This is the man who apparently sheltered Reina and his wife during their stay in Antwerp.[6] If he did not actually shelter them in his own home, he undoubtedly arranged somewhere for them to stay, and his connexions would provide the means for the next stage of Reina's journey.

Casiodoro was lucky. On 6 October 1563 a Genoese called Augustyn Boazio was caught by means of a letter intercepted on its way to England. He said he had come to Antwerp from Bordeaux two and a half years earlier and worked as a carrier between various foreign merchants in the city. In his possession were found a number of Spanish Protestant publications, of interest because they included the very ones on which Juan Pérez and Julián Hernández had worked during 1557 and 1558. He said they had been left in his shop by a certain Marc Antonio. He was sentenced to twelve years in the triremes.[7]

Reina next appears in Frankfurt as a member of the French Reformed Church, with which he had established contact in 1558 before going to England, and amongst whose congregation Juan Pérez had ministered briefly some years earlier. After his plans to settle in London had been so cruelly upset, Reina appears to have chosen Frankfurt as his base, and his fortunes from this time on were linked with that city. The choice was doubtless influenced by the fact that Frankfurt was the home of his father-in-law.

It is not clear what Reina's intentions were at that time. Perhaps he himself had no clear idea. He had a series of grave accusations hanging over his head, and he had a pressing invitation to visit the friend of his San Isidro days, Corro, from whom he might expect at least some sympathy, if not help. He had, we assume, temporarily lost the manuscript of his Bible translation, and he had no obvious means of support in Frankfurt or anywhere else.[8]

[3] Van der Essen, pp. 154, 158f.

[4] For Marcos Pérez, see A. Bernus; *Petri Rami Basilea ad senatum populumque Basiliensem* (Basle, 1571?), p. 33; *Bib. Wif.*, II, 213; L.v.d.Essen, 'Episodes de l'histoire religieuse et commerciale d'Anvers', *Bulletin de la Commission Royale d'Histoire*, 80 (1911), 529f.

[5] J. A. Goris, *Etude sur les colonies marchandes méridionales (Portugais, Espagnols, Italiens) à Anvers de 1488 à 1567* (Louvain, 1925), pp. 583-5.

[6] *Bib. Wif.*, II, 172, note 27; P. J. Hauben, 'Marcus Pérez and Marrano Calvinism', *BHR*, 29 (1967), 125.

[7] *Antwerpsche Archievenblad*, (Antwerp, undated) IX, 154f.

[8] *S. & V.*, p. 60.

In 1564 he was in Orleans, where Nicolas des Gallars, late French minister in London, was now exercising his pastorate. Reina must have felt that he was assured of a friendly reception there. He had attended the Colloquy of Poissy with des Gallars, and no doubt it was possible that news of the London scandal had not yet reached Orleans. But news travels fast, especially bad news, and it seems that des Gallars had already been informed of the situation. On 25 March 1564 he had written to Utenhovius in London praising God that Reina had been found out in time and asking Him to keep such harmful people away from His flock. Reina stayed in Orleans long enough to be able to write to Corro in south-western France and for Corro to obtain a six-weeks' leave of absence from his church and to travel north to Orleans to confer with both ministers for several months (well beyond the space of the leave he had).[9] It is hardly likely that Corro and Reina had met since the days of San Isidro (except perhaps briefly in Geneva). One supposes that on his way to see Corro in Bergerac Reina had made a point of calling on des Gallars, who was a highly respected Calvinist, and one of Calvin's most trusted lieutenants. If Reina could have convinced him of his innocence it would have gone a long way to restore his reputation. If he could have reached Orleans before the news of the accusation he might have succeeded. The outcome of the conference between the three men in Orleans is not clear; writing to Beza in 1571, Reina explained that des Gallars seemed friendly towards him, yet had a poor opinion of him and did not tell him so.[10] It could do no harm to Reina, however, to plead his innocence of the dreadful charges from which he had fled, even if des Gallars was not fully convinced.

Eventually Corro took Reina back with him to Bergerac, where they were at peace for only a few months. Corro's position there was anomalous: the Pacification of Amboise had expressly excluded all foreigners from exercising pastorates amongst Protestants in France, and the magistrates of Bergerac were breaking the law of France by allowing Corro to preach there. He had strong local patrons in a Huguenot nobleman, Jean d'Escodéca, Seigneur de Boesse (from whose château he had written the Bergerac letter), and in Jeanne d'Albret, mother of Henri IV. As Reina tells us later, he was admitted to communion by Corro and another minister named Broikius. MacFadden says this was after having signed a declaration of innocence of the charge of sodomy.[11]

---

[9] MacFadden, p. 201; Hessels, III, 1, 46:
Comme Cassiodore luy [Corro] auoit rescrit de . . . pour en sauoir la verité, nestant pas encor decidé . . . il prenoit congé de son église permettoit daller pour 6 sepmanes. Il trouua Cassiodore a Orleans et Monsieur de Saules quil ne se meslasse trop auant de cest affaire et contre la volonté de son eglise durant 6 mois pour traiter cest affaire. Il ne la peut defendre ni contenter.
MacFadden, p. 204; Hessels, II, 236f:
Quæ de Cassiodoro intellexi mihi fuerunt permolesta. Sed laudandus est Dominus qui in tempore talem fucam detexit. Potuisset enim temporis progressu ecclesiæ multum nocere. Non frustra sane in eo aliquid latere suspicabamur. Quorundam peccata præcedunt quorundam vero subsequuntur. Auertat Dominus tantas pestes a grege sua.
[10] Musée Historique de la Réformation, Geneva, Correspondence de Th. de Bèze (inédite), No. 656, Cassiodorus to Beza, 21 December 1571; Frankfurt docts., fol. 617-20.
[11] MacFadden, pp. 205, 211; Geneva, Bibliothèque publique et universitaire, MS. fr. 407, Corres. eccl., fol. 20r:

This period of calm, we suppose, was spent in discussion of those points raised by Corro in his Théobon letter and of the work which they both saw as their overriding task in life – the production of the Spanish translation of the Bible. No doubt Reina helped where he could in the work of preaching and pastoral care. But the calm was not to last. A royal commission under M. de Burie arrived in Bergerac in November 1564 and began to enquire into the religious situation. The entire civil magistracy and legal officers of the crown had been in Corro's congregation at the Temple in the 'Mercadil', and in this irregular situation they appealed to Renée de France who had passed through Bergerac on 12 November 1564. She tried to exercise her influence in favour of the town, but could do nothing about Corro, who was a foreigner. Corro apparently gained her confidence, and with it her patronage. When she left, he went with her as her chaplain, accompanied by his wife. With them also went Reina, to reside awhile in Montargis.[12]

On her progress northwards to her castellany, Renée had passed through Orleans, where she must have heard of Juan Pérez's situation. He too had been caught by the prohibition of the Pacification of Amboise, and was illegally exercising his pastorate in Blois. Corro would perhaps have been in touch with him; Reina had spent some months in Orleans nearby; but in any case Renée's interest in the Huguenot cause and sympathy with evangelical ministers in distress were well enough known for her to have been informed of his plight. Whatever the means, when she left for her château at Montargis, Pérez too had joined her train as a domestic chaplain. Renée lived at Montargis in defiance of the measures taken against the Huguenots. Her position as a princess of the royal blood rendered her immune from much of the law's severity.[13]

Reina cannot have been too comfortable in the presence of Juan Pérez, whom he had so irritated in Geneva, although he had at least the common interest of producing a Spanish vernacular version of the Bible. He did not stay long, although long enough to receive communion from both Corro and Pérez.[14] Early in 1565, probably in February, he left for Frankfurt again, where we suppose his wife was awaiting his return.[15]

Whilst in Frankfurt, early in 1565, he was approached by the French Strangers' Church in Strassburg, whose members wanted him to take up a pastorate amongst them. It is not clear whether they knew of the London affair or not, but they had apparently asked various leading Calvinist divines for their opinion of Reina.[16] Reina set off for Strassburg, and on his way he called on Gaspar Olevianus in Heidelberg. Olevianus was a leading Reformer in the Palatinate

---

Avant que de m'admettre a la communion de la S. Cene du Seigneur (comm'aussi je en suys esté depuis & a Londres & en france en l'eglise de Montargis soubs le ministere de Messieurs Pierius & Corranus & en Bergerac soubs le ministere dudz Corranus et Broikius).

[12] MacFadden, pp. 212f.

[13] *BSHPF*, 50 (1910), p. 211, where is given the text of a letter from Corro to Beza dated 3 September 1568.

[14] As note 11.

[15] MacFadden, p. 224; *Bib. Wif.*, II, 173.

[16] *Bib. Wif.*, II, 173; Hauben, p. 90.

and held the post of Court Preacher at the Holy Ghost Church.[17] Reina stayed in Heidelberg discussing matters with him, and with Johannes Sylvanus, Franciscus Mosellanus, Boquinius, and Ursinus, all theologians,[18] and a M. d'Honestis.[19] On Reina's departure from Heidelberg on 19 March 1565, the three first-ramed saw fit to send post-haste to Strassburg a letter condemning Reina's doctrines out-of-hand, but reserving judgment on his morals.[20] To this Reina saw the need to reply at length from Strassburg on 24 March 1565.[21] It is by collating both these letters with another written in August 1571 by Olevianus to Jean-François Salvard, minister of the French Church in Frankfurt, in which he went over the whole matter again, that we can piece together what happened.[22] Reina went to Heidelberg to tell Olevianus, whom he had known previously (where is not revealed) about his call to Strassburg, saying he was going to pull the French Church together. He was surprised not to be received so well as he had expected.[23] The fact was that news of the London accusations had reached Heidelberg and Olevianus was suspicious of him and began to interrogate him narrowly about his doctrinal standpoint, particularly in regard to the eucharist, since Marbach had persecuted the French Church of Strassburg because of this point in its doctrine. Olevianus claimed that at that time Reina had expressed ubiquitarian views on Christ's bodily presence (and therefore shewn a more Lutheran than Calvinist standpoint). Reina had asserted that he had preferred to quit London rather than spend his time unprofitably defending himself, since he had much more important and

[17] Gaspar Olevianus (1536-87), studied law in Paris and Orleans. He was a Calvinist divine, who helped to introduce the Reformation into the Palatinate and was one of the compilers of the Heidelberg Catechism of 1563. He went to the Holy Ghost Church in 1562, and remained there till his death.

[18] Johann Sylvanus began life as a R.C., progressed to Lutheranism, then to Calvinism, and was finally beheaded in 1572 for anti-Trinitarian views. In the light of his condemnation of Casiodoro (see below), his end is rather ironical. Zacharias Beer (Ursinus) (1534-83) had to leave Breslau as a result of the Lutheran-Calvinist eucharistic controversy. He found his way to Heidelberg, where he collaborated with Olevianus and lectured at the University. Beza sent his adopted son to Heidelberg to be instructed by him (Hessels, III, 631). Peter Bouquin (Boquinius) (?-1582), born in Guyenne and studied theology at Bourges, where he became a Doctor of Theology in 1539. He later became the prior of a Carmelite house, but left the order and France when he fully accepted the Reform. He was called to Heidelberg in 1557 by the Elector to be a professor of theology, and stayed there twenty years. His writings centre on the eucharistic differences between Lutherans and Reformed.

[19] An Italian, whom Olevianus later remembered as Modesti (see below).

[20] Geneva, MS fr. Corres. eccl. 407, fol. 6ʳ & ᵛ; Bib. Wif., II, 192f.

[21] Geneva, MS fr. Corres. eccl. 407, fol. 2ʳ-4ᵛ, 8ʳ-11ᵛ; Bib. Wif., II, 194-201.

[22] Van Schelven, 'Cassiodorus de Reyna', pp. 330f; Frankfurt docts., fol. 609.

[23] Van Schelven, p. 330:
Cassiodore est venu vers moy, Il y a quelques annees passe me declairant son intention de se vouloir laisser employer au ministère de l'église francoyse de Strassbourg pour la redresser.

Bib. Wif., II, 199; Geneva, MS fr. Corres. eccl. 407, fol. 3ᵛ:
Estant arrivé à Heydelberg, j'ai visité Olevianus pour communiquer avec lui ma vocation (car j'avois quelque cognoissance à lui de paravant), où je n'ai point esté receu de lui si amiablement que je persois a cause qu'on lui avoit rapporté de moi que j'avois esté deposé de mon ministere à Londres, et chassé de là à cause que j'avois soustenu publiquement les erreurs de Servetus.

useful affairs in hand.[24] Reina said that, after some discussion, he and Olevianus had parted amicably, but two days later, when they again met, Olevianus was most rude to him, accusing him of having deceived Beza, des Gallars and others. A sharp argument followed, in the presence of the Italian, d'Honestis, during which Reina accused Olevianus of being the enemy of the churches of Zurich, Geneva and France in the matter of the eucharist. Olevianus retorted that he was a 'proud ass' and threatened to write to Strassburg to warn them of Reina's heterodox views. It also appeared that someone had told Olevianus that Reina had been present at a lecture of Ursinus's at the University on the divinity of the Holy Spirit, at which Reina had shaken his head in disagreement. As Reina had not been present, this could not have been so, and eventually, by the intercession of M. d'Honestis, they had reached a friendlier frame of mind, and Sylvanus had even invited Reina to supper, which he had to refuse, but all parted amicably. The next day (according to Reina; a few hours later according to Olevianus) Reina came to Olevianus most affably to bid farewell and to ask whether he had any message for Johan Sturm. Olevianus offered financial help, as he had done in the past, but this was refused. They parted on good terms. Sylvanus had been at the first discussion by chance and then nearly at the end. Mosellanus had not been at the second. Neither understood French, so they must have signed Olevianus's letter in ignorance.[25]

[24] Johann Marbach (1521-1581), born in Lindau and studied in Strassburg and Wittenberg, where he was a house-guest of Luther. He went to Strassburg as a minister in 1545; represented that city at the Council of Trent; in 1552 became a teacher at the University and President of Strassburg Church Council. He was a theologian who loved controversy. In eucharistic ideas he supported the doctrine of the corporal presence of Christ. He was responsible for the expulsion of the Reformed theologian Zanchi from the city after a dispute over predestination. He was himself condemned for heterodoxy for accepting Flaccius's teaching on original sin.

Van Schelven, p. 330:

Or la desus d'aultant que Marbach a persécuté ceste église la a cause de la doctrine de la scene nous commençames à parler de la cène. La conference a duré plusieurs heures devant et àprês disne, avec papier et encre. Les propositions qu'il maintenoit estoit que le corps de Jesus Christ n'est point seulement en ung lieu a scavoir au ciel : et voyloit prouver cela par la dextre de Dieu. La desus estant interrogue sil croyoit donques que le corps de Jesus Christ fut maintenant en ce poile, ou nous estions, je ne sceu jamais tirer ny ouy ny nenny.

*Bib. Wif.*, II, 200:

Et que me voyant aussi pressé de nécessité de perdre mon temps en ma defense, j'ai esté d'advis de m'acquiter moi mesme de mon ministere, et pour enfuir les debats m'enfuir aussi de Londres pour vaquer es choses plus utiles a l'Eglise du Seigneur, que j'avois entre les mains.

[25] Van Schelven, p. 330:

Et moy voyant ceste suybite et impudente menterie luy dicts : Et ego protestor te esse superbum asinum Hispanum et tibi sancte promitto me statim scripturum ad fratrem Argentinenses Gallos de tuis hæresibus quas defendisti. Et iam habeo calamum in aure ut scias me esse in opere.

*Bib. Wif.*, II, 200f:

Deux jours après je l'ai visité derechef, et il m'a receu beaucoup rudement en me disant grandes injures, dont j'estois bien estonné, car je ne savois l'occasion de si grand changement en si peu de temps. Les plus petites estoient que j'estois ignorant, que je ne savois rien, etc. ; les plus atroces que j'avois trompé Monsr de Beze et Monsr de Saules, et tous les gens de bien qui avoient rendu bon tesmoignage de moi. Entre les injures me

Reina feigned surprise that such a letter of forthright condemnation should be waiting for him on his arrival in Strassburg. He had, after all, been warned. The letter merely contains strong assertions of Reina's heterodoxy, but without any detailed specification of the points at issue.

Casiodoro's reply begins with a lengthy doctrinal statement, asserting his undivided adherence to the historic creeds and particularizing his Trinitarian orthodoxy and his views on the eucharist. He went on to protest his innocence of the charge of sodomy, adding that he expected to receive very soon from London a declaration that he had been cleared of all the charges against him.[26] Finally he gave the explanation, already considered above, of the things that had passed between himself and Olevianus.

This reply was addressed to the Strangers' Church of Strassburg, but a copy of it must also have gone to Geneva. In fact, two copies of it are preserved in Geneva, in a longer and a shorter version. With it went a letter, signed by thirteen people in the name of the Strangers' congregation of Strassburg, testifying their support of Reina.[27] They indicated that they were fully satisfied with

---

amenaça de faire ce qu'il a fait, de estre mon adversaire partout etc. Donques nous ayant porté assez immodestement l'un avec l'autre, à la fin, par l'intercession de Monsᵣ d'Honestis qu'estoit present, nous nous sommes moderés, et y a eu lieu qu'il declairaist l'occasion de ce nouveau et acerbe courroux, disant qu'on lui avoit rapporté que le jour devant j'avois esté à la leçon de M. Ursinus, lequel traitant de la divinité du Saint Esprit, j'avois corné de la teste en signe que je ne consentois pas; et lui ayant certifié que je n'y avois jamais esté, il trouva son abus, et me certifia qu'on lui avoit dit, et que par ce nouveau rapport il avoit renouvelé tous les vieux rapports de moi, adjoustant que je ne convenois pas avec lui en l'interpretation du ciel etc., et que c'estoit pour cela qu'il m'avoit receu et traité si rudement . . . Quant aux autres qui sont soubsignés avec lui, soyes asseurés aussi que le Sylvanus n'a point esté à nostre premier colloque qu'à la moitié ou il est venu d'aventure, l'autre Mosellanus n'a point esté au second, afin que vous entendiez que ce n'a point esté une assemblée faite du propos pour disputer aveque moi, comme il semble qu'ils veulent donner à entendre par sa lettre, ains se sont trouvés à pieces ainsi qu'ils venoient à l'aventure, et le mesme Sylvanus (s'il voudra dire verité) pourra tesmoigner de l'amitié de laquelle je m'en suis departi d'Olevianus la premiere fois, et de la immodeste rudece, avec laquelle il m'a receu et traité la seconde fois à cause de ce nouveau rapport de sus dit, et comme ayant trouvé qu'ils avoint esté trompés, ils ont cogneu leur faute, et Olevianus a fait avec moi grand amitié, en laquelle nous nous sommes departis, ainsi que de sus est dit. Item, vous entenderez que les deuz soubsignés ne savent rien de françois, et par ainsi qu'ilz ont soubsigné ce que Olevianus leur a presenté, non pas ce qu'ils ont entendu.

[26] *Bib. Wif.*, II, 199:
Quant à ma vie, de laquelle les rapporteurs vous ont voulu aussi faire soupçon de moi, je ne tiendrai pas ici long propos pour en faire purgation, ayant celle que j'ai pres de moi laquelle pourra voir quiconque voudra, et attendant aussi celle que de tout je espere que me sera envoyé de Londres en brief.

[27] Geneva, MS fr., Corres. eccl. 407, fol. 3ʳ; *Bib. Wif.*, II, 201f:
Nous qui sommes au de soubz soubsignez, estants congregés au nom du Seigneur Jesus Christ et Son Eglise, testifions par ce present escrit qu'ayant oui la suscripte confession et response laquelle Cassiodore de Reyna, Espagnol, appellé de nous pour nous ministrer la parole du Seigneur, nous a presentée pour se purger de ces articles qui lui ont esté opposés par une lettre envoyée à nous de certains ministres de Heidelberge, nous recevons et advouons la response, et que nous sommes satisfaits de lui en cest endroit. Item, nous testifions que nous ne le renv. point pour blasme qui lui soit faite, sinon que lui mesme nous ayant prié au nom du Seigneur de nous desporter de lui jusques à ce

him and were not refusing him the pastorate; rather, he was asking them not to have him till the London matter should be satisfactorily settled.

In a letter written at the same time to the Rector and Scholarchs of Strassburg Reina revealed that he had by that time translated the whole of the Bible, and was now engaged upon making corrections and writing annotations, and that he hoped to be finished within a year. The letter was a request for admission to the ranks of pupils of the academy (which would seem to mean students of the university). He also referred to the request he had already made for citizenship or the right to live in Strassburg, and asks for their support of this application.[28] Johan Sturm was one of the scholarchs and the Rector of the Gymnasium. He became in time one of Reina's strong supporters.

After some days, Reina went back to Frankfurt, and on 22 April 1565 he wrote to Beza, going over the whole ground again in Latin.[29] Beza's support was desirable, since he had succeeded to Calvin's position as leader of the Geneva Church. Reina explained both the situation in London and that in Strassburg. He received a reply written on 23 June 1565, not wishing to condemn, but taking up various points that Reina had made in his Confession to the Strassburg Church, and in fact displaying some bias against Reina. Beza wrote again on 9 July, going over the doctrinal points in minute detail.[30]

Also on 22 April Reina had written to Marbach about the dissension concerning the eucharist, deploring the way in which those who held differing opinions wished neither to instruct nor to learn, but only to dominate. He praised the example of moderation shewn by Bucer, and assured Marbach that he himself wished to go to Strassburg not as a protagonist of any party in the dispute, but as a minister of peace and unity amongst the people of God.[31]

On 12 November 1565 Reina put in a second request to the Strassburg City Council asking for a resident's permit for himself and his wife, and for permission for his wife to carry on business in needlework to gain a livelihood. He gave

---

qu'il aie resolution de certains affaires qu'il a à Londres, et juste et entiere purgation de quelques choses qui lui ont esté opposées tant de sa vie que sa doctrine, afin qu'en la procedure de son ministere personne ne le puisse blasmer de quelque chose d'icelles comme n'estant pas sufisamment purgé, nous l'avons accordé, voyant sa petition estre juste; toutesfois avec telle condition qu'ayant la dite purgation, toutes et quantes fois il sera rappellé de cest'eglise, n'ayant nul autre just'impediment, il sera prest de ci venir, ce que lui nous a promis, etc. Et en tesmoignage de verité nous avons ici soubsigné de nos mains. Donné à Strasbourg, le jour que de sus, etc. Soubsignés 13. au nom de toute la Congregation. [13 signatures.]

[28] Strassburg, Bibliothèque publique, MS AST 48/29:
Textum omnem non sine ingenti labore Deo tamen vires suppeditente per sexennium integrum, exili difficultate remorante opus, iam verti: correctioni & annotationibus nunc incumbo, ac eo qui hunc animum indidit ut sacræ isti occupatione me totum addicerem, conatus meos benefortunante, intra annum prælo committendum opus spero . . . Consultum vero bonum ex parte hisce meis studiis arbitrarbor . . . si inter scholæ vestræ alumnos primum scribar, deinde si authores mihi fueritis ut illustrissimus ac prudentiss. huius inclytæ urbis Senatus me aut in numerum suorum civium admittat, aut si hoc minus fieri possit, habitandi saltem isthic licentiam tantisper mihi concedat.

[29] *Bib. Wif.*, II, 204; Geneva, MS fr., Corres, eccl. 407, fol. 12ʳ & ᵛ.

[30] *Bib. Wif.*, II, 205ff; Geneva, MS fr. Corres. eccl. 407, fol. 14ʳ-15ᵛ.

[31] J. Fecht, *Historiæ Ecclesiasticæ seculi A.N.C. XVI Supplementum* (Frankfurt, 1684), pp. 195f; Lehnemann, pp. 158f; see also Tollin, p. 396.

as reason that he wished to finish his work on the translation of the Bible and to publish it. The request was granted on the same date.[32]

Now began a time of busy movement between Strassburg, Frankfurt and Basle. These movements were occasioned by his work on the Bible, and by the silk trade in which he was engaged. In all three towns he gained the friendship of influential men. In Strassburg he became friendly, as we have seen, with Johan Sturm, with Conrad Hubert, a minister who also carried on various trading agencies, and with the Italian theologian, Girolamo Zanchi.[33] In Basle he had a friend in Theodor Zwinger, a doctor, and the support of two Lutheran ministers, Simon Sulzer and Huldrich Koechlein (Coccius).[34] In Frankfurt he established close ties with Matthias Ritter the Younger, an eminent Lutheran pastor of the city and the Superintendent of Foreign Churches there. As yet Reina was still a Calvinist, and, though not of the highest orthodoxy, he tried to maintain his place within the Reformed community. The enmity of Olevianus and Cousin, the coolness of des Gallars, and the intransigence of Beza must have disillusioned him, and cannot but have helped to ease his passage into the Lutheran fold. But at present he was a member of the French (Calvinist) Church of Frankfurt, and a visitor of Reformed assemblies in the towns through which he passed.

On 28 January 1566 Reina saw fit to write again to Beza from Frankfurt, this time in French. He elaborated the meaning of various passages in his confession which he felt might have been taken wrongly, striving to be an orthodox Calvinist, but driving himself deeper into the distrust of Beza and his friends.[35]

In Strassburg on 1 March 1566, he wrote again to Beza, enclosing two lists of objections extracted by his London accusers from his annotations to Isaiah and Ezekiel (these must have been notes intended for publication with his Bible). The notes are on the one hand rather 'modern' in tone (e.g. he understands Isaiah VII. 14, 'A virgin shall conceive . . . etc.' as referring to the prophet's wife and only by symbolism to Mary), and on the other hand they are very critical of the French translation. This letter pleaded once again his Calvinist orthodoxy in both his London and his Strassburg confessions, and used the extracts from his notes to shew just how petty his accusers were.[36]

The work of translating the Bible and its revision were now over and Casio-

[32] Archives de la Ville de Strasbourg, Procès verbaux des XXI 1565, fol. 397$^v$f:
Frauwen arbyt negen sticken und derglychen ernären konne so bitt er nachmals myne H[erren] wöllen Ime zu eynen innwoner ann nemmen . . . Erkannd. mann soll Ime ey Jarlang zu eynem Innwoner ann nemen doch auf syn wol halten.
There are no records of Reina's ever having been received as a full burgess of Strassburg.
[33] Girolamo Zanchi (1516-90) was born near Brescia. He became an Augustinian and taught at Lucca. After accepting the Reform, he went to teach theology in Strassburg from 1563 to 1568, but his Reformed views, although opposed to Calvin's doctrine of predestination, brought him into conflict with Marbach. He taught in Heidelberg from 1568 to 1576, when he went to Neustadt, where he died.
[34] Theodor Zwinger was the nephew of the printer Oporinus who printed part of Reina's Bible. At the age of twenty he had studied under Sébastien Castellio, whose chair of Greek in Basle he took over in 1564, although he had taken the degree of doctor of medicine at Padua in 1558. Sulzer and Koechlein were the ecclesiastical inspectors of Basle.
[35] Geneva, MS fr. Corres. eccl., 407, fol. 4$^r$f; Bib. Wif., II, 208f.
[36] Corres. eccl., 407, 16$^r$f, 24$^r$f, 25$^r$; Bib. Wif., II, 191f, 210f.

doro entered into negotiations with Johan Herbst, better known as Oporinus, for the printing of this work.

Oporinus, besides carrying on business as a printer, was a humanist lecturer at the University of Basle. We find out various details of his dealings with Casiodoro from his voluminous correspondence with Conrad Hubert, the pastor who appears to have been his agent in Strassburg.[37] Oporinus sent books in casks down the Rhine to Strassburg, and there they were off-loaded for onward transmission to their destinations elsewhere in Germany and France. Casiodoro also carried on a correspondence with Hubert, from which other details can be gleaned.

A letter dated 9 April 1567 to Beza from Reina in Strassburg speaks of the difficulties he was experiencing in finding a printer for his Bible. He really felt that Geneva would have been the best place to have the printing done, for several reasons : the cost was less, Crespin had the experience of printing Spanish, and Reina would have liked the opportunity of correcting his version from material available there. Two things prevented this : the difficulty of transporting his family so far, and the fact that people there who would have been able to help him were estranged from him.[38]

On 10 June 1567 Oporinus wrote to Hubert mentioning a pamphlet by Reina on the Spanish Inquisition.[39] Apart from another possible reference to it, nothing is known of this pamphlet.[40] Oporinus was not sure whether he ought to burn it or to publish it and thus add to the sum of knowledge about the horrible deeds of the Inquisition. He sent his regards to Casiodoro who was at Strassburg, having left Frankfurt to travel to Basle to supervise the printing of the Bible.

From Strassburg on 27 September 1567 Reina wrote to Diego López and

---

[37] Bibliothèque de Strasbourg, Epistolæ ad historiam ecclesiasticam vii, O-P, volume 160, fol. 188ʳ-196ʳ; *Bib. Wif.*, II, 211.

[38] Paris, Bibliothèque Nationale, MS Dupuy, ciii, fol. 73ʳf :

Etsi variis Satanæ oppugnationibus continenter impetiti, tamen Bibliorum versionem, quam nostris Hispanis iam dudum molimur, eosque perduximus, ut, adiuvante Deo conatus nostros ad proximas Francofordiæ nundinas typographiam adire meditemur. Ego vero ad id perficiendum nullum locum unquam existimavi Geneva commodiorem, tum ob minores sumtus, tum ob Crispini typographiam premendis Hispanicis haud infœliciter assuetam, tum maxime quod extremam tanti operis correctioni manum ex vestra collatione imponere consilium semper fuerit.

Tam ne id pro voto meo fiat duo imprimis obstant : alterum, quod alendæ familiolæ meæ Genevæ vix ulla appareat ratio; alterum, quod ut maxime appareret, tamen iis a me animo abalienatis, quorum opera imprimis ad operis correctionem uti debuissem, tentare id nimis stultum esset.

[39] Strassburg, Epist. ad hist. eccl., clx, fol. 190ʳ; *Bib. Wif.*, II, 211.

[40] In a PS to the letter referred to in the next note Reina wrote: 'Los mysterios dela Inquisicion estan impressos en latin creo q̃ por alla los veran.' Usoz y Río felt that this was the key to the problem of the real identity of Reginaldus Gonsalvius Montanus, the author of *Sanctæ Inquisitionis hispanicæ artes* (Heidelberg, 1567). Reginaldus could be a play on Reina (Regina), and Montanus could be a reference to Montemolín, Reina's birthplace. In addition, the author had clearly been a member of the San Isidro community. Menéndez Pelayo (*Heterodoxos*, V, 172) dismisses the idea with the statement that Montanus's Latin was definitely better than Reina's as seen in his letters. This judgement is open to question. Usoz's suggestion is interesting, and, if true, would give us Reina's real surname, but, although the date is right and the connexion with Heidelberg is proved, one feels that it is a little contrived.

Balthasar Gomes, both men who had been helping Juan Pérez in Paris in the preparation of his New Testament and other books for the press.[41] They had apparently stayed in Paris after Pérez's death. The letter to López has survived; we know of the letter to Gomes by reference to it in López's. When Reina last saw him (in Paris in 1564?) Gomes had promised to help in the preparation of the Bible for the press. Now Reina wanted him to come to Basle as quickly as possible to help as compositor. He would be paid the proper rate and would be assured of a job in the future.

Reina revealed that he had previously been in correspondence with López. He asked him to send the information in this letter to Gomes, in case the latter's letter did not arrive, and to find out what Gomes was being paid, so that he would know what to pay him in Basle.

The letter said that Reina and Oporinus had agreed that 1,100 copies of the Bible should be printed at a cost of over five hundred écus. Oporinus would have 200 copies for himself, and Casiodoro and the others would have 900 to distribute.[42] He also asked López and Gomes to bring with them a copy of the New Testament on which they had worked with Pérez.[43]

On his arrival in Basle, Reina was allowed to matriculate at the University, and began negotiations with the authorities for permission for the Bible to be printed.[44] Negotiations were particularly necessary because in 1550 the City Council had forbidden the printing of books in languages other than Latin, Greek, Hebrew, and German.[45] This had put an effective brake on Basle immigrants evangelizing their homelands in the same way that Genevan immigrants could do. Perhaps the law was a political safeguard; France and Spanish-held Germany were right on the borders. To print a Spanish Bible would require a special suspension of the rule, which the Council was not willing to grant without a recommendation from Johan Sturm.

On 28 October 1567 Casiodoro wrote to Hubert, asking him to use his influence to make Sturm expedite the matter of this certificate, which Sulzer and Koechlein, as Inspectors, wanted before they would move.[46] This is the first of

[41] Paris, Bibliothèque Nationale, MS Dupuy 103, MS latin 8582, fol. 103ʳff; full text published by E. Boehmer, 'Ein Brief von Cassiodoro de Reyna', *Romanische Studien*, 4 (1880), 483-6. See Appendix VI.

[42] But, in the Preface to his Bible (Amsterdam, 1602), Cipriano de Valera says that 2600 copies were printed (fol. *6ʳ).

[43] There has been considerable discussion about whether this New Testament was ever in fact printed. Boehmer argues strongly (p. 484) for the view that the whole impression was confiscated as soon as it was printed. The fact remains that no single copy of it has ever come to light.

[44] *Bib. Wif.*, II, 172 (reporting University of Basle Matriculation Book, an entry not in Reina's handwriting); II, 222; C. de Reina, *Expositio primæ partis capitis quarti Matthæi* (Frankfurt, 1573), fol. a2.

[45] N. Steinmann, *Johannes Oporinus* (Basle, 1967), p. 84 (quoting Basle City Archives, Ratsbücher A6, fol. 143ᵛ).

[46] Conrad Hubert (who sometimes used the humanist names Pulbarba and Ornithopogon) (1507-77) had been a friend and collaborator of Bucer. He studied in Heidelberg and Basle before becoming Œcolampadius's secretary. In 1531 he became Bucer's assistant at St Thomas's Church, Strassburg, and was one of the men responsible for the introduction of the Reform into that city. In 1562 Marbach engineered his expulsion from the

a series of letters from Reina to Hubert which are preserved in Strassburg.[47]

Oporinus wrote again to Hubert on 15 November 1567 with much the same request, asking him to prod Sturm to write his recommendation, since Oporinus had written to him three or four times without reply. The censors suspected everything they could not understand.[48] A similar point is again made by Reina in a letter dated 13 November. He was becoming irked by the delay and the Bible was being held up. His wife was still in Strassburg when this letter was written.[49]

Meanwhile Reina was consolidating his friendships with influential people in Basle. The two Inspectors, Sulzer and Koechlein, became sympathetic towards him, and he made a lasting friendship with Oporinus's nephew, the doctor, Theodor Zwinger.[50] He was lodging at the home of Marcos Pérez, who had fled to Basle in late 1566, when the situation in Antwerp became difficult.[51]

---

Strassburg Church Council on account of his Calvinist leanings. He spent his enforced retirement preparing an edition of Bucer's works.

[47] Strassburg, Bibliothèque publique, AST 161/83:

Ad promovendam nostræ versionis impressionem indigeo testimonio dnj Rectoris apud Inspectores Sulcerum et Coccium illud a dno Rectore per meas literas peto. Sed ut est crebris occupationibus continenter distractus vereor ne tantula ista illa excidat memoria. Te igitur oro ut ab eo extorqueas, ac primo quoq̃ tempore ad nos transmittas.

[48] Strassburg, Bibliothèque publique, Epist. ad. hist. eccl. vii, volume 160, fol. 191; *Bib. Wif.*, II, 211f:

Non potui differre longius quin te certiorem redderem de Biblia nostra Hispanica, in qua, ut tandem prelo subjiciatur, nihil impedit aliud quam ut D. Cassiodorus a Sturmio nostra bona testimonia consequatur, id quod hactenus et ipse, qui ter et quater jam scripsit ad eum, et nostri censores desiderant. Vellem itaque, mi D. Conrade apud D. Sturmium efficeres, ut eo accuratius D. Cassiodorum commendaret: plurimi enim id proverbii negotium, quia censores nostri omnia, quæ non intelligunt, suspecta habere judicantur.

[49] Strassburg, AST 161/84:

Orabam etiam ut Dominum Sturmium sollicitares ut primo quoque tempore me apud inspectores eorũ quæ imprimuntur, Sulcerũ et Coctium literis suis commendaret, quando ipsis ignorantibus quis ego sim, & Hispanice linguæ omnino imperitis eiusmodi commendatione adeo mihi opus esse video, ut ob illius unius defectu in promovenda nostra impressione nihil hactenus a me sit tentatum. Obsecro itaque ut, si ea in re hactenus nihil præstitit dominus Rector, eum ores meo nomine ut statim eas literas det, et a te acceptas primo quoque tempore ad nos differe cures. Quod si quidq̃ fortasse, accidit quod ne id prestetis impedimento sit, me q̃ primum potueris eius impedimenti certiorem facias, ut aliam rationem in tempore iniamus.

[50] *Bib. Wif.*, II, 213; Petrus Ramus (as note 4 above). Ramus, the philosopher, mentions in the same sentence as Reina several other people whom Reina must also have known.

[51] T. Geering, *Handel und Industrie der Stadt Basel* (Basle, 1886), p. 455. The situation in Antwerp had altered suddenly with the despatch of the Duke of Alba to put down heresy in the Low Countries. M. Pérez fled to Basle in October 1566, where he became a citizen. The transfer of his vast resources to that city enabled him to set up his business enterprises and to continue to help his refugee co-religionaries. In the Preface to his *Expositio primæ partis capitis quarti Matthæi*, fol. a2ᵛ, Reina wrote:

Illam ipsum erga relictos nequaquam intermissurum, indicium mihi certum erat Perezij mei domus, qui vt de me fuit semper egregiè benemeritus, ita etiam tunc charitate ac pietate insigni, neque à me aut quouis alio, qui illius beneficentiam sit expertus vnquam satis laudata me periculosè decumbentem, familiolamqué meam in domum suam transtulerat, curabatqué tum ægrotos, tum rectè valentes humanissimè.

Casiodoro's wife finally joined him there, and it was in Basle that his first son (or first surviving son) was born. He was named Marcus, and it seems unlikely that the reason for this name was anything other than gratitude to Marcos Pérez, who was also the child's godfather.[52]

Passing mention is made of Reina in letters from Oporinus to Hubert. One was written on 10 December 1567, according to which Casiodoro was to transmit a copy of the Plantin Hebrew prophets to Hubert for Oporinus.[53] The other was written at Christmas 1567, when Reina took a copy of an Old Testament commentary to Flaccius Illyricus for Oporinus.[54]

In January 1568 Reina was apparently still in Strassburg, for letters written on 7 January[55] and 12 January[56] sent greetings to him there. That of 7 January asks Hubert to tell Casiodoro that the Basle City Council had given permission for the Bible to be printed on condition that all notes were omitted, and that Casiodoro must hasten back to Basle so that the work might begin without delay. On 15 January the news was that Sulzer and Koechlein had managed to persuade the Council to allow grammatical notes in the Bible. As Oporinus was writing this third letter Casiodoro returned.[57]

By February 1568 the Bible was in production. On 6 February Oporinus wrote to Hubert saying that Casiodoro would tell him of the progress to date.[58] In view of Marcos Pérez's letter referred to in the next paragraph, this apparently meant that the type-setting had begun in earnest. On Easter Day 1568 Girolamo Zanchi wrote to Hubert from Heidelberg, asking him to transmit a letter to Casiodoro.[59]

Reina's letters to Gomes and López do not seem to have brought a response, and at this point Marcos Pérez tried to obtain a copy of the New Testament from Paris. In a letter dated 30 June 1568 from Basle he wrote to ask Diego López to send him one or two copies, whatever stage of completion they had reached, since the printing had not begun in Basle.[60] This letter also seems to

[52] Frankfurt City Archives, Bürgerbuch vii, fol. 179$^r$: 'Marcus Cassiodorus Reinius Basiliensis Pfarrherr alhir duxit filiam civis. Juravit dies 8 10bris Anno X 1597.'

[53] Strassburg, Epist. ad hist. eccl., fol. 188; *Bib. Wif.*, II, 212.

[54] Epist. ad hist. eccl., fol. 192; *Bib. Wif.*, II, 212. Matthias Vlacich (Flaccius Illyricus) (1520-75) was born in Istria and studied in Venice, Basle, and Tübingen. He went in 1541 to teach Greek and Hebrew in Wittenburg, and under the influence of Luther became an enthusiastic Reformer. His vehement opposition to Melanchthon's teaching led to his expulsion from Wittenberg, after which he wandered widely, to Magdeburg, Jena, Ratisbon, Antwerp, Strassburg, and finally to Frankfurt, where he died in poverty.

[55] Epist. ad hist. eccl., fol. 193; *Bib. Wif.*, II, 212.

[56] Epist. ad hist. eccl., fol. 193$^r$ & $^v$; this letter was not noted by Wiffen/Boehmer in *Bib. Wif.*

[57] Epist. ad hist. eccl., fol. 194; *Bib. Wif.*, II, 212:
Simul addens, esse a Coccio aliter primo quam post ab ipso Sulcero indicatum senatusconsultum nempe licere una cum annotationibus, grammaticalibus saltem, Bib. Hisp. edere. Et ecce, dum id molior, supervenit Cassiodorus ipse et tuas adfert literas.

[58] Epist, ad hist. eccl., fol. 196; *Bib. Wif.*, II, 212.

[59] *Bib. Wif.*, II, 212.

[60] A. Bernus, pp. 42f; MacFadden, pp. 244f; both quote a document from the Archivo General de Simancas, K1509 B22, entitled 'Del herege Marcos Perez al Español que imprimia la biblia en Paris':
Pesame del ynpedimento que ay en la ynpression del testamento nuebo y ansi ynperfeto como esta rreçiuire merced que con la primera opurtunidad v.m. me ynbie un exenplar

indicate that Marcos Pérez did not pay for the whole of the printing of the Basle Bible (in spite of claims that he did so) and that in fact Legrand had granted to Reina some of the Frankfurt fund set up by Juan Pérez.[61]

Some time in June 1568 Casiodoro fell ill on leaving Strassburg for Basle, and, as the journey proceeded, he felt worse. Arriving in Basle he went straight to bed, where he stayed for five weeks, gravely ill. On 4 August he was well enough to write rather shakily to Hubert to inform him that he was now on the road to recovery.[62]

During Reina's illness, on 6 July 1568, Oporinus had died, leaving his affairs in a very chaotic state and with debts amounting to some 15,000 florins. The four hundred florins he had apparently had from Casiodoro was a very small amount, lost in this huge debt, and Reina doubted whether he would ever see them again, since his name did not figure anywhere near the top of the list of creditors.[63] In fact, as he wrote on 25 August, in Basle the rule was that citizens always came first on lists of creditors. For this reason Reina wished Hubert to find out whether Oporinus had creditors in Strassburg or Frankfurt, and, if so, to get Reina's name entered quickly on the lists in those cities.[64] Probably, as a 'habitant' of both cities, he would have some preference over other creditors, and could recoup there something of the loss he faced in Basle.

Meanwhile Casiodoro addressed a request to Basle City Council, asking them to free the 400 florins he had already handed over on the grounds that it was really church property, since it had been brought together by charitable gifts. It was, as we have seen, part of the money that was held by Augustin Legrand in the fund started for the express purpose of paying for an edition of the Spanish Bible, and which Juan Pérez had been instrumental in setting up in Frankfurt. In this request Reina mentions the name of a printer, Thomas Guarin.[65]

---

o dos por vna parte o por otra lo de aqui no esta començado aun dizen me que se començara presto en lo que toca al autor la otra dara testimonio de su piedad o ynpiedad ynprimire solamente con las anotaçiones dela ley [sic=lengua?] y asi abra menos peligro den se estropeçar no me entremeto querria entremeterme bisto que no ay testamento de Juan Perez por donde conste de su ordenaçion de la muerte de ello me ha pesado mucho por la pedida que se ha halho en el pero Dios despertara a otros que suplan su falta . . . con el tiempo se podra en alguna manera aberiguar si es ansi que faltan dineros para ynpression deste testamento nuebo que es que el dinero se sacara de las biblias se saquen los 400. escudos o lo que faltara para complimiento de ese otro.

[61] T. Geering, (as note 49).

[62] Strassburg, AST 161/85:

Scis me inter ipse gravissimi imminentis morbi initia Argentorato dis cessisse: usque fefellit nos coniectura: nanqũ ex itineris agitatione morbus recrudescens adeo me acriter invasit Basileam ingressum ut post exactas in lecto quinque hebdomades vix tandem revizerim potius qũ convaluerim.

[63] Steinmann, p. 115; Reina, AST 161/85, said the figure was 10,000 florins.

[64] Strassburg, AST 161/86:

Superest ut si quid isthic noveris deberi Oporino illud primo quoque tempore intercipias. Si Argentinæ nihil ei debetur, in nundinis Francofortensibus aderunt haud dubie aliqui ex multis qui ipso debebant; cura igitur ea debita, si fieri potest, rescire ac primus occupare. id vero ut sũma diligentia fiat necesse est, ne a creditoribus huius urbis civibus.

[65] This letter is in German. The undated original is in Basle City Archives, Handel und

In a letter of 4 August he also says that the printer was holding back. It thus seems that Oporinus had already sub-contracted the work to Guarin, but that, since Oporinus was now dead, and funds might not be forthcoming, Guarin wanted some guarantee of payment before continuing the work. We know from the dedication inscribed in the copy of the finished Bible presented by Reina to Basle University Library that Guarin did finally print it.[66]

Thomas Guarin, or Guérin, was from Tournay. Born in 1529, he left his home town for religious reasons and settled first in Lyons, where he was a bookseller. In 1557 he moved to Basle and married the daughter of a printer named Isengrin. He set up as a printer in a small way, using a palm-tree as his device.[67] But the title-page of the finished Bible carries the device of Samuel Biener (Apiarius).

The latter was born in Basle and helped his father in his business as a printer in Strassburg, and from 1537 in Berne. In 1564 he was banned from Berne as a result of various conflicts. He tried to set up first in Solothurn, but in less than a year he went to Basle, in 1565, where he printed small pamphlets and often took on sub-contracted work. What is more important, it can be shewn that he sometimes worked in others' workshops. His device was a bear trying to get at a bees' nest in a tree, with bees flying all round. The bear represents Berne, and the bees are a pun on his German name, Biener. So we can suppose that Reina's Bible was set up by Apiarius for Guarin, either in Guarin's workshop or in Apiarius's own. This is to some extent conjecture, since neither the name of printer, compositor, nor translator appears on the Bibles (no doubt this was to facilitate their entry into Spain). Apiarius's device gives the Bible its distinguishing name : 'La Biblia del Oso'.[68]

On 23 December 1568 Reina asked Hubert's aid in the process of arranging the transfer of money from friends in Frankfurt by the agency of a Frankfurt silk merchant, Hans Wandenabelle, who would bring it to Strassburg. Casiodoro wished Hubert to receive it and forward it to Basle, since two hundred florins were urgently needed for the printer, who would brook no delay. Reina's letter of 16 January 1569 shews that the money had arrived, but that there was some difficulty in getting it handed over. Reina wanted to make use of an

---

Gewerbe JJJ 1, and is not Reina's autograph, as the signature 'Reimius' instead of 'Reinius' proves. See also A. Fluri, 'Die Bärenbibel', *Gutenbergmuseum*, 9 (1923), pp. 35-41, 82-90.

[66] The dedication reads thus:

Cassiodorus Reinius Hispanus Hispalens. inclytæ huius Academiæ alũnus, huius sacrorũ librorũ versionis Hispanicæ autor, quam per integrum deceñium elaborauit, et auxilio pietissimorũ ministrorũ huius Ecclesiæ Basil[sis] ex decreto prudentiss. Senatus typis ab honesto viro Thoma Guarino ciue Basil[si] excusam demum emisit in lucem, in perpetuũ gratitudinis et obseruantiæ monumentum hunc librum inclytæ huic Academiæ supplex dicabat. Ann. 1570. Mens. Jun. Cass. R. Quum sedero in tenebris, Jehoua lux mea est. Mich. 6.

[67] Fluri, p. 39.

[68] Fluri, p. 40; gives examples of this practice, including one where Apiarius is concerned. It might be said that Casiodoro's name does occur in the Bible, for the Preface is signed 'C.R.'.

Italian, Bartholomeo Versasca, as a messenger, as he had done several times in the past.[69]

On 15 May 1569 Reina informed Hubert of a recurrence of the previous year's illness, which was, however, now on the mend. This letter reveals that Casiodoro had hoped for the aid of a copy of the Spanish New Testament, which had not arrived. Apparently the copy of the Paris New Testament, which both he and Marcos Pérez had asked Gomes to bring with him to Basle, had never in fact been brought. The work of printing was proceeding apace, and he expected the last sheet of the Acts of the Apostles the following day. From II Corinthians to the end of the New Testament would take longer because of the lack of a copy of the Paris New Testament, nor could he recover from the printer his manuscript of the work already done.[70]

He referred to the money owed him from Oporinus's estate, and said that not a farthing had yet been received, even though his appeal to the City Council had succeeded in so far as his name had been listed officially as a creditor. Till this matter was settled, the printing was delayed, and there was a deficit of 250 florins. If anyone would lend these to him, he would in exchange sign over the debt of 400 florins. The hint is fairly strong that he hoped that the loan of this sum would be forthcoming from Hubert. Theodor Zwinger had suggested to him that, if Hubert did take over this debt, he could gain preference as a creditor much more easily than anyone else.[71]

In a postscript to this letter Reina mentioned a dedicatory letter he was considering printing at the beginning of his Bible. The next letter, dated 24 June, reveals that he had asked Sturm's advice about dedicating this translation to Queen Elizabeth, for which he needed Sturm's intercession.[72] Sturm carried on

[69] Strassburg, AST 161/87, AST 161/88.

[70] AST 161/89:
Quo die tuas accepi literas valetudinis ergo, quæ de ægritudinis præcedentis æstatis recursu erat valde suspecta, venam acideram triduo ante sumptis ad alios humores noxios evacuandos pharmacia. Utrũque per Dei gratiam non male cessit. Laboraveram per hosce dies, quos sæpe soleo, vehementi dolore capitis, titillante nonnihil continua febri . . . Excussis nostra procedit felicissime adeo ut Actorũ Apostolicorũ postremũ folium cras sim accepturus. Ceterum quin Novi Testamenti subsidio quod aliunde versũ expectabamus destitutus plusqũ duplicatũ laborem in eo ex integro vertendo adierim, qui poteram a typographo non assequi, currente hinc prelo, hinc multiplicato labore, difficiente hinc valetudine — Subsistendum itaque erit nobis quod ad prelũ attinet per aliquot dies, tantisper dum quod superest vertendũ Novi Test. hoc est ab altera Corinthiorũ ad finẽ usque.

[71] AST 161/89:
Cum ea de re consuluissem optimũ virũ doctorẽ Theodorũ Zvingerũ, respondit se nullam commodiorem rationem invenire, nisi ut divenditis commode pignoribus quæ apud te habes, confestam pecuniam dares fænuri fieri posse ut citius integrũ debitũ in de esses recepturus, q̃ hic creditores alii. Risi topicum remedium.

[72] AST 161/89:
Scribo ad dñ Sturmiũ quædam, ni fallor, tibi communicabit de nuncupatione nostro S. Bib. oro ut ad redendam nuncupatoriã epistolam, si consilium nostrum vobis probatur, sum solicites, ut quæ primũ fieri possit ad nos transmittetur.
AST 161/90:
obsecrabamque ut si prudentiæ vestræ maxime probaretur unas dispiceretis an e re foret ut versionis nostræ tutelam Reginæ Angliæ commandaremus . . . autoris nomine omnino suppresso ita enim expedire nunc videtur rebus meis quod si ita videtur.

a correspondence with the Queen and her secretary, Cecil, informing them of matters on the Continent. He did in fact commend Reina's translation to them in letters written in 1569.[73] His advice to Reina seems to have been not to dedicate to Queen Elizabeth, since in the end the translation appeared with a much more general dedicatory epistle. If Reina intended to circulate copies in Spain, it is difficult to see why he ever had this idea. Even the names of printer and translator were suppressed, and the Queen's name was far better known there than theirs.

In this letter he was still waiting for a reply about the money, although he had now received the whole Bible, both Old and New Testaments (this means, apparently, the proofs of the work). He mentioned that it would be better for his purpose not to have his own name on the translation, and this bears out the thought that he intended to circulate copies in Spain. The reason, however, may have been because the scandal, which had caused him to leave London, had not yet died down.

On 3 August 1569 he reported that he had received a satisfactory reply from Hubert and the return of his dedicatory epistle from Sturm. The matter of the money owed to him from Oporinus's estate was still dragging on, and, though the City Council now had funds, they appeared to be holding on to them so that the interest would mount up.[74]

We gather that Hubert must have supplied the money needed, for three days later, on 6 August 1569, Casiodoro wrote via Bartholomeo Versasca that Hubert should expect four great winecasks full of Bibles in the same ship and should store them in a previously arranged place. The rest would follow shortly.[75]

So the great work was finished. Although Reina's debt to other Spanish translators is undoubted, in the best humanist tradition he went back to the original Hebrew and Greek texts. He had been engaged on the work for ten years.[76] Whole committees have taken longer to produce vernacular versions, without having to battle against the sort of difficulties with which Reina had to contend. His achievement is all the more remarkable when one realizes that it has remained to the present day as basically the translation that is still in daily use

---

[73] E. Boehmer, *Q.F.F.Q.S.Viro summe venerando I. F. Bruch . . . Insunt Epistolæ . . . Johannis Sturmii* (Strassburg, 1872), pp. 26f; *Zurich Letters* (Cambridge, 1854), II, 175f.

[74] AST 161/91:
In Oporini negotio nihil innovatum, quod sciam: qui fiat, nescio, nemo hactenus quiquam recepit. Conflata pecunia apud Dominos asservatur, fortassis eo consilio ut ex ipsius usura intra tempus aliquod, puta decenniũ, quod nunc decesset satisfaciendo creditoribus, resarciri possit.

[75] AST 161/92. It is interesting that the date of this letter is August, since the completed Bible bears a colophon, 'Anno del Señor M.D.LXIX en Septiembre'.

[76] See note 64, and also the Preface to *Expositio primæ partis capitis quarti Matthæi*, fol. a2ᵛ, where Reina says:
quum in vertendis Hispanico sermone sacris Biblijs per integrum decennium laborassem. In the Preface to the Bible itself, however, he says:
La obra nos ha durado entre las manos enteros doze años. Sacado el tiempo que nos han lleuado o enfermedades, o viajes, o otras occupaciones necessarias en nuestro destierro y pobreza, podemos affirmar, que han sido bien los nueue, que no hemos soltado la pluma de la mano, ni affloxado el estudio (fol. ***vᵛ).

by Spanish-speaking Protestants throughout the world, although it has been through several revisions since 1569.

The *Biblia del Oso* has become a comparatively rare book, but, even so, many of the older libraries possess a copy. In 1602 Cipriano de Valera stated that it had become so difficult to obtain a copy that he felt a second edition was needed. This he published with some revisions to Reina's text. In spite of this, it appears that a stock of copies of the original printing of 2,600 remained at Frankfurt, since such copies exist with new title-pages bearing the dates 1602, 1603, and even 1622. Besides these, a number of different title-pages exist bearing the original date of 1569. In all of them, however, material other than the title-page remains the same. The format of this Bible is large quarto. It has a dedicatory preface in Latin, which occupies fourteen pages (foliated * [j] recto – [+vij] verso), and an introduction in Spanish, which takes up a further fourteen pages (foliated [+vij] recto – [***vj] verso). These are followed by 1,250 pages of text. The introduction has recently been reprinted in a modernized version by B. Foster Stockwell. To celebrate the fourth centenary of the original edition, a facsimile reproduction of it was published in June 1970 by the Spanish Bible Society.[77]

The dedicatory preface, although signed, 'Sacratissimae dignitatis vestrae observantiss. C.R.', is clearly the work of Johan Sturm, as the letters mentioned above indicate.[78] In spite of the talk of dedicating the Bible to Queen Elizabeth, it is addressed to the rulers and magistrates of the whole of Europe, and stresses their duty as Christians to afford their protection to this translation.

Besides the work of translation, Reina's own contribution is the introduction, which pleads the necessity of having vernacular Bibles, so that the common people will not be deprived of the Word of God. In it Reina explains the methods he used to produce the version, and the other versions of which he has made use.[79] He justifies his use of additional words when translating Hebrew, since a word for word translation does not produce readable Spanish. He ex-

---

[77] The title-page reads:
LA BIBLIA, | QVE ES, LOS SA- | CROS LIBROS DEL | VIEIO Y NVEVO TE- | STAMENTO. | *Trasladada en Español.* | [Device: a bear robbing honey from a bees' nest in a tree.] | רבר אלחינו יקות לצולם | *La Palabra del Dios nuestro permanece para siempre. Isa. 40.* | M.D.LXIX.
The variants and different editions are discussed at length in *Bib. Wif.*, II, 237-43, and in the British & Foreign Bible Society's *Catalogue of Printed Bibles*, III, 1431f. B. Foster Stockwell (editor), *Prefacios a las Biblias castellanas del Siglo XVI,* second edition, (Buenos Aires/Mexico, 1951).
[78] The argument is set out (with rather inaccurate references) by Menéndez Pelayo, *Heterodoxos,* V, 153, following Boehmer. See also notes 72 & 74 above.
[79] Reina names particularly the Latin version of the Bible made by Sanctes Pagninus, viz. *Biblia. Habes in hoc libro prudens lector vtriusq; instrumenti nouam translatione æditam a reuerendo sacræ theologiæ doctore Sancte pagnino lucesi concionatore apostolico Prædicatorij ordinis* (Lyons, 1527/28), which was the earliest Latin version of the Bible made in modern times from the original Hebrew and Greek texts. It was a literal rendering of the original. A new edition was brought out by Servetus (Lyons, 1542), using a copy of the first edition corrected by Pagninus himself. Servetus's marginal notes caused offence. It is interesting to speculate whether what Reina in fact used was a copy of Servetus's edition, in which, in any case, the books are arranged in the same way as they are in Reina's version

plains why he has used 'Iehoua' rather than 'Señor' for the tetragrammaton, and why he has used other words in preference to those usually employed previously for certain Hebrew words. He has introduced the new words 'reptil', 'esculptil', and 'esculptura' because there seemed to be no suitable alternative Spanish words.

He says that, although he himself has not attempted an authoritative version, he puts forward an idea for the production and continuous revision of such a version. Let an official committee of pious men, learned in Latin, Greek, and Hebrew, be set up that would produce two translations, one in Latin for students, and one in Spanish which would be the canonical translation for the country, declared authoritative by a national synod, that would also watch for errors that needed correction, and would make sure that a sufficient number be printed each year to ensure a free supply, to be produced in turn with care by a single authorized printer. Such a practice would establish a norm of reference in ecclesiastical disputes, and would eliminate corrupt texts. It is noteworthy that this is almost exactly what happened in 1611 with the production of the English Authorized Version. If a practice of constant revision such as that suggested by Reina had also been accepted, the effect would have been better over the long term.

The arrangement of the books of Reina's Bible is that of earlier Catholic Bibles in that the books of the Old Testament and the Apocrypha are not separated, but are intermingled. One of the main changes introduced by Valera was to re-arrange the Old Testament books according to Protestant usage.

As for the notes, Reina is at pains to explain that the majority are explanations of Hebraisms, the best Spanish translation being given in the text, and the literal Hebrew in the margins. Notes of a doctrinal nature were omitted, for reasons of space, claims Reina, but the attitude of the authorities in Basle must have been as important a consideration. Cassiodoro says that he hoped to print these in a separate work at a later date. In fact, a few lengthier notes which would not fit into the margins were printed on two leaves (one page being blank) and bound into some copies of his Bible. One supposes that the two commentaries, on John's Gospel, and on Matthew IV, published in 1573, were the only parts of this project that ever were produced.

# IV

# From the Completion of his Bible
# to his Arrival in Antwerp

His great task accomplished, Casiodoro set out with his family from Basle for Frankfurt, calling at Strassburg on the way. From there he wrote to Theodor Zwinger on 13 July 1570, returning the thirty florins he had borrowed from him, since Marcos Pérez had given him a more than adequate provision for the journey.[1] He was in Frankfurt before the end of the month. On 1 August 1570 he requested the grant of citizenship from Frankfurt City Council, which was refused for the time being, although the right to live there was granted.[2] On 7 August he wrote to Hubert explaining this and describing the rigours of the journey. He mentioned that his weaker children had not stood up to the journey very well. From this we deduce that already he had more than the one son he is known for certain to have had. Of these, only Marcus appears to have survived infancy in any case.[3] Otherwise, the letter is concerned with the difficulty of finding accommodation at reasonable cost, because of the many travellers and the influx of refugees from Cologne, and with a detailed request for a large supply of tallow candles together with a careful explanation of how to convey them to him via Joseph Heidelberger, a customs official.

Friends in Frankfurt, presumably of the Reformed Church, had received him well, but in view of the opposition of well-known Calvinists such as Beza, Cousin, des Gallars, and Olevianus, they were hesitant about allowing him into the full fellowship of the church, and they were particularly reluctant to allow him to take communion before they had once more investigated his morals and his doctrine.[4] The pastors of the French Church, Jean Salvard and Théo-

[1] Basle Public Library, Fr. Gryn., ii, 26, fol. 42; *Bib. Wif.*, II, 224.

[2] Frankfurt City Archives, Bürgerbuch 1570, fol. 58ᵛ:
Dienstag der 1 Augusti Anno C. 1570. Als cassiodorus Reynius um die Bürgerschaft gebetten. soll man Ime sein bitt abschlagen.

[3] Strassburg, AST 161/94:
Appulimus tandem Francofortum incolumes, Xto ductore, licet pueri teneriores ex molestia itineris eiusque incommodis nonnihil ægrotarunt.
In Reina's Preface to *Expositio primæ partis capitis quarti Matthæi*, fol. a2ʳ, a similar passage, referring to several of his children alive during the period of his stay in Basle, leads to the same conclusion, that only Marcus survived from this time:
quum me gravissimus ac plane letalis morbus Basileam cum uxore et familiola recenter ingressum corripuisset? . . . Uxoris et parvulorum liberorum memoria.
His family was well-documented as its members grew up in Frankfurt, and Marcus is the only one not listed as born in that city.

[4] Strassburg, AST 161/94:
Exceperunt nos amici Francofortenses qua solent charitate, qua quidem & nunc etiam commodum utimur.

phile de Banos, made enquiries about him in various quarters. They received replies from Cousin in London, together with the documents of the Bishop's commission of enquiry held in 1563 (which Reina carefully copied); from Nicolas Balbani, Italian minister in Geneva, from Olevianus, and from Beza. Against the wishes of the last named, they finally decided to admit Reina into fellowship, issuing a certificate to that effect on 12 July 1571.[5] Olevianus's letter is the one which we have already considered, concerned with Reina's visit to Heidelberg.

Accordingly, on 12 July 1571, so that he could be received as a full member by the French Church of Frankfurt, Reina addressed a doctrinal declaration to Beza.[6] It goes over exactly the same ground which had been gone over before in the declaration of faith made at Strassburg. This does not seem to have satisfied Beza, for, on 25 November 1571, Reina wrote again to him, apologising for the petition in his favour that had been sent in the meantime, about which he had known nothing.[7] This letter makes clear that the French Church had accepted Reina to take communion in spite of Beza's opposition.[8] The members had insisted on his writing to Beza to attempt to put matters right between them, which he did willingly, although he felt that there was nothing more that needed to be said. They had insisted too on a declaration of innocence of the charge of sodomy, which he also wrote out formally and deposited in the archives on the same date.[9] It is a categorical denial of the charge, declaring it

---

[5] O. Fatio & O. Labarthe, *Registres de la Compagnie des Pasteurs de Genève* (Geneva, 1969), III, 30, 211f; Jean-François Salvard, dit Dupalmier, was sent from Geneva to Frankfurt in the spring of 1571 and stayed till 1576; Théophile de Banos was originally from Bordeaux, studied in Paris and Heidelberg, going in 1570 to Frankfurt and staying till 1580, when he went to the University of Basle. Their enquiry is the origin of the file on Reina which has been called the 'Frankfurt documents'. The certificate is transcribed in Appendix III, together with other items from these documents.

[6] Geneva, Corres. eccl., MS fr 407, fol. 18ʳ-19ᵛ; *Bib. Wif.*, II, 216.

[7] Geneva, Corres. eccl., MS fr 407, fol. 21ʳ; *Bib. Wif.*, II, 219:

Ces jours ici estant au point d'aler à la communion de la Cene du Seigneur, le Consistoire de l'Eglise françoise de ceste ville, ayant entendu qu'il y a eu par le passé entre vous et moi quelques differents, par l'esgard de leur office et de ma conscience m'ont requis qu'avant que d'aler à la Cene j'eusse à vous escrire quelques lettres de reconciliation, ce que je fais mantenant volontiers, veu qu'en cela je ne suis pas requis que de mon devoir, encores que j'aie desja a mon advis souffisanment acquitté ma conscience en cest endroit . . . Quant à la lettre que quelques uns de mes amis, à ce qui semble, de par deça ont envoyée à Geneve, dont j'entens qu'il y en a eu plusiers offenses, vous veus que je aussi certifier devant Dieu qu'elle n'a point esté faite ne de ma volonté ne de mon conseil ne de mon seu, et que mesmes il m'a despleu et desplait encores, qu'elle aie esté faite.

[8] See also Hessels, II, 372f:

Cassiodore ayant beaucoup tournoyé, et non, comme ie croy, sans quelque efficace enuers ceulx quj ne ueulent croire conseil, dit en fin qu'il ira pardela pour se purger. Dieu uielle le lauer si a tort on luj a mis ceste tache, sinon, le plonger du tout et noyer en son ordure affin qu'il n'en infecte des aultres plus auant. J'en ay aduertj ceux quj m'en ont escrit. Ils en feront ce qu'ils uouldront (letter of Beza to Jean Cousin, 1571).

[9] This declaration exists in two autograph copies made by Reina. One was sent to Beza, and is preserved in Geneva (Corres. eccl. MS fr., 407, fol. 20ʳ); the other was kept by the French Reformed Church of Frankfurt (Frankfurt docts., fol. 615ʳ). It was published by Boehmer (*Bib. Wif.*, II, 220f).

to be pure calumny; he was innocent of both the act and the desire. It includes a clinical analysis of just what he had meant when he had used the word 'pollution'. He had made similar declarations before, including several outright denials made to the consistory of the French Church in London. As a result of them he had been admitted to communion in London, Bergerac, and Montargis.

Beza continued to be unconvinced, and on 21 December Casiodoro wrote to him once more, protesting his innocence with regard to both doctrine and behaviour. He felt that he had made abundant satisfaction on this score and he was rather hurt that Beza and des Gallars seemed still to be unconvinced.[10] Beza replied on 25 December 1571, and it is difficult to decide whether his letter was ironic or sincere. He insists that it was high time that Reina had himself officially purged of the crime of which he was accused; when this was done he would embrace him with true charity. Reina's friendship with Corro was a further reason for continuing suspicion.[11] There must have been another letter from Reina to Beza which has not survived, for on 9 March 1572 Beza wrote once more in a very similar vein, though rather more sharply, revealing an animosity against Spanish refugees, but none the less hoping that eventually Reina would be cleared.[12]

Meanwhile, in August 1571, another son was born to Casiodoro's wife. He was baptized Augustus, on 16 August 1571.[13] His godfather was Augustin Legrand, and ever afterwards he was called Augustino. One is justified in supposing the entry of Augustus in the register to be a slip of the pen.

On the same day as the baptism Casiodoro's request for citizenship of Frankfurt was finally granted. He remained proud of this right to the end of his life.

In 1573 Reina's only daughter, Margarethe, was born.[14]

This year also saw the publication of two commentaries by Reina on parts of the New Testament. Both are of exactly the same format, and all copies so far found have been bound together in one volume. Both are in Latin. The gospel text printed is a Latin translation made direct from the Syriac version by Tremellius, of which Reina apparently had a manuscript copy.[15]

---

[10] Frankfurt docts., fol. 617-20.

[11] Frankfurt docts., fol. 631f.

[12] Frankfurt docts., fol. 623-6 :

Vous avez trotté, comme vostre compagnon Corran, d'Orient en Occident, et quoy que soit, vous aultres trouvez tousjours moyen d'eschaper là-où les aultres demeurent . . . Je serai bien aise d'entendre que vous en soyez bien purgé plustost que conveincu . . . le bien vostre quand vous servirez à Dieu bien droictement.

[13] Most of the Frankfurt records of births and deaths were destroyed during the 1939-45 War. Herr Georg Itzerott had, however, made extensive extracts from the registers for his genealogical studies, and these remain. Thanks are due to him for the generous manner in which he made his transcripts available for this study. All references to births and deaths in Frankfurt which carry no special note must be assumed to come from Herr Itzerott's materials. The registers are unusual, in that the dates of birth and dates of death as such are not recorded, but the dates of baptism and burial respectively, which normally took place a few days later.

[14] Frankfurt City Archives, Bürgerbuch, vi (1540-85), fol. 235ʳ :

Hispalis. Cassiodorus Reinius Hispalensis Ist frembt zum Bürger angenommen worden. Iuravit Iovis 16ᵃ Augusti anno 71.

Herr Itzerott has no day or month for this birth/baptism.

[15] See the Preface to Reina's book, fol. a2ʳf. John Emmanuel Tremellius was born in

One of these works is a commentary on John's Gospel entitled, *Evangelium Ioannis: hoc est, justa ac vetus Apologia pro æterna Christi Divinitate, atque adeo, quatenus unum cum eo est, Æqualitate cum Patre: adversus impietatem Iudæorum, Cerinthi, Ebionitarum, Arrii, Mahumethis demum, & illorum scholæ, cum veteris, tum novæ. Ex Novo Testamento Syro a Viris doctis nuper Latinitati donato: cum diversa lectione ex Græcis, si quando illa secus habeant, ad marginem apposita: & argumentis capitum, & annotationibus in quibusdam locis selectioribus. Nonnula insuper adiecta sequens pagina indicat. Per Cassiodorum Reinum Theologiæ studiosum.* It is a well-printed quarto book, consisting of a ten-page dedicatory epistle (numbered a 2 recto – [b 3] verso); a twelve-page preface (numbered 1-12); the commentary occupying 163 pages (numbered 13-177); and a personal apostrophe to the opponents addressed by the work, occupying three pages (numbered 175, 176, 180 instead of 178-180). As its title indicates, the aim of the commentary is particularly to prove the divinity of Christ against the Jews, the Moslems, and a variety of Christian sects which hold the contrary view. The dedicatory epistle is addressed to Johan Sturm, and is particularly interesting because of the biographical detail it provides, especially about the short period of Reina's life that was spent in Strassburg.

In the commentary itself, Reina's insistent Trinitarianism makes one wonder why it was ever possible to accuse him of contrary views. Yet, in refuting and rejecting the doctrines of Jews, Ebionites, Moslems, Arians, and Roman Catholics, he is never abusive or violent. His eirenic spirit is evident in the courtesy with which he deals with views different from those he is putting forward. He specifically mentions Servetus's ideas to refute them, although it is to be noted that he does not condemn them as impious. Another point worthy of notice is that Reina several times refers to the Hebrew of the Old Testament and to the Hebræo-Syriac forms behind the translation of Tremellius that he is using, in such a way as to demonstrate his familiarity with the languages. This makes nonsense of Menéndez Pelayo's claim that Reina knew very little Hebrew.[16]

The other book was a commentary on the fourth chapter of Matthew's Gospel, entitled, *Expositio primæ partis Capitis Quarti Matthæi, commonefactoria ad Ecclesiam Christi, De periculis piorum Ministrorum Verbi in tempore cavendis. Per Cassiodorum Reinium Theologiæ studiosum.* This short work is really an integral part of the above-mentioned commentary. It contains twenty-two pages, consisting of a three-page dedication (on unnumbered pages 3-5), and the commentary, which occupies pages 6-22. The dedicatory epistle is addressed to the Basle professors, Simon Sulzer and Huldrich Koechlein, and it is interesting for the autobiographical detail it gives concerning Reina's con-

---

1510, the son of a Jew in Ferrara, and therefore he was possibly a Spanish-speaker, since this was a centre of the exiled Sephardim. He became a Christian and joined the Reformed Church. After some time in Strassburg, he became a lecturer in Hebrew at Cambridge, but had leave under the Marian persecutions. He spent time in Heidelberg, Metz, and Sedan. He published a Syriac New Testament in Paris in 1569, and died in 1580. Reina apparently had access to the manuscript of a Latin version made by Tremellius directly from the Syriac.

[16] *Heterodoxos*, V, 154f; see, for example, in the Commentary, pp. 21, 23, 32, 33f, 54, 61, 73, 75, 120, 150.

nexion with Basle at the time of the production of his Bible. Great tribute is paid to the two ministers for their help and advice at that time.

The commentary follows the same pattern as that on John's Gospel. The intention of the work is, as its title shews, to make ministers aware of the dangers attendant upon the ministry. The Temptations of Christ are used by analogy to warn of the temptations that beset the Christian pastor. It began, according to the preface, as annotations on the Bible, but got too long, and so he issued it as a separate book.[17]

Both commentaries were printed by Nicholas Bassée, originally of Valenciennes. Elsewhere we are told that Reina translated Spanish works for Bassée.[18]

It is not very clear how Reina earned his livelihood at this stage, but he appears to have continued to be active in the silk and the book trades.[19] The spring and autumn fairs at Frankfurt were great centres for the supply of books in the unbound state. He mentions the sale of some of Oporinus's books in a letter to Theodor Zwinger and Adam Petri, dated 9 March 1574.[20] Zwinger was Oporinus's nephew and apparently had the task of disposing of his library to help to pay his debts. Further mention of these books is made in letters to Zwinger, dated 24 September 1574, 27 October 1574, 23 November 1574, and 6 April 1575.[21]

In a letter to Hubert, dated 12 April 1574, Reina spoke of a plan to publish a life of Bucer, which was apparently well-advanced. In fact Beza's letter of 23 June 1565 had spoken of the plan in vaguer terms. No trace remains, in any case, of such a book by Reina, if one was ever published. However, in 1577 Hubert published in Basle a book in memory of Bucer, entitled, *Martini Buceri Scripta Anglicana fere omnia Iis etiam, quæ hactenus vel nondum, vel sparsim, vel peregrino saltem idiomate edita fuere, adiunctis A Con. Huberto . . . Adiuncta est Historia de Obitu Buceri . . .*, which has two dedications, one by Hubert to Grindal, and a second one by Johan Sturm to Francis Walsingham, and bears testimonies to Bucer by Marbach, Matthias Ritter, Johan Sturm, and others. This book could well be the one referred to; at least, there is sufficient in it to suggest the possibility. In the letter of 12 April Reina mentions a recent visit to Strassburg, and that he was now sending a copy of his *Evangelium Ioannis* to Hubert by Theodosius Richelius.[22]

The letter to Zwinger, dated 27 October 1574, also gives the information that Reina was preparing an edition of the *Bibliotheca Sacra* of Sixtus Senensis, to which he was adding a 'theological antidote'. This edition appeared in two volumes printed by Bassée in 1575, with no sign of the antidote, and, indeed, only a four-page appendix in Latin at the very end which can be attributed to Reina.[23]

---

[17] Preface to this Commentary, fol. a3.
[18] A. Dietz, *Frankfurter Handelsgeschichte* (Frankfurt, 1910), III, 34.
[19] *Evangelium Ioannis,* fol. a2$^r$.
[20] Basle, Fr. Gryn. II/26, fol. 43$^r$f; *Bib. Wif.*, II, 224f.
[21] Fr. Gryn. II/26, fol. 44-47; *Bib. Wif.*, II, 225-8.
[22] Strassburg, AST 161/95.
[23] *Bib. Wif.*, II, 226, 303. *Bibliotheca Sancta a F. Sixto Senensi . . . ex præcipuis catholicæ ecclesiæ autoribus collecta. Secunda editio, in qua adiecta est tabula Chrono-*

On 22 October 1575 another son, Servas, was baptized. His godfather was Servas Marell, a Walloon merchant.

Further mention is made of the sale of books in a letter to Zwinger, dated 22 April 1576, and again on 7 April 1577.[24]

Some time in mid-1557, a chance arose for Reina to go to Poland. From a letter to Zwinger dated 23 September 1577, it appears that he had put in a request to be considered and wished for a recommendation from Zwinger.[25] The matter is further mentioned on 1 April 1578, where it appears that a Pole named Nicolas Firlei had some part in the negotiations. After this no further mention is made of that country, and, since Casiodoro stayed in Frankfurt, we must suppose that the negotiations came to nothing.[26]

In 1577 Reina printed in Frankfurt an edition of the Spanish Confession of London of 1559. It would seem that this was the first time it had appeared in print. Boehmer reports a copy of it in the University Library of Frankfurt, but it is no longer to be found there, and no other copies of it seem to have survived.[27]

There are in the City Archives of Frankfurt, amongst the legal documents preserved there, the records of a long legal battle between Reina and Helias von Offenbacs, a Licentiate in Law. In August 1577 Reina had rented from Offen-

---

*graphica.* Copies of this edition which contain the leaves signed Qqq, by which Boehmer established Reina's connexion with the edition, are not to be found.

[24] Basle, Fr. Gryn., II/27, fol. 212-3; *Bib. Wif.,* II, 228f.

[25] Fr. Gryn., II/26, fol. 48; *Bib. Wif.,* II, 229:
Quod attinet profectionem meam in Poloniam, res adhuc sub deliberatione est. Neque enim tam difficilem et multis nominibus laboriesam provinciam temere suscipiendam arbitror, in hac præsertim ætate, quantumvis conditio sit amplissima et valde honorifica. Cæterum, si Deus ita disposuerit, ut abeam, senties in illo tuo negotio haud frustra te meam coluisse amicitiam, atque de bono successu nihil dubito, cum sciam negotium tibi esse cum viro bono.

[26] Basle, Fr. Gryn., II/33, fol. 241; *Bib. Wif.,* II, 229f:
De mea profectione in Poloniam nosse cupis? Quiesco. Idque non sine Dei providentia, ut semper alias, qui meas sortes in manu habens, et quidem valde commendatas, eas gubernat pro sua voluntate. Si illuc venissem, sensisses fructum commendationis tuæ cum D. Firleio in illo negotio, de quo intelligo nundum tibi satisfactum.
Ersch & Gruber, *Allgemeine Encyklopädie* (Liepzig, 1846), ad loc. The Firley family owned lands at a place in Poland of the same name. Johann Firley accepted the Reformation, and filled the livings he controlled with Protestant incumbents. His son became a Roman Catholic in 1569 and reversed Johann's policy, giving the livings to Roman Catholics as they became vacant.

[27] Boehmer gives its title in *Bib. Wif.,* II, 232, *Declaracion, o confession de fe hecha por ciertos fieles Españoles, que huyendo los abusos de la iglesia Romana, y la crueldad de la Inquisicion d'España hizieron a la Iglesia de los fieles para ser recebidos por hermanos en Christo. Declaranse en este perqueño [sic] volumen los principales Fundamentos de la Fe y Religion Christiana necessarios a la Salud conforme a la Diuina Escriptura de donde son sacados con toda fidelidad y breuedad.* The Library of the University of Halle has a later edition with a parallel German translation, *Confession de fe Christiana, hecha por ciertos fieles Espannoles, los qvales hvyendo los abvsos de la Iglesia Romana, y la crueldad de la Inquisition d'España, dexaron su patria, para ser recebidos de la Iglesia de los fieles por hermanos en Christo* (Cassel, 1601), and the British Museum has a German translation, *Christlich und in Gottes Wort wohlgegründtes Glaubensbekäntnuß Der verfolgten Evangelischen Kirchen in und ausser Hispanien* (Amberg, 1611).

bacs a store in the Haus der Groll to keep books to be sold at the fair. Offenbacs had locked the books in the store and would not release them. Reina naturally wanted them for sale. The case was still dragging on on 13 May 1579, with no apparent progress being made.[28]

On 15 December 1577, another of Reina's sons, Johan, was baptized. His godfather was Johan Bode, another Walloon merchant of Frankfurt.

There is a further letter to Zwinger, dated 13 April 1578, dealing with book matters.[29]

On 22 September 1578, Casiodoro acted as Augustin Legrand's agent in the sale of a house, the Haus Braunfels, on the Liebfrauenberg, at the corner of the Neue Kräme. This was sold to the patrician, Nikolaus Greiff, for three thousand florins. This is of interest because in later years Reina had an apartment in that massive four-storey, arcaded, stone-built gothic town house, with great court-yards and large warehouses. In 1578, French services were held in the house, presumably before the sale.[30]

Up to this point, Casiodoro seems to have remained a member of the French Reformed Church, and to have preached occasionally in French, and possibly even in Spanish, although he was not officially one of its ministers. He had, of course, been a minister, and had never been removed from the ranks of the ministry – except that his situation with regard to the London scandal had still not been regulated. There are signs, however, of his growing sympathy with the Lutheran party, and at this time he became extremely friendly with Matthias Ritter the Younger, the (Lutheran) Superintendent of Foreign Congregations in Frankfurt.[31]

Hence, when an opportunity arose in 1578 for him to become a French preacher of the Lutheran Church in Antwerp, he shewed interest. This church called itself the Evangelical Church of the Confession of Augsburg, and its Calvinist opponents called it 'Martinist' or 'Confessionist'. This was a serious offer, and Reina, who had never ceased to desire the full-time ministry, was determined to accept. Lutheran refugees from Antwerp, who had been in Frankfurt since 1567, and who were returning now that the situation was easier, asked him to go with them as their pastor. It became imperative to have a settlement of the London matter, which had been hanging over his head now for some fifteen years. Leaving his family in Frankfurt, he set out for England to present himself in London for a trial of his case.[32]

He travelled to England in late 1578. On the way he passed through Antwerp, from where he wrote to Matthias Ritter on 6 November. He had had an eigh-teen-day boat journey, but had been well received by the brethren. The church in Antwerp was in a poor way and short of ministers. The harvest was great, the labourers few, the difficulties many. If he could return from England

---

[28] Frankfurt City Archives, Judicialia R 226, Acta Cassiodori Reinij Contra Heliam von Offenbacs der Rechtenlicentiater.

[29] Basle, Fr. Gryn., II/26, fol. 49; *Bib. Wif.*, II, 230f.

[30] Dietz II, 62, 67; *Baudenkmäler in Frankfurt* (Frankfurt, 1914), III, 62; *Bilder zur Frankfurter Geschichte* (Frankfurt, 1950), p. 32, has a picture of the house.

[31] *Allgemeine Deutsche Biographie*, article entitled 'Cassiodorus Reinius'.

[32] H. Dechent, *Kirchengeschichte von Frankfurt* (Frankfurt, 1913), I, 235.

cleared of the long-standing charges, he would attack the work with vigour.[33]

On Saturday, 13 December 1578, Grindal, by now Archbishop of Canterbury, sent out a letter to all foreign churches of London : because a position in Belgium was being offered to him, Casiodoro had come of his own free will to have his case examined, so that he might with a clear conscience accept the proposal. Any who had anything against him were called to testify on Thursday, 18 December 1578 at 2 p.m. at Lambeth Palace.[34] The minutes of both the French and the Dutch consistories were sent for (and as a result the relevant sections of both were lost to posterity). Cousin and Utenhovius were both now dead, otherwise the affair might not have gone so well for Reina.

The French Church was now under the pastorate of Robert le Maçon de la Fontaine, and its members were not happy at this turn of events. Their main contention seemed to be that Reina had now drawn closer to the German Lutheran position and was to take up a ministry in Antwerp in opposition to the Calvinist churches.

On 15 January 1579, Bernardo de Mendoza, the Spanish Ambassador to England, wrote to Gabriel de Zayas, the Secretary to the King of Spain, that Casiodoro had returned with letters from Johan Sturm, one of the heresiarchs of Germany, in consequence of which he was being favoured by some of the principal people in London. On 22 February a further letter informed the same addressee that Reina had been boasting that he had brought with him numerous copies of his version of the Bible, which he intended to send to Spain. Mendoza said he would try to discover what ships were taking them there.[35] Reina must have brought certain copies for presentation as well, and this was no doubt the time when he made presents of various copies of his two commentaries.[36]

The affair dragged on, till finally, on 13 March 1578/9, in the presence of the Archbishop, Dr William Lewin (Luinius) put five questions to Reina concerning his understanding of the eucharist.[37] He answered satisfactorily in a completely Calvinist manner, and signed a declaration stating that what he had

---

[33] Lehnemann, p. 101; ZHT, 50 (1870), pp. 286f :

Post diuturnam et valde molestam navigationem appuli tandem Antuerpiam 18 die a meo a vobis discessu. Exceptus amantissime a fratribus, incepi ex eisdem cognoscere de huius ecclesiæ statu, non malo sane, nisi tanta penuria ministrorum laborarent. Res est plane digna lacrymis, videre fruges, ad messem præmaturas, in tanta copia propemodum perire ob messorum fidelium paucitatem, cum præsertim neque in ea paucitate omnes pro officio sint frugi . . . Quod ad me attinet, ad novam eamque multo difficiliorem profectionem iam accingor, in Angliam nimirum, veteres ibi in me calumnias olim congestas præsentia mea depulsurus, ita exigente ministerii mei conditione. Ab his si, (uti de Deo et mea innocentia spero) liber revertar, supponam hinc oneri libens humerum, cum magna etiam atque certa spe fructus.

[34] Hessels, II, 629f.

[35] CSP(Sp), II, 630, 635; Col. doc. inéd., XCI, 311; J. B. Avalle-Arce, 'Dos notas', Filología, 8 (1962), p. 22.

[36] For the Bible, see note 72 to Chapter II. Copies of the commentaries in Lambeth Palace Library and Sidney Sussex College, Cambridge, bear the inscription 'Ex dono Cassiodori Reinii'.

[37] William Lewin (d. 1598) was an advocate, and held the appointments as Dean of Peculiars and Judge of the Prerogative Court of Canterbury from 1576 till his death. He was a friend of Johan Sturm (Zurich Letters, II, 276, 281, 285).

answered should be understood to conform to the Helvetic Confession, and to the confessions of the Church of England and of the London French Church. On 19 March he further signed a document in which he accepted the Helvetic Confession as orthodox and in conformity with the word of God.[38] One cannot help feeling, as did the London French, that the signature in London of a Calvinist confession of faith was a strange prelude to acceptance of a Lutheran pastorate in Antwerp!

That Casiodoro was living in comparative indigence at this time is indicated by an entry in a disbursement book of the period; on 10 March 1578 he was paid ten shillings by Robert Nowell, brother of Alexander Nowell, the Dean of St Paul's. The book also records sums given about the same time to Corro, and from this we can suppose that the two had some contact.[39] Nevertheless, it is rather significant that when, at the end of the trial, Casiodoro wanted a helper, it was Valera, not Corro, who came forward.

Antonio del Corro had come to London some time early in 1567 and had found the Spanish Church, of which Reina had been the pastor, disbanded and its members split into two factions. The pro-Reina party, whose protagonist was the ex-prior of San Isidro, Francisco Farías, worshipped at the Italian Church, and the anti-Reina party worshipped with the French, their main spokesman being Balthasar Sánchez. Corro tried to call the Spanish Church together again with some success, but, after considerable upheaval in the Strangers' Churches on his account, he had despaired of his position in the Calvinist ranks and had passed into Anglicanism. After a period as reader at the Inns of Court, he was now beginning a period as lecturer in theology at Oxford. It may be that his duties did not permit him to be with his friend at this time. In any case, the bitter opposition of the Strangers' Churches to Corro might have increased Reina's difficulties, had he stood with him.[40]

The trial of Reina's case was formally over at the end of March, and had turned out to his entire satisfaction. At least, he had an official clearance (or purgation) of the charges, and was theoretically in good standing with the Calvinists. Accordingly, he presented himself to the French Consistory on 22 March 1578/9 with three witnesses, two of whom were Cipriano de Valera and Antonio Giustiniano, saying that he had pressing reasons to return to Germany

[38] These questions and declarations were published later in Antwerp by Reina's opponents in a trilingual text (Latin/Flemish/French), presumably with the intention of harming him in some way. A unique copy exists in Leyden University, Catalogus van pamfletten 303, *Confessio in articulo de Coena, Cassiodori Reinii Hispani, Ministri in ea Ecclesia quæ Antuerpiæ se Augustanam Confessionem profiteri dicit, quam si eius Symmistæ sincerè profitentur, sublata erit inter eos & Ecclesiarum reformatarum Ministros controuersia* [? 1579] fol. A2ᵛ:

Ie Cassiodore Reine Hespaignol bourgeois de Francfort, Ministre de la parolle de Dieu, ai leu ceste Confession des Eglises de Suisse, laquell i'approuue comme Orthodoxe, conforme & accordante à la parolle de Dieu, & à icelle ie soubscri de coeur en tout & part tout, à Londres ce 19. Mars 1579. Et dessoubs estoit escrit: Cassiodorus Reinius.

[39] A. B. Grosart (editor), *The Towneley Hall MSS: The Spending of the Money of Robert Nowell* (Blackburn, 1877), p. 62. Robert Nowell was the brother of Alexander Nowell, who became Dean of St Paul's after a period as a Marian exile in Strassburg and Frankfurt.

[40] MacFadden, pp. 298-345.

65

(his wife was ill) and that he wished to be reconciled, on the terms of the Archbishop's judgement, with the church that had caused him so much trouble.[41] The French refused entry to his friends, and were unwilling to accept his terms, which they saw as a demand, almost a threat, whereas they considered that he ought to have adopted an attitude of respectful humility.[42] As he saw it, he had made sufficient gestures in that direction before being admitted to communion in Frankfurt, and also the Archbishop's judgement gave him certain rights. To their objections that he was now going over to the Lutherans, he replied that the Lutheran Church was just as much a church as theirs, and, if they did not accept him, he must go where he was accepted. He had expressed his reserves on various eucharistic points, viz. impanation and ubiquity, and was still acceptable to the Lutherans. In any case, his appointment in Antwerp was still not mutually decided.[43] The French Consistory was disposed to insist on an expression of repentance, which Casiodoro was not prepared to make, as he did not consider it necessary. He said he was not content. The reply was that he would have to be so, because that was all they were prepared to do. On that unsatisfactory note the matter ended, and Reina left for the Continent.

It seems that he went to Frankfurt first, to visit his sick wife, and, because she was sick, he left her there, and went on to Antwerp to take up his appointment.

[41] Schickler, II, 232-5:

Il nous requérait lui faire cette faveur, et aussi lui semblait bien raisonnable, vu la sentence qu'il a obtenue, d'avoir bonne opinion de lui et le tenir en même rang et estimation qu'il avait eus auparavant . . . Il ne demandait rien sinon que nous le voulussions tenir et reconnaître pour inculpable et innocent et, pour l'écrire en peu de mots, pour frère et homme de bien.

[42] Schickler, II, 235:

Incontinent après nous n'avons pas failli d'estre importunés de l'admettre et recognoistre comme frère, premièrement par quelques-uns de la cour qui ont trouvé fort mauvais nostre refus, puis par Mgr. l'archevesque, lequel ayant de bonne heure faict advertir de ma résolution par s'estre animé et remonstré le danger qui en pouvoit venir néantmoins m'appela pour ce faict, mais ayant bien entendu nos raisons, je l'en rendis fort content . . . Cassiodore puis après se présenta en ma compagnye, demandant, voire la verge à la main, que nous eussions à le tenir en pareil rang et degré qu'il avoit esté auparavant. Nous luy parlasmes à bon escient de la reconnaissance de ses faultes, puis luy deslarasmes avec la conclusion pourquoy ne le pouvions nullement admettre. Ce ne fut pas sans de grandes complaintes : mays peu de jours après touttefoys il repartit sans nous molester davantage. J'ay eu aussi quelques craintes qu'il se voulût icy nischer (letter of the French minister, Le Maçon de la Fontaine, to Beza).

[43] Schickler, II, 234:

Sur ce il remarqua que ce n'était pas ce qu'il requérait de nous, car ce serait une chose inique et injuste que nous fussions autrement, mais qu'il avait estimé que, par la sentance des juges, si nous avions conçu quelque mauvaise opinion de lui, le tout maintenant devait être effacé. Puis, déclarant qu'il ne lui était rien advenu que ce qu'il pouvait avouer à tout homme, dit qu'on lui ferait tort si on pensait qu'il aurait besoin de telle avertissement qu'icelui qu'on lui avait fait; et, poursuivant son propos, dit quant à M. de Bèze qu'il a eu son consentement et par l'avis de gens graves la chose avait été débattue, il avait depuis été admis à la Cène à Francfort. Que n'étant reçu de la communion de l'Eglise française [that is, as a minister] il fut contraint de s'adresser à ceux de la Confession d'Augsbourg qu'il reconnaît aussi bien Eglise comme la nôtre, et parlant aux ministres (dont il ne se repent point) il aurait nommément résisté l'ubiquité et impanation. Quant à ceux d'Anvers, qu'il avait voirement été appelé d'eux pour les enseigner, mais qu'il n'avait encore rien résolu avec eux (quoting the Minutes of the French Consistory, French modernized).

# V

# From Antwerp till his Death in Frankfurt

Circumstances in Antwerp had continued their erratic course, as far as religion and politics were concerned. The great reversal of Protestant fortunes in 1568, which resulted in the loss of 10,000 inhabitants out of a total of 90,000 when it capitulated to the Spanish troops in the Duke of Alva's campaign, and during which time Marcos Pérez had been expelled, had been followed by Alva's governorship of terror and the 'Spanish Fury' of November 1576, and further depopulation.

On 8 November 1576 the States-General accepted the idea of a religious peace settlement, known as the Pacification of Ghent. Although this favoured the Roman Catholic religion, it tolerated the presence of Protestants in such places as they were already established. In the two northern provinces, exceptionally, the Roman Catholic religion was banned altogether. It insisted on the removal of Spanish soldiers, and the suppression of the laws against heresy and the repeal of Alva's criminal ordinances. Philip II sent his brother, Don John of Austria, as governor with a mission of peace, to counteract Alva's excesses.[1]

On 12 February 1577, at Marche-en-Famenne, Don John of Austria signed an act, called the Perpetual Edict, by which he approved the Pacification of Ghent, and promised the removal of Spanish troops within twenty days, and of foreign soldiers as soon as they had been paid; and the States-General promised to obey the king, to maintain and propagate the Roman Catholic faith, and to pay off the troops. Don John did not like having to do this, and thus the king dismissed him. The suggestion was made that the Archduke Matthias, brother of the Emperor Rudolph, would be an acceptable substitute, provided that Maurice of Nassau was Lieutenant-Governor.[2]

On 10 December 1577 the States-General began to collect signatures for what is known as the New Union of Brussels, which was based on the Pacification of Ghent. Signature of the New Union implied acceptance of the Pacification. Although it gave a very privileged position to the Roman Catholic religion, it also gave limited recognition to Protestants, who promised not to 'violer, grever, ou endommager ceulx de ladite Religion Catholique Romaine ou par aulcun destourber lexercise dicelle'.[3] On 17 December 1577 the Archduke Matthias accepted the New Union of Brussels. Thereafter conditions improved for the Protestants, to such an extent that on 16 March 1578 there were fifteen Protestant preaching places in the city, and these were apparently not enough. On 18 May 1578 the Calvinists had the temerity to seize churches for them-

---

[1] E. Gossart, *La Domination espagnole dans les Pays-Bas* (Brussels, 1906), pp. 37-47.
[2] A. C. de Schrevel, *Recueil de documents relatifs aux Troubles* (Bruges, 1921), pp. 120f.
[3] De Schrevel, p. 123.

selves and to help to expel the Jesuits and Friars Minor from the city for their refusal to accept the Pacification of Ghent. On 29 August a provisional religious peace was declared in the city, under the terms of which the Calvinists got four churches for their use, including the cathedral nave, the Roman Catholics being relegated to the side-chapels. On the same date the Lutherans signed an agreement of twelve articles with the Antwerp City Council, and on 6 September to the above-mentioned churches held by Protestants were added three for the use of Lutherans, viz : St Michael's Convent, the Droogscherders' (Drapers') Guild chapel, and the Hessenhuis. On 18 September 1578 Prince Maurice and his brother Jan van Nassau entered the city. On 20 October the Lutherans asked for larger premises, and on 22 October they were granted additional places for the exercise of their worship, the Carmelite refectory and the nave of St George's Church.[4]

In May 1579 there began the religious consultations of Cologne, which caused great concern amongst the Protestants of Antwerp, so much so that the Ascension Day procession on 28 May in which the Archduke Matthias was taking part was dispersed by armed Calvinists and the Archduke locked in a church.[5]

The situation settled down somewhat when on 12 July 1579 a religious peace-settlement was drawn up and published by Prince Maurice in Antwerp, under the terms of which freedom of religion was granted to Roman Catholics, Calvinists, and Lutherans : each had schools, churches, and hospitals, the right to preach and teach, and to conduct weddings and funerals, etc. A commission of nine (three Roman Catholics, three Calvinists, and three Lutherans) was set up to watch over matters of religious peace.[6]

The assembly in Cologne went on till January 1580. It is claimed that Casiodoro and some of his congregation went to Cologne to attend the meetings and to know what went on there. Certainly on 27 June 1579 Reina wrote to Matthias Ritter from Cologne. This was in any case before his official appointment to the pastorate of Antwerp.[7] There is evidence that he stayed in Cologne to wait for a call from his Antwerp congregation, and that he began to preach in December 1579. When he did arrive in Antwerp, he exercised his ministry in the refectory of the Carmelite convent. A copy of the Antwerp Lutheran articles of 1578, which all ministers were expected to sign on appointment, had been published. Presumably, therefore, in accordance with these, Reina signed his acceptance of the Confession of Augsburg and that church's discipline.[8]

[4] E. de Moreau, *Histoire de l'Eglise en Belgique* (Brussels, 1952), V, 154; F. Prims, *De Groote Cultuurstrijd* (no date or place), I, 53, 78, 81; J. C. Diercxsens, *Antverpia Christo nascens et crescens* (Antwerp, 1773), V, 302.

[5] M. Lossen, 'Aggäus Albada unter der Kölner Pacificationscongreß', 5th series, Year 6 (Liepzig, 1876), p. 280.

[6] Diercxsens, V, 364; F. Prims, 'Incident uit de Religionsvrede', *Bijdragen tot de Geschiedenis*, Reeks III, Year 5 (Antwerp/Ghent, 1953), pp. 14-16.

[7] *ZHT*, 50 (1870), p. 288.

[8] *Bib. Wif.*, II, 180; Lehnemann, p. 82; F. J. D. Nieuwenhuis, *Geschiedenis der Amsterdamsche Luthersche Gemeente* (Amsterdam, 1856), pp. 23-26; J. B. Blaes & A. Henner, editors, *Mémoires anonymes sur les troubles des Pays-Bas* (Brussels/Ghent/Leipzig, 1859-66), III, 58 :
En celuy temps de décembre 1579, commencha à precher ung dict Cassiodore, de ladicte nation d'Espaigne, en ladicte ville d'Anvers, au lieu du cloistre des Carmes, où

A letter dated 11 July 1579 and signed by Jean Taffin went to London from the Antwerp Calvinists, expressing a certain dismay at Reina's intention of settling in Antwerp, and asking for the help of the London French in averting this, assuring them that the writers would do their best to see that he was kept away. They did not succeed, since on 6 August his appointment was officially ratified by the City Council. It may be that Taffin's letter had some effect, in that the exact substance of Casiodoro's declarations before the Archbishop of Canterbury arrived in Antwerp and was soon circulated by his opponents in an attempt to discredit him.[9]

---

avoient paravant presché lesdicts martinistes ou confessionnistes d'Ausbourg. Lequel Cassiodore Reyne se disoit ministre de l'Eglise d'icelle confession, dont il faisoit profession, oires que se disoit avoir paravant presché en Angleterre, à Londres, et y a enseigné la doctrine de ladicte religion réformée; mais s'en estoit retiré en ces Pays-Bas et soy tenu audict lieu de Collongne, jusques ad ce que lesdicts martinistes d'Anvers le mandèrent.

[9] See note 38 to Chapter IV above; *ZHT*, 50 (1870), p. 291; *Mémoires anonymes sur les troubles des Pays-Bas*, p. 59, Hessels, III, 1, 558:

Messieurs et honnorez freres, Nous auons entendu que Cassiodoro Espagnol estant allé a Londres a obtenu de l'Euesque quelque justification des crimes dont il a esté chargé de long temps. Et que sur cela ayan requis tesmoignage de vostre Eglise il luy a esté refusé. Or il est de retour en ceste ville et practicque auec les Ministres de la Confession d'Ausbourg auec apparence tresmanifeste que leur intention est de lestablir icy au Ministere en Langue Françoise: et que mesmes a ces fins ils font instance dauoir encore vn temple. Nous craignons que, venans a bout de leur dessein il nous sera icy vn instrument dangereux et pernicieux. Pour donc destourner ce mal de nous nous vous prions quil vous plaise nous enuoyer par le premier vn Acte de sa demande faicte a vostre Eglise et du Refus dicelle auec les raisons. Ensemble si vous auez autre conseil et ayde pour ce fait, nous en vouloir assister. Cependant nous faisons et ferons de nostre coste nostre mieux pour obuier a ce quil ne soit receu.

F. Prims, *Register der Commissie tot onderhoud van de Religionsvrede te Antwerpen* (Brussels, 1954), pp. 75f:

De gecommitteerde . . . gesien hebben de certificaten hem representeert van leven ende conversatie van Jacobus Bernardes, Cassiodorus Reynius, Merardus Swarte, Thyman Brakel ende Jacobus Bender ende hem geinformeert hebbende op de qualitat van deselve ende van dem persoon van Johannes Leonisie, om geadmitteert te wordene totte predicatie van de confessie van Augsburch bynnen dese stadt, en bevinden egeene oosaken omme hennen dienst te wederleggen. Actum in de vergaderinge der gecommitteerde 6 Aug. anno 1579.

*ZHT*, 50 (1870), p. 291:

Dum in eo negotio nullum lapidem non movent, effecerunt tandem ut responsiones quasdam meas ad quosdam de Cœna Domini articulos (quas reverendissimo archiepiscopo Cantuariensi, qui ex commissione Consilii regii de mea causa cognoscebat, præterito anno mea manu subscriptas dederam, ut me demum ex illo labyrintho extricarem, bona tamen conscientia) effecerunt (inquam) ut has eruerent ex Anglia, et hîc vulgarent typis, tribus linguis, meo nomine, me inscio atque inconsulto, qui tamen autor dicor, rationes pacis ineundæ prætexentes, revera tamen ut me nostri ecclesiæ suspectum redderent, existimationem meam elevarent apud nostros et denique ministerium meum (tam illis grave) interciperent atque infringerent.

*Mémoires anonymes sur les troubles des Pays-Bas*, p. 59:

L'on disoit que lesdict confessionnistes d'Anvers l'avoient ainsy mandé sa résidence de Francfort audict Anvers affin de y gaigner de ceulx allans ès esglises franchoises desdictz réformez en icelle ville d'Anvers; lesquelz feirent imprimer ladicte confession de Cassiodore faict audict Londres par lettres au Rme évesque de Cantourbéri, affin de veoir de sa confession qu'il enseignoit présentement audict Anvers.

The assembly at Cologne finally ratified the Pacification of Ghent, the New Union of Brussels, and the Perpetual Edict. Its terms were published on 18 July 1579, and were not at all to the liking of the Antwerp Lutherans, who published on 4 August, in Dutch and French, their objections, which they addressed to the Archduke Matthias. They disliked particularly those parts which established the Roman Catholic Church with special privileges.[10] There has been some speculation on how much a part Reina had in the compilation of this document. Since he was not officially appointed till 6 August, it is doubtful whether he had any part.

On 28 August 1579 Ursula López, widow of Marcos Pérez, asked permission for herself and her children to return to live in Antwerp. This was granted, and she had returned by 28 September. It is interesting to ask oneself how far this was attributable to Casiodoro, given the amount of time he had lodged with that family in Antwerp and in Basle.[11]

There are letters to Ritter extant dated 8 December 1579 and 18 December 1579. In the former Casiodoro speaks of his sick wife, still in Frankfurt. The latter deals with the situation in Antwerp, and speaks of the opposition there has been to his working there. This letter also asks Ritter to translate into Latin the Frankfurt *Agenda,* and to send it to him by Michel Bode. Reina will then translate it from Latin into French for use in his own congregation. A letter of 11 January 1580 to Ritter indicates that opposition to him came mainly from the Calvinists.[12] They were up in arms that he should be working there, though he himself had said nothing at all to provoke them. He refers to the publication without his knowledge of his replies to the Archbishop of Canterbury. The Calvinists had pretended to be doing this for reasons of peace, but, in fact, had succeeded in that which they really intended, namely to hinder his ministry. This was, of course, not really surprising, for he was demonstrably a Lutheran-Calvinist – or a Calvinist-Lutheran – a position not easy to maintain in those

[10] Antwerp Public Library has two pamphlets: *Protest vande Christelijcke Ghemeynte binnen Antwerpen, toeghedaen der Confessien van Ausborch, op de Articulen vande Pacificatie van Nederlant, Ghemaect tot Ceulen den xviij Julij* (Antwerp, 1579), and *Protestation des fideles en la ville d'Anvers dediez a la Confession d'Ausborg, presentée au Conseil des Estats, sur les Articles de la Pacification du Païs-Bas: Faict à Coulogne le xviij. Iuillet, &c.* (Antwerp, 1579).

[11] F. Prims, *De Groote Cultuurstrijd* (no place or date), I, 31of.

[12] *ZHT*, 50 (1870), pp. 289ff:

Tentat per suos Satanas firmitudinam ecclesiæ nostræ multis modis, mea in primis causa, quem multi ad transtra quam hic potius esse vellent. Sed quia Christi promissione firmo utique fundamento nititur, frustra tentatori est omnia opera atque erit demum, præsertim si iuvemur vestris precibus . . . Ii, quos vulgus hic Calvinistas, sese vero ipsi Reformatos vocant, tam graviter ferunt meum huc adventum atque ministerium, ut ferre nullo modo aut velint aut possint, idque ne uno quidem verbo hactenus a me lacessiti. Queruntur etiam apud exteros, illorum ecclesiæ meo huc adventu grave vulnus esse inflictum. Cui querimoniæ ego soleo respondere, illos, qui ita de me conqueruntur, imprudenter satis prodere cuiusnam ecclesiæ ipsi sint, quippe ego ecclesiæ Christi non vulnera infligo, sed inservio, idque non omnino inutiliter per gratiam Christi, Satanæ vero et Antichristi ecclesiæ vulnera infligo quam possum duriter, cuius rei testes cito omnes meos auditores.

*Agenda* is the name still given by German Protestant Churches to the book used by pastors in the conduct of public worship. It corresponds to the *Book of Common Order* of the Church of Scotland.

days of strife and bitterness between the two factions. In England this might have been possible, but it made him very suspect to all his flock and to many others in strife-torn Antwerp.

He had now written, in three parts, a reply against his detractors. Firstly, he had unmasked his adversaries' intrigues; secondly, he had set forth the terms of the Wittenberg Concord, which he himself had signed, and stated that, if the Calvinist ministers would do so too, there was a hope that the long-drawn-out strife over the eucharist might be ended. This was followed by a consideration of the replies to the Achbishop, which he undertook to explain privately to anyone who should ask him; and thirdly, he expressed a grave admonition to the man who was leading the Calvinists against him, Loiseleur de Villiers, and to the magistrates of Antwerp, together with an offer to leave of his own free will if his own flock did not want him as their pastor. He doubted very much whether the magistrates would allow this to be printed and circulated. He would have sent Ritter copies of the London replies if he had suspected that either Michel Bode or Bernuy had not already shewn him them.[13]

At this point comes the one reply of Ritter to Reina that we possess. Although dated 28 December 1580, it replied to Reina's letter of 11 January 1580, and Boehmer argues the case carefully that Ritter wrote 'December' instead of 'January', a mistake everyone has made at the beginning of a new year. Ritter says that Bode had shewn him a copy of the London articles signed by Reina, and these caused Ritter a certain amount of concern. The articles were just not Lutheran enough for him; for instance, the bread of the eucharist must be more than just a symbol. We have noted earlier how strange it was for Reina to sign a Calvinist declaration as the prelude to a Lutheran ministry. In London he had declared that the Lutherans did not mind his reservations on the points of impanation and ubiquity. Ritter at least was not happy, and was not surprised that the document could be used against Reina. In fact, he seemed amazed that Reina could be so naïve about it. Reina's eirenic spirit, which might have found a very ready response in twentieth-century circles, was far too generous for the sixteenth-century temper. In a postscript to this letter, Ritter indicated that he was sending a copy of the Frankfurt *Agenda* already translated into French,

---

[13] *ZHT*, 50 (1870), p. 291:
Huic remoræ occurrere statui mea publica responsione et declaratione, quæ in summa constat tribus partibus: prima, detectione consilii autorum seu autoris huius editionis; secunda, confessione mea ingenua de Dominica cœna, quæ est ad verbum formula illa concordiæ inter Lutherum piæ memoriæ et Bucerum et reliquos Witebergæ inita cum suis subscriptionibus, desumpta ex historia confessionis Augustanæ Chytræi, regesto adversariorum aculeo in eos ipsos istis verbis in fine confessionis: Huic confessioni verbis in sua simplici significatione acceptis sincere absque ulla fraude aut dolo malo Cassiodorus subscribit, cui, si eadem sinceritate Ministri Ecclesiæ, quæ in hac civitate Antuerpiana Reformata appellatur, velint addere suas subscriptiones, spes erit controversiam de cœna Domini sublatam fore non solum in hac civitate, sed fortassis etiam quacunque illa viget. Hanc partem præcedit mea de illis responsionibus Anglicanis declaratio, qua ingenue illas agnosco pro meis, quas tamen non putem huic præsenti confessioni ullo modo esse contrarias, quod cuivis private rationem a me poscenti planum facere suscipio. Tertia pars constat admonitionibus, duabus valde (ni fallor) seriis, altera ad autorem huius editionis, altera ad huius urbis magistratus . . . Alterum, de quo dubitamus, est, an magistratus permissurus sit evulgari hanc meam responsionem.

which was more than Reina had asked of him. This would be sent on when it had been polished up. Casiodoro replied to this letter on 5 February 1580, indicating that he was rather hurt that his articles had caused Ritter consternation, for he had taken great care to see that they conformed to the Wittenberg Concord.[14]

Meantime, the *Agenda* must have arrived, for in a letter dated 1 March 1580 Reina remonstrated that he had merely asked for a quick translation into Latin, and that he would have had it translated into French in Antwerp. (Possibly, in view of the trouble over the articles, Ritter was taking no chances!) They already had in Antwerp a French catechism, and French hymns set to German tunes, but common prayer and an *Agenda* were totally lacking. In fact, as long ago as 1567 a German Lutheran *Agenda* and a Latin version of the Confession of Augsburg were provided from Frankfurt for use in Antwerp, under the guidance chiefly of Flaccius Illyricus (Matija Vlacich), with whom Reina had had some contact in Strassburg.[15]

Opposition to Reina flared up again when a young minister left the Calvinists to become a Lutheran. After the customary declarations, he was admitted to the pulpit, but the Reformed churchmen got the burgomaster to forbid this. Such events caused Casiodoro to despair, and almost made him give up his pastorate. On 17 April, however, he wrote to say that he had decided to stay, won over by the entreaties of his flock and the challenge and needs of the situation. This decision was apparently made in the face of financial hardship, for he asked Ritter to arrange through Patiens the sale to the Elector Palatine of a Plantin Bible for some seventy-five to eighty florins.[16]

Reina had decided to ask his wife and children to join him in Antwerp, but did not wish this action to prejudice his rights of citizenship in Frankfurt, and

[14] J. B. Ritter, *Evangelisches Denkmal der Stadt Franckfurth am Mayn* (Frankfurt, 1726), pp. 427f; *ZHT*, 50 (1870), pp. 293f.

[15] *ZHT*, 50 (1870), pp. 295f:

Vellem summopere Agendam vestram ad me transmissam. Neque ego, si recte memini, petieram ut Gallice nobis eam ipsi verteretis, sed Latine, et perfunctoria ac festinate opera, ut citius nos habere potuissemus, Gallice hic vertendam. Habemus iam psalmos et catechismum Gallice; psalmos . . . ad musicam Germanorum psalmorum. Hæc iam ut prelo committantur in procinctu sunt. Desunt communes preces et Agenda tota deest.

The British Museum has, *Kirchenagend, oder Form und Gestalt, Wie es mit den Sacramenten un Ceremonien gehalten wird, in der Kirchen der Augspurgischen Confession zu Andorff* (no place, 1567), and the library of Amsterdam University has, *Confessio ministrorvm Iesv Christi, in Ecclesia Antuerpensi, quæ Augustanæ Confessioni adsentitur* (no place, 1567).

[16] *ZHT*, 50 (1870), pp. 295, 297f:

Constitui tandem his manera, piis precibus fratrum expugnatus, sed inprimis ecclesiæ istius necessitate quæ, ut Dei beneficio et benedictione augetur in dies, ita summam sibi invidiam ab iis conciliat qui, si veri Christiani forent, deberent potius de illius incremento summopere gaudere . . . Biblia illa magna Plantini quæ apud nostrum Bodium asservari iussi, tibi commendo, ut videas an per dominum et carissimum fratrem nostrum Patientem divendi posset Palatino Principi. Nam neque illis valde indigeo neque, si maxime indigerem, illis uterer tam sumtuose compactis. Si aliquid effeceris, facies mihi rem valde gratam. Pretium erit ab 80 ad 75 florenos vestrates.

Tollin, p. 293; *Mémoires anonymes sur les troubles des Pays-Bas*, III, 145f. Patiens is probably Petrus Patiens, who published a revision of Luther's German Bible at Frankfurt in 1596.

he asked Ritter to check for him that these would not be jeopardized. It might seem risky to bring small children into such a situation, he wrote on 17 May 1580, but it was either that or see nothing of them, and he hoped they would soon be able to join him.[17]

The work was hard, partly because of the continued bitter opposition of the Calvinists, and partly because there was in Antwerp less than half the number of Lutheran ministers really needed. Those who did come were untrained and unwilling to suffer hardship for the gospel and often did not stay long.[18]

Indeed, for much of the time that Reina was in Antwerp the Lutherans were divided over a theological point concerning original sin. Flaccius had some point which was at variance with the orthodox Lutheran teaching, and carried many along with him. The point was of great subtlety, in the sixteenth-century theological tradition, and caused much harm and tumult in the church. A certain Peter Eggerdes was a particularly troublesome character on the Flaccian side, and eventually on 13 May 1580 the Deputies of the Church of the Confession of Augsburg in Antwerp wrote to Martin Chemnitz, Superintendent of the (Lutheran) Church of Brunswick, a long letter of explanation of the quarrel that was raging, but also giving some informative details of the state of their church in Antwerp. They had barely four German preachers and two French, one of whom was Casiodoro, who was particularly praised. Mention is also made of an edition of their catechism (modelled on the Strassburg catechism), which had been printed in German, French, and Dutch, and was shortly to be issued in Spanish.[19] This accords with the 'Privilege' printed at the beginning of a 1582 Dutch edition of this catechism, stating that the Archduke Matthias had given permission on 25 April 1580 for the printing of a four-language edition.[20] Reina must have been concerned with the Spanish, if not the French,

---

[17] *ZHT*, 50 (1870), pp. 297ff.

[18] Lehnemann, p. 101.

[19] Lehnemann, p. 101; J. G. Leuckfeld, *Historia Spangenbergensis* (Quedlinberg/ Aschersleben, 1712), pp. 87-97:

Ausserhalben unserer Frantzösischen Kirche, welche uns der liebe Gott aus Gnaden gegeben hat, und auch mit zweyen feinen und tüchtigen Predigern versorget hat, (welche herzliche Sorge tragen für die Gemeinde Gottes allhier und besonder der Herr Cassiodorus unser lieber Vater, der feylich Gelehrt und Gottfürchtig ist, und nach seinen Eyfer und Gottfürchtigkeit auch gegenwärtiglich dieser Sachen halber an E.a.w. schreibet) zwar gar übel mit Predigern versorget seyn . . . So senden wir . . . ein Exemplar von unserm Catechismo in Niederländischer teutscher Sprache itzund neuliches gedruckt, welcher vor etlichen wenigen Tagen in Frantzösischer Sprache auch ist gedruckt worden, und ingleichen in Lateinischer Sprache wird gedruckt werden, wie wir denn denselben auch künfftig in Hispanischer Sprache übergesetzt zu thun drucken vermeyen, und derowegen das Straßburgischer Exemplar (welches wir gefolget haben) an etlichen Orten ist vermehret (pp. 94, 96).

[20] *Catechismus Dat is: Corte onderwijsinge vande voornemste Hoofstucken der Christelijker leere: Op Vraghe ende Antwoort ghestelt, Alsoo in-de Christelijke Kerkë ende scholen der nederduytscher landen, de Confessie van Ausborch toe-gedaan synde, gheleert ende gheoffent wordt,* Second edition, (Antwerp, 1582); inside the title-page the privilege granted by Archduke Matthias reads:

Seyne hoocheydt heefte toe-gelaten Arnout s'Conincx, te moghen drucken oft doen drucken desen teghenwoordighen Catechismus in vierder-hande spraken, te weten Latijn, Hoochduyts, Franchoys ende Neder-duyts: Ende verboden allen anderen Persoonen, den-seluen den tijt van drij naestcomende iaren ghedurende, binnen dese neder-

edition, and, authorities agree that he was concerned with the compilation, not merely with the translations.[21] Two of the signatories to this letter to Chemnitz were Jacques and Michel Bode, who are known to have been friends of Reina, both at that time and later in Frankfurt.

Meanwhile, in the face of opposition and difficulties, the Church of the Confession of Augsburg continued to increase. On 5 March 1580 they requested another school in St George's Church, and a house to go with it. On 24 March the request was for yet more room, consequent upon the appointment of two more preachers, Michiel Peschard and Bernard Arnoldi. For services in French they asked for the Vrouwenbroeders' (Carmelites') Church, and, since they needed a place large enough to hold synods, etc., they requested the whole monastery. This seems to indicate that Reina's ministry was more successful than his letters indicate, since he had begun in the refectory, and now the church and the whole convent were being asked for. On 22 August another German preacher was appointed, and on 12 September two more. But these, no doubt, were amongst those for whom Reina expressed ill-concealed contempt in his letters to Ritter. Several churches in the city were in use by the Lutherans at this date : St George's, St Walburga's, the Carmelites', the Chapel of the Drapers' Guild, St Michael's, the Hessenhuis, and the Burchtkerk (in the castle), and yet on 27 September a further request went to the Archduke for still larger premises.[22]

On 17 August 1580 Reina wrote of the lack of pastors for the Lutherans. They were hoping to get Chemnitz to come to Antwerp to be their Superintendent. If Chemnitz would not come, he earnestly requested Ritter to seek out some other suitable man to fill the office, since the church in Antwerp was almost entirely lacking in church order and discipline. At this time, Reina's wife had not left Frankfurt.[23]

---

landen na te drucken; oft elders ghedruct sijnde te versoopen: Op-de pene begrepen in-de Originale priuilegie, daer-af ghegheuen den 25. dach April. Anno 1580. Gheteekent Matthias.

It is noteworthy that no mention is made of a Spanish edition in this permission, and it is quite possible that in fact none was ever published.

[21] *Bib. Wif.,* II, 180; J. C. S. Jacobi & F. J. D. Nieuwenhuis, *Bijdragen tot de Geschiedenis der Evang.-Luthersche Kerk in de Nederlanden,* 2 volumes, (Utrecht, 1843), I, 43; II, 64; G. Langemack, *Histor: Catecheticæ, oder Gesammleter Nachrichten Zu Einer Catechetischen Historie* (Stralsund, 1729), p. 545.

[22] F. Prims, *De Groote Cultuurstrijd,* I, 207f, 320, 323, 330f; Lehnemann, p. 101; *ZHT,* 50 (1870), pp. 286f, 299 :

Res est plane digna lachrymis videre fruges ad messem maturas in tanta copia propemodum perire ob messoreum fidelium paucitatem. Cum præsertim neque in ea paucitate omnes pro officio sint frugi . . . Petunt undique juvari a nobis. Nos neque nobis ipsis habemus vel mediam partem Ministrorum, qui nobis essent necessarii, & hos (ut apud te unum tantam vastitatem deplorare mihi sine ulla mea fraude liceat) juvenes, imperitos, nihil ferre doctos. Accersivit hæc Ecclesia præterito anno ex Osterlandia, deinde duos alios. Tres illi plenis loculis redierunt in patriam periculum hic vitantes & desiderio patriæ victi, neque revera, si mansissent, melius habituræ essent hujus Ecclesiæ res, quam in eorum absentia. Duo alii erant prorsum inutiles.

[23] *ZHT,* 50 (1870), pp. 300f. Many areas which accepted the Reformation with a Lutheran pattern retained an episcopal structure, but for anti-Roman reasons rejected the title of bishop, which they replaced by that of Superintendent or Inspector. The latter title is still in use in the Eglise Luthérienne de France.

It was in 1580 that a native of Montbéliard was appointed to the French Lutheran ministry in Antwerp. His name was Antoine Serray (Antonius Serrarius). Later, in Frankfurt, he and Reina were to work together again.[24]

There is a letter to Ritter dated 'prid. Kal. M. . . 1581'. This must of course be March or May. Casiodoro still complained of the lack of a Superintendent. Another German minister had arrived, whose salary was to be twelve hundred Flemish florins (i.e. seven hundred Frankfurt florins). This, we therefore suppose, would be approximately the amount that Reina was receiving at this time. Someone meanwhile had sent to Heshusius a copy of Reina's Antwerp catechism, and he had written a condemnation of it, which added to Reina's difficulties, but by the date of this letter Reina's wife and children were with him in Antwerp.[25]

Letters by several people written in 1581 to Conrad Schlüsselburg, a German Lutheran pastor in Antwerp, make mention of Casiodoro, mostly to send greetings.[26] One, however, written by David Chytræus, dated 18 July 1581, suggests that Casiodoro would make a very suitable superintendent for the Antwerp Church of the Confession of Augsburg. This suggestion does not seem to have been acted upon. It nevertheless speaks highly for Reina's standing in certain people's estimation.[27] This letter and another dated St Catherine's Day, 1581, mention a French translation of Chytræus's *Historia Augustanæ Confessionis,* which eventually appeared in 1583, printed in Antwerp.[28]

Up to this time Reina continually complained of the difficulties he experienced because of the unfriendliness of the Calvinists. The situation may have improved after the Antwerp City Council issued a decree on 5 August 1581 to protect the Lutherans in the city in the same way as the Calvinists were protected. It is also worthy of note that one of the extant copies of Reina's Bible of 1569 bears an autograph dedication to Jean Taffin, the Calvinist preacher who had expressed concern when Reina was first appointed.[29]

A letter to Ritter dated 9 January 1582 devotes most of its contents to enquiring about the method of administering the eucharist in Frankfurt and elsewhere, asking in particular whether, when insufficient bread and/or wine had been consecrated, a new supply should be consecrated by a repetition of the

[24] *Naamroll der Predikanten* (Amsterdam, 1777), p. 86.

[25] *Bib. Wif.,* II, 182; *ZHT,* 50 (1870), pp. 303-5. Tilemann Hesshusen (Heshusius) (1527-88) was a rather hot-headed defender of Lutheran orthodoxy. He was a pastor or a professor in various German towns, and was several times dismissed for his outspokenness.

[26] *Conradi Schlusselburgii . . . epistolarum volumen* (Rostock, 1624), pp. 224-8, 264-78, 426-35.

[27] *Conradi Schlusselburgii,* pp. 224f:

De Superintendente, quod vobis in primo articulo propositum est, existimo sine conscientiæ offensione recipi posse. Hortatus sum deputatos, ut inspectorem ministerio præficiant, et Cass^m., cujos doctrinam et studium pacis mihi prædicasti, nominavi.

David Chytræus (Kochhafe) (1531-1600) was a Lutheran theologian, from 1550 onwards a pillar of Rostock University. He had a great influence on the course of the Reformation in Sweden, Austria, and Antwerp.

[28] *Conradi Schlusselburgii,* pp. 226f.

[29] *Bib. Wif.,* II, 301; J. W. Pont, 'De Belijdenis van de Luthersche Gemeente te Antwerpen', *Niewe Bijdragen tot Kennis van de Geschiedenis en het Wezen van het Lutheranisme in de Nederlanden* (Schiedam, 1907), I, 163f.

words of institution being murmured over it. The letter also mentions a sister, who might just possibly have been Casiodoro's own sister, living in Frankfurt. But, in view of the custom of using the terms 'brother' and 'sister' for fellow-members of the church, it is perhaps unwise to make this assumption too firmly.[30]

The year 1582 also saw the publication of a Dutch version of the Antwerp catechism. This is the publication in which the 'Privilege' issued by the Arch-duke is printed, and both Boehmer and Jacobi bring evidence to shew that there had been earlier editions, including a possible Spanish one. The Dutch edition of 1580 was completely sold out in two years, thus necessitating this revision and reprint of 1582.[31] A further revision of this catechism, made by another French pastor of the Lutheran Church in Antwerp named Allard, in 1585, be-came the standard adult catechism of the Lutheran Church of Holland, and remained so for several centuries.[32]

In late 1582 French troops under the command of the Duke of Brabant en-tered Antwerp. On 17 January 1583 an outbreak of violence by those troops, afterwards known as the 'French Fury', broke out. Much of this fury was directed against the Protestants, but Casiodoro, with his flock, weathered the storm. Indeed, later in the same year, on 5 April, there appeared in Antwerp the French translation referred to above, David Chytræus's *Histoire de la Con-fession d'Auxpourg*. Schutz is categoric in attributing the translation of this to Reina, and others have followed his lead. The book itself gives the name of Luc le Cop as its translator, but Rahlenbeck asserts that this name had been Reina's pseudonym as far back as 1563. Pont argues that this was not so; and, since we can point to the existence of a Savoyard called Luc le Cop in Antwerp in the late sixteenth century, there seems to be no case in Reina's favour. The book bears a preface signed by the Elders and Deputies of the Antwerp Church of the Confession of Augsburg, and there is no clear mention of Reina in the whole publication.[33]

No trace of Casiodoro's activity can be found for 1584, but his time in Antwerp was running out. Spanish troops under Alexander Farnese, Duke of Parma, occupied the city on 17 August 1585, and their hostility to Protestants was evident from the first. On 18 August a treaty was signed, permitting Protes-tants to remain in the city for four years without harm, but the writing on the wall was clear. A massive exodus from the city began, which was to reduce a population of 83,000 in 1582 to one of 53,000 in 1589. Once more, as earlier in Geneva, Reina played Moses, and he and Serrarius and a large part of the

[30] *ZHT* (1870), 305f.

[31] *Bib. Wif.*, II, 180, 305f; Jacobi & Nieuwenhuis, I, 43f; Langemack, II, 552, states that when Wittenberg had expressed doubts regarding the orthodoxy of the Antwerp Catechism, 'hierauf schrieb Cassiodorus Reinius als autor des Catechismus; eine apologie desselben, so 1583, einer neuen edition seines catechismi angehenget ist'.

[32] Jacobi & Nieuwenhuis, I, 44; J. W. Pont, 'De Catechismus van Franciscus Alardus', *Nieuwe Bijdragen*, 2 (Amsterdam, 1909), p. 146.

[33] O. F. Schütz, *De Vita Davidis Chytræi* (Hamburg, 1720), II, 360; C. Rahlenbeck, *L'Inquisition et la Réforme en Belgique (Anvers)* (Brussels, 1857), p. 191; J. W. Pont, 'De Luthersche Gemeenten in de Zuidelijke Nederlanden', *Nieuwe Bijdragtn*, 3, second edi-tion, (Haarlem, 1911), p. 413; Luc le Cop did in fact exist. He was a Savoyard and signed the 'Album Amicorum' of Abraham Ortelius in Antwerp in the later sixteenth century (*De Gulden Passer*, 45 (Antwerp, 1967)).

French-speaking congregation went en bloc to Frankfurt already well before the Spanish occupation.[34]

On 31 May 1585 Casiodoro was instrumental in setting up, after preaching a sermon on the subject, a charitable foundation for the relief of any poor Lutherans from the Low Countries who were in Frankfurt. It had the effect of keeping together the members of Reina's congregation, who felt themselves to be a corporate whole, long before they were officially recognized as a church. In fact, the charitable foundation still exists long after the congregation as a church has vanished, and amongst its prized possessions is a portrait claimed to be of Casiodoro.[35]

By 28 September 1585 there was a request, signed by ten members of the ex-Antwerp congregation, before the City Council of Frankfurt, asking for permission to hold services in French and requesting the appointment of Casiodoro as their preacher. The City Council passed this for their observations to the Consistory of German ministers (known as the Predigerministerium). The latter were extremely reluctant that the request should be granted, saying that Casiodoro was old and difficult to understand (whether they meant in German, in French, or just in general, is not clear), and one gains the impression that they really did not trust the theology of the newcomers enough to make them fully independent. Although they considered the matter on 21 October 1585, their answer was delayed till after the Fair, and apparently conveniently overlooked, for a further request was submitted on 8 March 1586, with nineteen signatures, and a third on 21 June 1586, followed by a fourth on 30 August 1586. None of these requests received a satisfactory answer, and there the matter had to rest for the time being.[36]

About this time it was recorded that Reina paid tax on a property assessment

[34] *Articles et Conditions du Traicté fait & conclu entre l'Altesse du Prince de Parme, Plaisance, &c, Lieutenant, Gouverneur & Capitaine general és pays de pardeça au nom de sa Maiesté comme Duc de Brabant, & Marquis du Saint Empire d'une part, & la ville d'Anvers d'autre part, le xviij iour d'Aoust, l'an M.D.LXXXV.* (Antwerp, 1588), article vi, p. 7; E. de Moreau, *Histoire de l'Eglise en Belgique* (Brussels, 1952), V, 331; R. Boumans, 'Le dépeuplement d'Anvers', *Revue du Nord,* 115 (Lille/Arras, 1947), p. 190.

[35] F. Scharff, 'Die Niederländische und die französische Gemeinde', *Archiv für Frankfurts Geschichte und Kunst,* New Series, 2 (1862), p. 275; T. Schott, 'Frankfurt als Herberge', *Jahresbericht des Vereins für Reformationsgeschichte,* 3 (1886), p. 275; Lehnemann, pp. 169f, gives the foundation document in full, and the frontispiece to his book is a reproduction of the portrait in a line-engraving made by Peter Fehr (1681-1740), who also offered for sale separate copies of the engraving, thus giving rise in time to the belief that he was the painter of the original.

[36] Lehnemann, pp. 125f; Scharff, pp. 263f; *Franckfurtische Religions=Handlungen Welche zwischen Einen Hoch=Edlen und Hochweisen Magistrat und denen Reformirten Bürgern und Einwohnern . . .* (Frankfurt, 1735-45), II, 371:
Wo denn also, so wäre sich desto weniger Conspiration unter ihnen, oder sosten Neuerung und dergleichen zubefahren, wie dan ohne des unter so wenigen Hause-Gesässen nicht zu besorgen ist, und zwar zu dessen Versicherung dienet, unsers Bedünckens nicht wenig, daß sie zu ihren Frantzös[n] Prediger keinen frembden, unbekanten, sondern H[rn] Cassiodorum Reins, dieser Stadt von vielen Jahren her Burget, nominiren und fürschlagen, welcher bißher mäniglich nicht anders, dann sittig und friedsam erkannt hat, vernehmen auch, daß er zu Antorff in drey Jahrlang, sich nicht anders gehalten habe, wie dessen ihn & andern der reinen Christlichen Kirche daselbsten ihre Widersacher selbst Zeugniß geben.

of 1,500 florins, and again, presumably later, on a sum of 3,500 florins. We suppose, therefore, that the business ventures, which he once more entered into, were a financial success.[37] But this was not his real desire, however well he prospered in business. It may be supposed that these commercial activities required him to travel away from Frankfurt from time to time. A small piece of evidence of this exists in the dedication of a book by Jean de Léry, published in 1586, and describing the author's travels in America. He states that Reina had earlier been at the court of the Landgrave of Hesse-Cassel, who had indicated his interest in the book. Reina had, in fact, written to inform the author, who now dedicated to the Landgrave the Latin translation of the French original.[38]

In 1587 the press of Nicolas Bassée brought out a second edition of Antonio del Corro's *Dialogus Theologicus,* a commentary on Romans. It is apparent that Reina supervised the printing of this, as the dedication makes clear, if he was not entirely responsible for its production.[39] Otherwise, nothing at all of Casiodoro's life during the years 1587 to 1591 seems to have survived. During these years the Antwerp Lutheran congregation held together without a proper meeting-place, despite the City Council's apparent neglect of it. It is inconceivable that Reina should not bear much of the credit for its survival during those years, and it is not unlikely that some form of conventicle existed, albeit unofficially, with some kind of preaching and/or Bible study in its own language.[40]

On 10 January 1582 the Antwerp Lutherans' patience was finally rewarded when the City Council appointed Serrarius, who had not settled in Frankfurt, but had returned to his native Montbéliard, where he was pastor of Héricourt, as the first French preacher for the refugees. That Casiodoro was not appointed was ostensibly because Serrarius could understand German as well as French, which was true enough. A native of Montbéliard would be well-placed in that respect, (the area was in the possession of Ulrich, Duke of Wurtemburg, who had early accepted the Reformation, and its pastors were at that time trained in Germany). It was also hoped that a Frenchman would attract the French Calvinist refugees into the Lutheran fold. There are suggestions, however, that the Frankfurt pastors generally were still very suspicious of Reina's earlier adherence to Calvinist beliefs.

The services of the now officially reconstituted Antwerp Church were held at first in the Spitalkirche (Church of the Holy Ghost Hospital) in the shambles area between the cathedral and the River Main, but the worshippers quickly complained that the stench from the butchers' shops was most upsetting, especially in summer, and so they were given leave to hold their services in the

[37] F. Bothe, *Frankfurts wirtschaftlich-soziale Entwicklung* (Frankfurt, 1920), II, 115; A. Dietz, *Frankfurter Handelsgeschichte,* II, 35.

[38] Jean de Léry, *Historia navigationis in Brasiliam quæ et America dicitur* ([Geneva], 1586).

[39] MacFadden, p. 345; *Dialogus in Epistolam D. Pauli ad Romanos, Antonio Corrano Hisp. in Academia Oxoniensi Professore, Theologo, autore.* The Frankfurt edition has in the dedication these words, not contained in the original London edition:
cvm hisce diebus è Germania accepissem quendam dialogum in Epistolam Apostoli Pauli ad Romanos, olim à me conscriptum, nunc verò amicorum opera iterum typis expressum, suis tamen præfationibus atque appendicibus mutilatum (p.* [1]).

[40] Lehnemann, pp. 126f.

Bärfüsserkirche (Church of the Discalced Carmelites), what at that time was the main Lutheran church of Frankfurt. We can suppose that they would hold their services in French at times that avoided the hours of the main German services there.[41]

A legal document concerning Reina at this time is extant in the Frankfurt City Archives. It consists of the papers of a case begun on 5 April 1592 against Jacob Rasür of Leipzig, concerning a barrel full of goods (presumably books, but possibly silk) worth one hundred and thirty-one florins, which had been deposited in the Nicolauskirche. The case dragged on till June 1593.[42]

On 10 February 1594 Casiodoro wrote a long letter to Adolf Fisscher, Lutheran minister in Amsterdam, to commend a former Antwerp Lutheran named Populerius. In this letter he tries to play down the controversy concerning original sin which was raging at that time amongst Lutherans.[43] Reina, like his friend Corro, was well in advance of his time in his desire to reduce to a minimum theological controversy on minor points, when the tendency of the day was to argue endlessly about details, which, at this distance of time, seem barely comprehensible. In this respect he contrasts strongly with Juan Pérez and Cipriano de Valera, who remained blameless Calvinists all their lives.

Serrarius was physically weak, and the Antwerp Lutheran refugees were still determined to have their old pastor, Casiodoro, reinstated officially. Thus, once more, in March or April 1593, they requested the appointment of Reina as Serrarius's assistant, describing him as 'fine, respectable, peace-loving, learned, experienced, and willing', and they offered to bear all the costs of his salary themselves, if the City Council was not willing to pay it. On 29 March the council accepted the request on condition that two citizens stood surety for Reina, and pending a satisfactory report on trial sermons that he would preach in French. On 17 April Schadeus gave his report on two sermons preached by Reina, recommending his acceptance as a pastor.[44] On 20 April the Prediger-ministerium informed Reina by letter that his appointment had their official approval, subject to satisfactory replies being received from him on points of Lutheran orthodoxy, in addition to his making personal undertakings. It seems that many of these statements were those required in any case from a candidate for the ministry; others, however, were clearly designed to control Reina personally. He was required to signify assent to the Apostle's Creed, the Nicene

---

[41] G. Florian, *Franckfurt am Mayn. Chronica* (Frankfurt, 1706), II, 66; Lehnemann, pp. 128f; G. Guaitta, *Merckwurdiges Verzeichniß derer . . . zu Franckfurt am Mayn gestandenen Evangelischen Predigern* ([Frankfurt], 1774), p. 6; H. Dechent, *Kirchengeschichte von Frankfurt am Main seit der Reformation* (Leipzig/Frankfurt, 1913), I, 278. This church has now been replaced by the nineteenth-century St Paul's Church.

[42] Frankfurt City Archives, Judicialia R 283, Acta Herr Cassiodori Reinig Clagers Contra Jacob Rasür zue Leiptzig Beclagten 1592.

[43] F. J. D. Nieuwenhuis, *Geschiedenis der Amsterdamsche Luthersche Gemeente* (Amsterdam, 1856), pp. 19-22.

[44] Lehnemann, pp. 133f; F. Scharff, II, 274f:

Ein feiner, ansehnlicher, friedfertiger, gelehrter, wohlerfahrener und beredter Mann . . . Und soll man Beschluß von denjenigen, so ihn nicht zu besoldem sich erboten, vernemen, was sie ihm zu geben gedacht; auch ihnen untersagen, daß sie solches stipendium hinter E. E. Rath oder dessen Scholarchen erlegen, und daß derselben Hand ihn Cassiodoro gereicht werde, andere präjudicirliche Consequenz zu verhüten.

Creed, the Athanasian Creed, the Confession of Augsburg, the Wittenburg Concord, the Six Articles of Schmalkald, Luther's Catechism, Bucer's Accord made for the pastors of Frankfurt, and the Formula of Concord of Melanchthon. Then he had to condemn those who did not agree to the Formula of Concord, and all who adhered to the Pope, the Anabaptists, the Flaccians or neo-Manichæans, the Schwenkfeldians, Sacramentarians, Zwinglians, Calvinists, and all who resembled them. He had to accept Andreas's defence against Beza, and to declare his London Confession abolished, revoked, and extinguished by his Antwerp Confession. Next, he had to undertake to exercise the office of pastor zealously and to remain content with it; to accept from the brethren advice, warnings, and reproaches; to introduce no innovations; to keep the peace with Serrarius and to consider him his equal. And finally he had to condemn strife between Lutherans and Calvinists as the blackest monster that had reared its head since the Reformation. (One can imagine that he did this last very willingly!) This declaration, dated 8 May 1593, was followed by a long explanation of the trilingual *Confessio in articulo Cœnæ* which had caused him so much trouble in Antwerp. Even at this point the past was raked up against him: his erstwhile supporter, Théophile de Banos, minister of the French refugee congregation, tried to bring it up now, but he does not appear to have had much success, and, when Reina had made this satisfaction, he was finally appointed by the City Council on 20 July 1593.[45]

During 1593 also, the Weissfrauenkirche (former Church of the White Ladies, Cistercian nuns), which had earlier been used in turn by the English and the French refugee congregations, was made available to the Church of the Antwerp refugees. Now they had a church and pastors of their own – although they still had to celebrate baptisms and weddings in the Bärfüsserkirche.[46]

But, after becoming a minister for the third time in his career, an office to which he felt surely called by God, and which he had never willingly quitted, Reina was not to live long to enjoy this reinstatement. He died on 15 March 1594, and was buried on the 17 March. His wife was to survive him by eighteen years, and his descendants can be traced in Frankfurt well into the eighteenth century.[47]

Two more sets of legal documents exist in the Frankfurt Archives, which indicate that Reina did not entirely abandon his business activities because he had re-entered the sacred ministry. One is the Acta of the creditors of Jacob Cehnets, which Casiodoro's widow signed on 31 March 1594, and in which Cassiodorus Reinius † (=deceased) is listed as being owed 49 florins, 3 pounds and 18 batzen.[48] The other is a list of the creditors of Dieterics von Beferfort and his wife of Cologne, in which Michel Bode takes over the debts of Casiodoro to the

---

[45] Lehnemann, pp. 163-8; G. Florian, II, 66; Tollin, p. 297.

[46] H. Dechent, I, 278; This building remained the church of the former Antwerp congregation till its destruction during the War of 1939-45.

[47] Frankfurt City Archives, Sterbebuch (1579-96) & Sterbebuch 4 (1612-26); Herr Itzerott is not more precise. See also my article, 'Cassiodoro de Reina & his Family in Frankfurt am Main', *BHR*, 32 (1970), pp. 427-31.

[48] Frankfurt City Archives, Judicialia Z 57, Acta Creditorum Jacob Cehnets Contra Jacob Cehnets.

extent of 603 florins and 15 batzen.[49] Presumably Bode paid Anna Reina the sum and then had his own name entered as a creditor, much in the same way as had been done when Reina himself urgently needed money from the estate of Oporinus.

[49] Judicialia W 236 II, fol. 35ʳ, 284ʳ.

# VI

# Some Consideration of his Theology and Learning

It is clear that Reina lived well before his time. In the twentieth century not many eyebrows would have been raised by his mild personality and basically undogmatic theology, which, despite his signing many downright dogmatic statements in his career, remained eirenic and syncretist, in the sense of trying to unite various facets of non-Roman Christianity. Whilst remaining firmly on the Protestant side of the fence, he appears to have felt at home both in the Calvinist and the Lutheran folds, nor did he feel it necessary to reject the one to be in the other; and he avoided the extreme positions and hair-splitting arguments that threatened to divide both of them from within. His inclusiveness seems to have stretched as far as Anglicanism on the one hand and Unitarianism on the other – for we must suppose that his troubles sprang at least in part from an unwillingness to condemn anyone who sincerely felt himself to be a Christian. It is noteworthy too that, unlike Juan Pérez and Cipriano de Valera, he never wrote, so far as we know, any doctrinal polemic against the Roman Church (though he might well have written a pamphlet against the Inquisition).

Much of the opposition to Casiodoro came from the fact that he was friendly with people who were not acceptable to the champions of orthodoxy, particularly those of the Calvinist persuasion. It was also taken amiss that he had expressed disagreement with the execution of Servetus; whereas the successors of Calvin and his companions have since erected on the site of Servetus's martyrdom an expiatory monument. Detached from the strife of the period, we can readily understand that someone, who has escaped the risk of a like fate for similar reasons, would be horrified to find that what he thought to be a haven of gospel religion was capable of the same savagery as his native Spain. Casiodoro evidently had expected to find that the spirit of the Prince of Peace was dominant in Geneva, and, when he found otherwise, he lost no time in leaving for a more congenial place in which to live.

During his stay in Geneva, however, there is evidence that he made an approach to Sébastien Castellion, which would have to be done by correspondence, since by then Castellion was living in Basle, having become very much *persona non grata* in Geneva.[1] Castellion's views on the freedom of the conscience in the state had brought him into sharp conflict with Calvin, his former tutor. It is noteworthy that, when Reina stayed in Basle, those who had been friendly towards Castellion became his friends. Indeed the very choice of Basle,

[1] Frankfurt docts., fol. 591, Deposition of Angel Victor, paragraph 7.

82

and the presses of Oporinus, seems to have been connected in some way with Castellion, for, although the latter had died in 1565, he had taken refuge in Oporinus's home and had worked for him when he had had to leave Geneva. Oporinus was known not to be altogether in favour of Calvin's more extreme doctrines. Sulzer and Koechlein had both been supporters of Castellion, as they later were of Reina. Zwinger, besides being a nephew of Oporinus, had also been Castellion's pupil, and succeeded him in the chair of Greek in 1564. Oporinus had also given refuge to Francisco de Enzinas (Dryander), and had printed the notice of the treacherous murder of Bartholomeo Diaz. Oporinus's wife and Sulzer were amongst the godparents of Castellion's children.[2]

Another link with Castellion was that his doctrines had triumphed over Calvin's in Montbéliard (this was before Wurtemburg had opted for Lutheranism), and Reina's assistant in both Antwerp and Frankfurt was a native of that region.

An aspect of the matter of Reina's theological standpoint that does not seem to have received sufficient consideration, is that it is possible for a man's beliefs to undergo considerable modification during his lifetime, a fact not unnoticed when the thought of other men is discussed. Hence, it is not inconceivable that in his early days in Geneva and London Reina had had leanings towards the doctrines of Servetus and others who questioned the traditional view of the Trinity. Corro's letters indicate that Reina had at least considered them, and we know that he did not feel that such views should result in their holders being excluded from the fellowship of the church, but the Confession of Faith that he drew up for the Spanish Church of London gives no indication that he wished to question seriously the doctrine of the Trinity, even though the French Consistory wished Reina to amplify the statements on that doctrine. The Confession does not appear to equivocate on this doctrine when, having mentioned in Chapter I (De Dios) the Father, the Son, and the Holy Spirit, it sums up the doctrine thus:

> Creemos hallarse estas tres personas en la misma substancia, naturaleza, y essencia de vn Dios, de tal manera distinctas, que el Padre no sea el Hiio, ni el Espiritu sancto : ni el Hiio sea el Padre, ni el Espiritu sancto : ni el Espiritu sancto sea el Padre, ni el Hiio. Esto sin derogar a la vnidad y simplicidad de vn solo Dios, por no auer en todas tres Personas mas de vn ser diuino y simplicissimo, segun que la hallamos auersenos declarado el mismo Dios en su sancta Palabra, por la qual enseñados lo conocemos, adoramos, y confessamos ansi   (Chapter I, Section 3).

Nevertheless, in admitting the need for the words 'Trinity' and 'Person', the Confession points out that the words are not taken from Scripture, and this may well be the section that the French objected to:

> Y aunque entendemos que todo hombre fiel se deue conformar con las maneras de hablar, que Dios en ella usa mayormente en la manifestacion de mysterios semeiantes a este, donde la razon humana ni alcança, ni puede,

[2] F. Buisson, *Sébastien Castellion sa vie et son œuvre* (Paris, 1892), I, 234, 251; II, 257, 275, 277.

empero por conformarnos con toda la Iglesia de los pios, admittimos los nombres de Trinidad, y de Persona, de los quales los Padres de la Iglesia antigua vsaron vsurpandolos non sin gran necessidad para declarar lo que sentian contra los errores y heregias de sus tiempos acerca de este articulo   (Chapter I, Section 4).

It is certainly these last words that receive considerable attention in the depositions regarding Reina's doctrines that were laid before the Bishop's commissioners. As Angel Victor put it :

Finalement Sa confession de foy m'est fort suspecte en l'article de la Trinité et des troys personnes lesquelles il n'admet rondement, mais pour se conformer avecque les eglises. Le mesme dict du Baptesme des enfans. Ce qu'il ne debuoit pas fayre, comm'il semble, en vne petite confession de foy on debuoit estre brieff, clair, et rond   (Deposition 15 Sept 1563, Section 13).

Reina's honesty in stating that neither the Trinity nor infant baptism is mentioned explicitly in Scripture seemed to be a treacherous admission, which would have been better left unstated. It is indeed probably his honesty in speaking his mind, rather than any real deficiency in his beliefs, that brought disaster in the end. To admit that it was the writings of a condemned heretic that had been responsible for enlightening his mind about God, to state that since the Apostles nobody had spoken better than that same heretic, and to assert that it was a lack of Christian charity that had been responsible for his death at the stake in Geneva, was merely to add fuel to the flames of suspicion that had already been kindled. And, as if such unconcealed admiration for Servetus and condemnation of his murderers were not enough, Reina's friendship with men who had been notoriously antipathetic towards the extremes of Calvin's doctrines was further evidence. His goodwill towards Acontius and his familiarity with Adriaan Haemstede and Castellion were not calculated to endear him to the more rigid Calvinists, any more than was his insistence that Anabaptists were not excluded from God's scheme of salvation.[3]

We have seen how Casiodoro moved during the course of his life from Roman Catholicism into the Calvinist Church and finally into the Lutheran fold. We have quite a lot of material on which to base our knowledge of his theology, since he bore the main responsibility for the production of two confessions of faith during his lifetime, one moderately Reformed and one claiming to be Lutheran, and the accusations to which he was subjected in London resulted in the production of a number of declarations of his doctrinal standpoint, some of which have survived, whilst his final trial in London in 1579 produced another doctrinal statement about the Lord's Supper (although the published form was, admittedly, put out by his opponents). Besides these there are a number of letters containing doctrinal matters, most of them written to Beza, and one very lengthy one to Adolf Fisscher, a Lutheran minister in Amsterdam.

If one takes all the above together, one can see that Reina, having been convinced of the centrality of the Bible and of the doctrine of justification by faith,

---

[3] Frankfurt docts., fol. 592f, Depositions of Angel Victor, Francisco Ábrego, Balthasar Sánchez, and Jeremias Ackerman.

found the papal Roman Catholic form of Christianity very much wanting, and wished to move to a grouping of believers amongst whom he would feel at home, since the papacy refused the kind of Reformation demanded by the Reformers. He appears to have had an extremely enquiring mind and a truly Christian temperament, that is, one which, though willing to condemn the sin, did not condemn the sinner. He was able to distinguish between a man and his ideas, not refusing to befriend those whose ideas he found unacceptable, and very unwilling to accept one set of ideas to the exclusion of all others. This is what led him into trouble from the earliest days of his arrival in Protestant territory. It is clear from the evidence that he felt the monolithic system of Geneva quite uncongenial. He was willing to condemn evil where he saw it, even if it meant criticizing Calvin for his intolerance, as demonstrated in its extreme form by the execution of Servetus.[4] This gave him from the outset a reputation for 'unsoundness', which was reinforced by the friendships mentioned above.

When Reina finally wrote the Spanish Confession of Faith of London, it was condemned by several people, as outlined above, for being too vague on certain points which were in dispute.

Reina's spirit of peace kept him from fruitless denunciation of others' beliefs, where these were not clearly anti-Biblical. When pressed in Heidelberg to be precise about his attitude to Servetus, he was, but the words were another's that he accepted :

> Et pour s'en plus asseurer de moi en cela, [Ursinus] me demanda derechef, me conjurant par le Seigneur, si de cœur je detestois les erreurs de Servetus, et je lui ai testifié devant le Seigneur mesme, qu'ouy, et que je n'avois autre chose en mon cœur   (*Bib. Wif.*, II, 200).

Rarely at all does Reina voluntarily condemn a denomination by name; in fact, only in one extant book is this done, his *Evangelium Ioannis,* where various anti-Trinitarian heterodoxies, as well as the Anabaptists and the Roman Catholics, are expressly refuted. If he had been able to stay in England, one feels that he would perhaps have found in the end a home within the Church of England, as Corro did some time later, to be followed by Saravia and Texeda.

Reina's first doctrinal protestation after his departure from England, made at Strassburg on 24 March 1565, contains extremely forthright Calvinist statements. After a general acceptance of the ancient creeds, he says :

> Quant à la doctrine en général, ie aduoe et reçois pour fidele et chrestienne doctrine tout le corps de la doctrine que i'ai ouye en l'Eglise de Geneve, en les Eglises Francoises à Francfort et à Londres, en lesquelles i'ay conversé comme membre d'icelles, et en lesquelles i'ay aprins et profitté par la grace du Seigneur après ma venue d'Espagne; du consentement desquelles ie proteste en saine conscience que ce n'est pas n'y a esté mon intention de me separer touchant les principaulx points de la doctrine   (paragraph 2).

The cautious insertion of the words 'principal points of doctrine' is perhaps significant, especially when we learn elsewhere that he had said that at Geneva the preaching tended to concentrate on a condemnation of monasticism to the

---

[4] Frankfurt docts., fol. 591, 593, Depositions of Angel Victor and Balthasar Sánchez

exclusion of teaching on charity and mortification, that Calvin had written a book against the burning of heretics, and then, when he had captured Servetus, had written another of a totally contrary opinion, and that he had himself said masses in Spain that had been of much more use than many of the sermons he had heard in London.[5] Reina's idea of where liberty of interpretation began and where rigid definition ended was in fact not that of the majority of Calvinists, and, in trying to be eirenic, he ended by displeasing many at least of those amongst whom he wished at first to live and work.

The paragraph in this Strassburg declaration which concerns the Lord's Supper is moderately Calvinist, that is, it interprets the sacrament in neither a transubstantiationist nor in a consubstantiationist manner :

De la Cène . . . ie confesse, qu'à tous les fideles y approchants en vraye foy en est rendu tesmoignage que toute la vertu de la mort du Seigneur leur est appliquée pour la remission de leurs pechez, at pour certaine, et ferme asseurance de leur reconciliation avec son Pere. Item, que pour estre faitz participans de l'incorporation avecque luy, et en estre faictz os de ses os et char de sa char, leur est donné presentialement et sustantialement son vray corps et son vray sang en viande et breuvage de leurs Ames par le moyen de la foy et par l'efficace du Sainct Esprit, par une façon toutesfoys admirable et incomprehensible à nostre humaine raison   (paragraph 3).

It is to be noted that Reina here avoids coming down strongly on the Calvinist side, whilst definitely avoiding the Roman and Lutheran statements. He is content to leave certain areas of faith indefinable, or, at any rate, undefined. He does go further, in the following paragraph, to make the point that the body and blood of Christ are not to be sought in the bread and wine :

. . . n'est pas de besoing, et si ne doibt pas faire de chercher ce sainct corps, et sang dedans les terriens elements du pain et du vin, comme estans là enclos et ataches necessairement pour estre prins tant des Infideles que des fideles, ou pour estre mangé corporellement auec la bouche corporelle . . . ( . . . car ainsi on ne prend pas que le sacrement exterieur . . .) ains que luy se donnent es sacres symboles, ainsy qu'il a esté dit, doibt estre cherché par foy plus hault, c'est àscavoir . . . où il sied à la dextre de Dieu son Pere   (paragraph 4).

In this statement he rejects by implication the Lutheran position of ubiquity, which leads to consubstantiation. But he goes on to make this quite clear, by mentioning ubiquity specifically in the sixth paragraph, saying that it is 'une question outrepassant les bornes de la modestie chrestienne'. He quotes Bucer,

---

[5] As note 4. Calvin's first book was indeed *L.Annei Senecæ . . . libri duo De Clementia . . . I. Caluini cõmentarij illustrati* (Paris, 1532), which, since Seneca's treatise was written to persuade Nero to be more benevolent to his subjects, is generally supposed to have been written in the hope of bringing Francis I to consider a policy of clemency towards the Protestants he was persecuting, although F. Wendel (*Calvin* (London, 1963), pp. 27ff) maintains that the work cannot be taken in this sense. After Servetus's execution, Calvin wrote *Defensio orthodoxæ fidei de sacra Trinitate, Cõtra prodigiosos errores Michaelis Serueti Hispani, vbi ostenditur iure gladu coercendus esse . . .* (Geneva, 1553), to defend his attitude to Servetus's trial and the principle of repressing heresy by capital punishment.

whose Calvinist orthodoxy was not in question, in support of this rejection, and goes on to discuss the matter at length, ending with a good Calvinist statement of the real presence :

> Doncques d'enquerir du lieu, et de la maniere comment le Seigneur est au Ciel, c'est chose irreligieuse, et estrange de la pieté de la foy, laquelle laquelle [twice] doibt simplement croire, et confesser que le Seigneur Jesus demeure en ceste celeste et inaccessible gloire du Pere, et que, demeurant en icelle, il se donne à nous en sa Saincte Cene, et y est vrayement.

In paragraph twelve of the same declaration Reina makes a plea for sanity in treatment of others for statements that they make on theological points which are not of the essential basis of the faith, rather in the spirit of Richard Baxter's, 'In necessary things, unity; in doubtful things, liberty; in all things, charity'. He says :

> En un temps si bien plein de calumniateurs que d'erreurs et sectes il est merveilleusement expedient à toute l'église et à chacun fidel en particulier de faire distinction entre les articles fondementels de nostre foi et les privees declarations et sentences lesquelles ont esté tousjours libres en l'Eglise, sauve la verité de la foi.

He points out that, whereas Calvin speaks highly of Luther, there are some Calvinists who condemn the latter as a heretic; furthermore, œcolampadius has not been condemned by them for very similar views to Luther's, nor have Bucer and Capito for having the same views as Luther, nor Zwingli for not stating his eucharistic doctrine in exactly the same terms as Calvin; and Calvin wrote well of Melanchthon. When one reads such sentiments, it becomes easier to understand how Reina could pass eventually from the Calvinist camp to the Lutheran, for one sees that he did not consider himself bound to one system to the exclusion of others. The effect of the intransigent attitude of Beza and other Calvinist leaders towards him, in the years between 1564 and 1578, contrasted with the friendship of various Lutheran leaders, is also a factor which cannot be ignored.

Further, it is very difficult to understand how Reina could have acquired the reputation for Servetism. Rather, it ought to have been easy for people to have checked his views on the Trinity after they had become suspicious of him for befriending men with reputedly Servetan views. Besides the London Confession of Faith, he made sufficient forthrightly trinitarian statements in his life for this suspicion to be dismissed as groundless. For instance, in his declaration to the Frankfurt Church, dated 12 July 1571, he states expressly, and clearly in refutation of the suspicions about him :

> perseverant en l'approbation . . . des trois symboles receus de toute l'Eglise, à savoir celui qu'on appelle des Apostres, celui du Concile de Nicée et celui d'Athanase, et rejettant tous erreurs et heresies à iceux contraires (pour l'esgard principalement de la doctrine contenue et declairee es deux derniers touchant l'unique essence de Dieu et trinité de personnes).

This declaration also makes clear his view of the real presence in the sacrament:

> mon intention n'a jamais este et n'est encores de confondre . . . la chose
> spirituelle qui nous est presentee au sacrament de la s$^{te}$ Cene, à savoir la chair
> et le sang du Seigneur et tous ses benefices, avec le moien par lequel nous en
> sommes faits participans . . . ces mots 'presentiellement et substantiellement'
> . . . je les ai [utilisés] . . . pour signifier la vraie presence et substance du corps
> et sang de Christ; protestant que je n'y recognoi toutesfois autre presence
> que celle que nostre foi y apprehende spirituellement, demeurant son dit
> corps au ciel.

Despite all the cavilling with which Beza and others bombarded him, this was
the position on the Trinity and the Lord's Supper which he retained right up
to the eve of becoming officially a Lutheran minister. Of course, the position
regarding the Trinity remained the same after that time. When Reina returned
to London to be cleared of the charges that had hung over him for many years,
he made a declaration on the Lord's Supper that the Calvinists felt was so
orthodox that it would remove all controversy between Lutherans and Calvinists, as the title of the pamphlet they printed and circulated in Antwerp indicates:

> Confession (en l'article de la Cene) de Cassiodore Reine Hespaignol, ministre
> en icelle Eglise qui se dict faire profession de la confession d'Ausbourch en
> Anuers, laquelle si ses compaignons veulent confesser en sincerité, le different
> entre eux & les ministres des Eglises reformees sera osté.

In this interrogation, according to the pamphlet, Reina made a fully Calvinist
declaration about the sacrament, although his first answer contains a vague
hint of the Lutheran position:

> Quel est le sens des parolles de la Cene, & si les parolles de la Cene doibuent
> estre entendus proprement ou par figure? Repons. A raison des Sacremens leur
> definition & nature, estans icelles actions mysticques figuratiues & significa-
> tiues, mon aduis est qu'il est necessaire de confesser qu'il y a figure és parolles
> de la Cene, si non que nous voulions confondre les signes auecq les choses
> figurees. Toutesfois il faut tellement conioindre les choses auecq les signes, que
> nous facions entendre que nous ne voulons proposer des signes nuds & vuides
> des choses, ainsi i'enten'le pain en la saincte Cene du Seigneur *signifier* &
> aussy estre en sa maniere le corps de Iesus Christ & le vin le sang d'icelluy.

These declarations were sufficiently on the Calvinist side for Ritter to remon-
strate with Reina about them, and, although the Lutherans of Frankfurt were
fairly willing for him to be a minister in the Antwerp Church, for which they
had taken responsibility, when eventually he moved to Frankfurt itself it was
a different matter. His ministry was resisted for a long time, but when finally
he was allowed to become a minister of his old congregation, now in exile, it
was only after signing all the formularies of the Lutheran Church, and making
a declaration in terms dictated to him by the Consistory of Frankfurt. One feels,
on reading it, that such a declaration went somewhat against the grain for

Reina, requiring him, as it did, to condemn so many people, and in it he is at pains to point out that he makes his declaration in terms put to him by others :

> eam fidei meæ Confessionem, quae à me jure optimo exigitur, nimirum, apertam atque ingenuam, veluti in conspectu Dei, cordium inspectoris, neque id voce solùm, sed etiam scripto : & ut petitioni Vestræ commodius satis-faciam, Vestro ordine, imò, quoad fieri poterit, Vestris etiam verbis  (Lehne-mann, p. 164).

After a whole-hearted acceptance of the ancient creeds and various Lutheran formularies, he abjures the errors of certain non-Lutheran and heterodox Lutheran groups (Roman Catholics, Anabaptists, Flaccians, Schwenkfeldians, Zwinglians, Calvinists), but not without again inserting the 'your' several times :

> sed etiam in Antithesi Vobiscum consentio, id est . . . omnes eos Errores & Hæreses . . . veterum aut recentiorum hæreticorum, verè & ex animo Vobis-cum damno & execror   (p. 164).

In this document he has to wriggle somewhat to escape the difficulties into which he was brought by the declarations he had made before the Archbishop's court in England in 1579. He pleads the fact that the pamphlet was put out by his opponents, who had not printed the whole of what had transpired, and that, in any case, he had been a Lutheran for fourteen years since that date, without causing any scandal by wrong beliefs or evil living.[6]

To sum up, it can be said that Reina was a man whose orthodoxy on the cen-tral evangelical truths held by all Protestants cannot be doubted, but that he wished to avoid strife at all costs, understanding that it was the Church's duty to put the Gospel into practice rather than to dissipate its energies in fruitless wrangling over minute points of non-essential doctrines. Not that he ignored the discussion of such points, but he preferred, when allowed, to make a simple Scriptural statement that might well be capable of several divergent interpreta-tions, and he was unwilling to condemn, unless pushed, views which did not entirely coincide with his own, that is, provided always that they did not contra-dict the Gospel truths. The last extant letter of Reina's is an excellent illustration of all this. Writing to Adolf Fisscher, a Lutheran minister in Amsterdam, who had been with him in Antwerp, on the subject of the Lutheran debate on original sin, he refers to those writers who obscure truths by spiteful and falla-cious craftiness :

> tamen quia negotium tibi nunc est cum literatis hominibus, qui maligna et captiosa versutia disputationem obscuriorem reddant quam ipsa sit.

The method adopted at Antwerp would be far better, in a question where there was raging controversy over a minute point which threatened to do great dam-age to the Church, namely, to ask all ministers to avoid all mention of it, and by this means to build up the Church :

> Populerium . . . intelligo virum . . . bonum ac simplicem, et qui sua verborum simplicitate ædificet Ecclesiam. Quapropter mi Adolphe vehementer illum

---

[6] Lehnemann, pp. 163-7.

tibi commendo. Videlicet ut si de rebus ipsis bene et orthodoxe nobiscum sentit . . . et abstinere velit ab omni contentione eorum verborum quæ non intelligit, illum cures Ecclesiæ restituere. Quia vere fieri potest, ut haec perniciosa contentio Ecclesiam jam Vexare inceperit, memineris qua ratione Antverpiæ non tam incipientum quam magna vi jam grassantem eam Deus optimo sanctissimo et prudentissimo consilio compescuerit, prohibitis videlicet Ministris, ut ab omni ejus quæstionis mentione abstineret, contentis res ipsas diligenter docere verbis in ipsis sacris litteris traditis et in Ecclesia usu receptis atque usitatis. Scis . . . quanta cum Ecclesiæ tranquilitate, quanto cum fructu pietatis hujus sancti consilii beneficio per Dei gratiam, Ecclesiam continuerimus atque auxerimus adversus diaboli insidias et pessimorum illorum hominum.[7]

In spite of his reverence for the Word of God, Casiodoro had a critical attitude to the text of the Bible and was certainly no slavish literalist, but brought his historical and philological knowledge to bear on the problem of interpretation. Mention has already been made of Reina's understanding of Isaiah VII. 14, 'A virgin shall conceive . . .', as referring to the prophet's wife, and only by analogy to Mary, and a similar freedom may be discerned in the other annotations on Isaiah and Ezekiel. In his *Evangelium Ioannis* he studiously avoids naming the author of Hebrews, writing several times 'Autor epistolæ ad Hebræos', and even separating the author from the Apostolic epistle-writers.[8] He recognizes in John's Gospel the element of commentary by the Evangelist himself, where the speeches of Jesus and of John the Baptist merge almost imperceptibly into theological statements about Christ :

Non sunt (quoad ego iudico) verba Baptistæ, vt nonnulli autumant, qui illa ijs quae in fine præcedentis versiculi præcesserunt, coniungunt decepti interpositionne illa 15. versiculi in sententiæ medio : sed sunt Euangelistæ ipsius declarantis vsum illius opulentiæ Christi, de qua dixit in fine 14. versiculi, versiculus enim 15. omnino est interiectus in illa sententia, cuiusmodi interpositiones frequentissimæ sunt cum in sacris omnibus scriptorib. tum maxime in hoc nostro Euangelista, quas nisi quis diligenter obseruet ac deprehendat, falli sæpe in contextu necesse est. Itaque reiecto ver. 15. inter 18. & 19. qui illius est proprius locus, decimum sextum decimo quarto subiungemus in paraphrasi nostra in hos 18. primos versiculos, quam mox subijciemus, vbi videre erit, quomodo ista cohæreant   (p. 23).

Reina is also willing to suggest that verses are out of place in other chapters. He admits allegorical interpretations, but firmly tries to see a passage as it struck the writer and those who first read it.[9] He relies considerably on other parts of the Bible to provide interpretations, and quotes freely from both the Old and the New Testaments. Occasionally, to explain what he wishes to say, he finds

---

[7] F. J. D. Nieuwenhuis, *Geschiedenis der Amsterdamsche Luthersche Gemeente* (Amsterdam, 1856), pp. 19-22.
[8] *Evangelium Ioannis*, pp. 9, 12, 22.
[9] *Evangelium Ioannis*, pp. 32, 40, 48, 53ff, 83, 173.

it useful to use Spanish, French, and Italian, alongside the Hebrew, Chaldean, Syriac, and Greek of the sacred text.[10]

Reina's learning is amply shewn by the good Latin style of his letters, and, in spite of his self-deprecatory remarks in the introduction to his Bible, by his skill in translation into Spanish from Greek and Hebrew. Of Reina's version of the Bible Menéndez Pelayo says that 'el escritor a quien debió nuestro idioma igual servicio que el italiano a Diodati era . . . Casiodoro de Reina', and, 'como hecha en el mejor tiempo de la lengua castellana, excede mucho la versión de Casiodoro, bajo tal aspecto, a la moderna de Torres Amat, y a la desdichadísima del Padre Scio'." Menéndez Pelayo is less complimentary when he comes to remark on Reina's ability as a translator :

> Como trabajo filológico no es el suyo ninguna maravilla. Sabia poco hebreo y se valió de la traducción latina de Santes Pagnino (muy afamada por lo literal) recurriendo a la verdad hebraica sólo en casos dudosos (*Heterodoxos*, V,155).

It is evident that the eminent author of *Heterodoxos* had never compared in Reina's Bible the literal renderings given in the margins with Casiodoro's considered final version as it appears in the text; nor had Menéndez Pelayo any knowledge of the two commentaries of 1573, in which Reina's familiarity with Hebrew, Syriac, and Greek is demonstrated very well.

Reina's education began at University in Spain and continued during his time as a priest and a monk there, and it was certainly not interrupted throughout his years in exile, despite the many difficulties which this brought. The two short commentaries mentioned above display quite well the width of his reading (and its depth, since he claims to have read John's Gospel more than one hundred times).[12] Although, apart from his Bible translation, Reina's published work is not extensive, an analysis of authorities cited by him in his three extant works is instructive. In the Amonestacion to his Bible he quotes seven books of the Old Testament, nine books of the New Testament, and the Tridentine Decrees, besides shewing familiarity with the Septuagint, the Vetus Latina, the Chaldaic Paraphrases, the Syriac New Testament, the Ferrara Spanish Version of the Old Testament, and Sanctes Pagninus's Latin version of the Bible. In his *Evangelium Ioannis* he quotes sixteen books of the Old Testament, nineteen books of the New Testament, Suras 2, 5, 11, 12, and 13 of the Koran, the Muslim 'Alfurca', the Talmud, Eusebius, Cato, Aristotle, Schwenkfeld, Erasmus, Zanchi, and he shews familiarity with Servetus's edition of the Bible and with the Antwerp Polyglot. In the *Expositio Primæ Partis Capitis Quarti Matthæi*, a very short work indeed, he refers to four books of the Old Testament, one from the New Testament, he quotes Horace, and discusses the Donation of Constantine and the opinions regarding it of six Roman Catholic scholars, viz., Nicholas of Cusa, Jacobus Volaterranus, Antonino, Bishop of Florence, Hieronymus Paulus Cathalanus, Laurentius Valla, and Aeneas Sylvius. This reveals a breadth of scholarship and interest equal to that of cultured Spaniards of his

---

[10] *Evangelium Ioannis*, pp. 88f.
[11] *Heterodoxos*, V, 150, 197.
[12] *Evangelium Ioannis*, fol. b[1].

day.[13] Further evidence of this is his lively interest in contemporary theology; besides his interest, already mentioned, in theologians who were not in the main stream of Protestantism, he displays in his letters an easy familiarity with the writings of Luther, Calvin, Bucer, Œcolampadius, Zwingli, Melanchthon, and Capito.[14]

Reina was a Spaniard and proud of the fact. The immense time and trouble he expended in the production of a vernacular Bible for Spain is alone proof of this. This Spanishness can be surmised from the portrait preserved in Frankfurt, and by the extant descriptions of his character.

---

[13] From so few published works, none of them lengthy, this list is not unimpressive. A similar list, established from Cipriano de Valera's *Dos Tratados* alone, contains 136 authorities, Classical, Jewish, Fathers of the Church, Mediæval, and contemporary Roman Catholic and Protestant scholars (my unpublished Ph.D. thesis, Sheffield University, 1971). Valera was considered by himself and by his contemporaries as Reina's subordinate, and it is not likely that the master would be less well-read than his disciple.

[14] *Bib. Wif.*, II, 197f.

# Appendix I

# Request for a Spanish Church in London 1560

The text of Reina's request to the Bishop of London and the Queen's Secretary, Sir William Cecil, for the Spanish Protestant refugees to be allowed their own place of worship. The original is in the British Museum, Lansdowne MSS., Vol. 4, Art. 46, and is in Reina's own handwriting. It was printed in *Bib. Wif.*, II, 190f.

Summa prioris cujusdam scripti illustrissimis Dominis Episcopo Lond. et Secretario primario Regiæ Majestatis exhibiti, quo ostendimus, quibus jam rationibus cogamur ad petendam facultatem ad sacras preces et contiones publice conveniendi : eosque per Christum obsecramus, ut nostris hisce rationibus animadversis hujus rei curam ex animo suscipiant.

Hactenus prudenti atque pio vestro consilio usi, Domini Amplissimi, intra privatas ædes ad preces et contiones convenimus. Jam necessitate urgemur ad petendam facultatem publice conveniendi in templo aliquo ex multis quæ a piis Ministris hujus urbis ad id nobis offeruntur. Qualis vero nos urgeat necessitas, ex subsequentibus rationibus apparebit.

1. Primo. Dum in privatis ædibus convenimus, retardari experimur Regnum Christi, dum multi a nostro Coetu se subducunt, alii nobiscum convenire omnino non audent, quod periculum sibi et rebus suis creent in Hispania, ubi commercia sua habent. Notantur quippe facile, qui sese adjungunt nobis, ab adversariis hac in parte oculatissimis : id quod non fieret in publico aliquo loco, ubi cuivis ingredi est impune.

2. Secundo. Intra privatas ædes tam diu convenientes, præsertim in civitate Dei beneficio Christianis conventibus libera, ansam præbemus adversariis et nos et doctrinam nostram fœdius quam antea traducendi. Aperte enim dicunt, nos portenta quædam intra nos alere ipsis quoque Lutheranis (ut vocant) invisa, quando in civitate maxime Lutherana in publicum prodire haud ducamus nobis tutum. Neque dubito quin, ut hac calumnia impudenter nos istic impetunt, literis quoque in Hispania traducant, hac utique apparenti ratione conflaturi nobis ingens odii pondus non solum apud adversarios, verum etiam apud amicos et fratres. Rationem haberi velim hac in parte Evangelii Christi sincere a nobis annuntiati, quod hanc contumeliam haud dubie subire cogitur nostra hac ratione conveniendi.

3. Neque si, quod petimus, nobis concedatur, verendum erit ne majorem inimicitiarum cum Rege Hisp. occasionem demus : nam simul atque id noverimus, libentius cedemus tota Anglia, quam Regis patiemur nostra causa tumultuari. Neque pudet nos tanto nostro periculo hanc quam petimus emere facultatem : caritas enim Christi urget nos, cujus hoc periculo injuriam propulsamus. Quod vero Legatus Hisp. huic actioni sit intercessurus, vix in animum induco. Primum, quod ultra annum hic jam egerimus, habuerimus coetus titulo Ecclesiæ Hisp. Legatus resciverit, prohibuerit etiam suis ne nostris coetibus interessent, neque ullo modo hactenus intercesserit. Certe id aut quia non possit, aut quia nolit. Si primum, non est quod timeamus ab invalido; si alterum, gratulari etiam debemus ipsi saniorem mentem. Addo etiam quod post duodecim dies idem ipse ingenue fassus est, se nobis hactenus nunquam fuisse adversatum neque si ecclesiam velimus constituere, adversatum iri, quod neque tale quippiam habeat in

mandatis, neque nobis prorsus male velit. Omitto alia quæ si e sincero pectore prodierunt, spem etiam faciunt ampliorem; sui minus, necessitas demum cogit ut periculum faciamus. Tantum obsecro, viri Amplissimi, ut in mentem veniat quantula vestra opera insigniter promoturi sitis negotium Christi, si pro fide vestra officium præstetis.

Amplitudini vestræ addictissimus.

Cassiodorus Hisp.

[Endorsement] 1560 for the Spaniardes p[ro]fess. relligiõ in Lõdon Cassiodorus hispanˢ. To haue a publick place for yᵉ exercise.

# Appendix II

# Corro's Letters to Reina from Thèobon and Bergerac

Antonio del Corro's letter from Théobon to Reina, dated 24 December 1563, reproduced from *Acta consistorii ecclesiæ Londinogallicæ, cum responsio A. Corrani* (London, 1571). Corro gives both Latin and Spanish versions, of which the latter seems to have been the original.[1]

La gracia, paz, y consuelo que Iesu Christo nuestro solo Redemptor pretendio dexar y dexo a sus verdaderos discipulos en tanto que biuiessen en este mundo, sea con v.m.

Señor y amado hermano, yo auia pensado que multiplicar mis cartas, seria causa de recebir alguna de v.m. Pero auiendo quatro meses esperando respuesta suya, no puedo conjecturar otra cosa, sino ô que mis cartas no sean venidas a sus manos, ô que las suyas no pueden facilmente pasar para venir à las mias. Yo tengo tal apprehension de la prouidencia del Señor, que creo su Magestad darà orden en esse negocio, y se empleará de tal suerto, que nos podamos communicar, ô por palabra, ô por escrito. Lo primero que me haze esperar esto, es veer que el Señor ha despertado en mi tal desseo desta communicacion, que creo auiendo el despertado el apetito, no lo dexarà sin hartura. De mas desto veo, que mi intencion en buscar este contento, se desnuda de dia en dia de los interesses que la carne podria buscar. Lo tercero, considero leyendo y releyendo su carta, que este mismo desseo està arraygado en su coraçon. y ansi me certifico, que este negocio se menea por la poderosa mano del, que junta las dispersiones de Israël, quando viene la hora de su voluntad. Resta que lo mas dulçamente y passo à passo que sera possible esta nuestra junta le haga en alguna parte, sin violentar los medios que podriamos tomar para ponerla en execucion. De mi parte es verdad (poniendo por testigo el Espiritu del Señor) que si estuuiera libre de compañia (la qual de tal manera me es compañia, que es vna parte de mi mismo) mas ha de tres años que vuiesse bolado par alla, desde el dia que vide y conosci quan impossible me era biuir sin v.m. Pero pues Dios lo ha querido assi, que yo no pueda andar mas de priessa que al passo de buey (como dizen) y aun atado al yugo con cojundas y lazos, esperarè al Señor de tal orden que serà agradable à su Magestad. Con todos estos contrapesos el año passado auia determinado de hazer my hato, y irle à buscar, sin saber aun adonde estaua. Pero auiendo andado treynta leguas, començaron por aca à condemnar tanto mi liuiandad y mudança, que fue constreñido à hazer posa, y dilatar mi viaje. En el qual tiempo recebi su carta casi milagrosamente. y viendo lo contenido en ella, assi de su desseo de vernos, como de la impression de la Biblia, determinè de esperar este inuierno su determinacion, la qual holgaria saber de cierto y con breuedad, para que yo pudiesse poner orden aqui à mis negocios, y dar respuesta assegurada à los que se pretenden seruir de mi. Porque si v.m. determina de venir por aca, yo no harè mudança alguna, antes entretendrè los amigos de por aca, afin que ayuden en algo à nuestras deliberaciones. Tocante à la impression, creo tendremos buen recaudo, y à escoger solamente aurà alguna difficultad en la correction. Y por esto, si v.m. no piensa em-

[1] See the first paragraph of Corro's Bergerac letter below.

plearse: traygale al Señor Cypriano en su compañia.[2] Su viaje podrà ser passandose en Flandres: y de alli venirse en las vrcas Flamencas hasta la Rochelle, y hasta Bordeaux. Y en las cosas que tuuiere necessidad de encaminar hazia aca, fieze de vn mercader de Bourdeaux, que llaman Pierre du Perrey, del qual le embio aqui vna carta, para que vea mi diligencia en escreuirle, y su voluntad en hazernos plazer. Y si poruentura deteminare de venir por tierra, y no se atreuiere à cargarse de los dineros de la impression, dexelos en manos seguras de algun mercader de Anuerez que aqui hallaremos respondente para recebirlos por poliza de cambio. Y si el Señor Iaques Fixer le dixere que este mercader de Bordeaux tiene por alla correspondencias, fiese que si à el viene adereçada la poliza, nos hara todo el plazer possible, y es bien rico, que no dilatarà por pobreza el pagamiento.

A este mismo rogue, como vera en su carta, que hiziesse dar à v.m. quatro escudos, para que me comprasse algunos tractados ô libros, que piense me haran prouecho. Entre los quales querria auer los libros de don Gaspar, y de Valentino Crotoaldo, y de otros que tractassen la doctrina de nuestra Religion, con edificacion de nuestras consciencias.[3] Porque cierto ya estoy fastidiado de Hebraismos y Helenismos, y los luengos commetarios no me dan gusto ni sabor alguno. Estos libros me podrà v.m. adereçar al dicho mercader de Bordeaux, y el pagarà el flete.

Holgarme ya mucho, de que en sus primeras cartas me hiziesse vn discurso sobre vna demanda que estando en Losana le hize, conuiene à saber, Del conocimiento que vn Christiano deue tener de Iesu Christo, segun los tres tiempos diuersos de su ser, es à saber, En que manera podremos contemplar la palabra prometida de Dios, por remedio del hombre, antes que tomasse nuestra carne, y en que essencia aparecio à los Padres del viejo Testamento. Item del segundo estado, Como estando enel mundo, residia à la diestra de su Padre, *iuxta illud, Et nemo ascendit in cœlum nisi qui descendit de cœlo, Filius hominis qui est in cœlo, &c.*[4] Item tocante al tercero estado, Despues de su glorificacion, holgaria saber que residencia haze Iesu Christo en los fieles, y por que comparaciones se puede esto entender. Y para este effecto querria me buscasse y embiasse los libros, que Osiandro escriuio De la Iustificacion del hombre Christiano, donde prueua, que essencialmente Christo se communica à los fieles. Y sobre este punto querria que me declarasse vn lugar de S. Iuan 17. *Vt omnes vnum sint, sicut tu Pater in me, & ego in te, vt & ipsi in nobis vnũ sint, vt credat mundus quod tu me miseris, &c.*[5]

Item holgaria mucho saber, que opinion se tiene por alla de Velsio,[6] y del Señor Aconcio Italiano, de los quales vn ministro de sancta fee me dio nueuas, meneando la cabeça.[7] Y preguntandole por v.m. mostrò auerse contentado muy mucho. Y entonces yo dixe entre mi: *Si scires donum Dei, & quis est qui loquitur tecum, &c.*[8] Dizeme este, que essa gente ha mal entendido vn librico de Pedro Martyr *De Christi natura,* escritto contra la Vbiquidad. Sobre el qual punto holgaria saber, lo que v.m. siente, *Sit necesse, nec ne, Christum esse vbique secundũ humanam naturam.* Y de que seruiria al Chris-

---

[2] That is, Cipriano de Valera.

[3] That is, Caspar Schwenkfeld and Valentin Krautwald. See note 40 in Chapter II.

[4] John III. 13, Vulgate version (this differs in one word only from Erasmus's translation, 'de' in the former becomes 'e' in the latter).

[5] John XVII. 21, Erasmus's translation.

[6] That is, Justus Velsius. See note 41 in Chapter II.

[7] The place is Saint-Foy-la-Grande (Gironde) on the Dordogne.

[8] Writing to Corro in 1569, Beza refers to this conversation thus, 'Hoc uero quinam Antoni uel de te sentire, sine extrema arrogantia, uel de tuo Cassiodoro scribere, absque intolerabili adulatione potuisti?' (Hessels, II, 73).

tiano la affirmacion d'esta doctrina y presencialidad. Y sobre este punto holgaria de veer vn librico impresso en Alemaña, cuyo argumento es, *Christum esse vbique, &c.*[9]

Item holgaria saber, que edificacion puede dar à vna anima Christiana, de saber, si Christo glorificado sea creatura, ô no. Porque en la Religion Christiana, donde todas las cosas se deuen endereçar à edificacion, no introduzgamos questiones superfluas y sin fructo. Porque veo que el Señor Don Gaspar toma tanto à pechos este negocio, que *existimat actum iam esse de Christiana pietate veroque Dei cultu, ni ambabus, quod aiunt, vlnis hanc doctrinam recipiamus.*

Item desseo mucho saber, que manera de celebracion de Cena tienen en vso las yglesias, donde reside el Señor Crotoaldo, y que interpretacion dan à las palabras de Christo. Porque en estos tratadicos mas emplea su tiempo en impugnar la falsedad, que no en mostrar lo q̃ entiende de la verdad.

Viendo v.m. tantas demandas juntas, bien sé que hallara difficil el responder à todas de vna vez. Pero mi intencion es prepararle para quando nos veamos, y que en el entretanto en cada carta de las que me embiara no se oluide de poner vna añadidura. Seruira tambien de auisarle que manera de libros yo queria que me embiasse. Porque los escoja segun la necessidad que vee en estas demandas.

Resta que le auise de mi deliberacion, que es, de no escreuirle cosa que sea mas nueua que esta, antes pienso hazer tres ô quatro traslados desta misma.

Este dia de la feria vino aqui vn Imprimidor, à hazer concierto conmigo, de lo que podria constar la impression de la Biblia. Antes todas cosas demanda Corrector, para que se pueda bien sancar de su negocio. Y dize, que si le damos el papel, y Corrector sustentado à nuestro gasto, que nos dara mil y dozientos volumines in folio commun imprimidos con distinction de versetes, por quatro reales y medio cada exemplar. Y si el pusiere el papel, pide por cada exẽplar seys reales. Quanto à la commodidad de papel, aqui la ay grande, porque estamos cerca de tres ô quatro molines. Ofrece el Imprimidor de assentar la prensa, donde nosotros quizieremos. Y para este effecto la Reyna de Nauarra nos prestarà vno de sus castillos que sera mas commodo. Y assi sera menester que v.m. embie respuesta de su determinacion, lo mas presto que sera possible, para que yo hable à la Reyna, antes que se vaya à Francia. Y seria lo mejor que el mismo viniesse en persona, y que ambos diessemos orden al negocio. Y aun que quede algo por trasladar, entretanto q̃ se adereça la prensa se podra hazer. Porque entienda que para poner los negocios en astillero, son menester mas de dos otros meses. Item es menester adelantar dozientos escudos al Imprimidor. Sobre todo esto me embie respuesta lo mas presto que sera possible. Hare sin embiando encomiendas à todos essos Señores juntamente, y à cada vno en particular. De Teobon à 24 Deziembre de 1563

*Tuus ex animo,* Antonio d'el Corro.

Corro's letter from Bergerac to Reina, dated 25 March 1564, reproduced from Hessels, III, 1, pp. 32ff.

Monsieur et tresaymé frere. Il me seroit presque impossible de uous pouuoir raconter les grandes diligences que i'ay fait de huict moys en ça à fin d'entendre quelque nouelle certaine de vous. Ce que ne m'a esté possible : et vous certifie que ne tient pas à lettres. Car voycy la vint et vniesme, et estant ia las d'escrire en Espagnol pour me soulager i'ay usé de la main et langue d'autruy, et ay deliberé de continuer en la sorte, iusques à ce qu'il uous plaise de m'enuoyer response.

La somme de toutes mes lettres passées est telle, uous faire entendre comment le moys de Septembre passé ie receus vne lettre vostre qui m'adressastes par mons[r] le Blanc aduocat de Bourdeaux : me faisant mention d'une autre, laquelle ie ne receus

---

[9] A letter of Cousin to Monsieur de St Pol identifies this book as being by Johann Brenz (Brentius) (1499-1570), the Swanbian Reformer (Hessels, II, 50).

point: ny autre aucune quatre ans a. Vous me fistes entendre de vostre deliberation touchant à la Bible Espagnole: laquelle i'approuue grandement, et m'amployeray de toute mon affection en tout ce que sera en ma puissance. Je trouue icy assez bonnes commoditez pour le tout. Si vous en aués de meilleures ie uous suyuray. Mais pour ce faire il faudra que vous venez part deça. Et ce pendant que nous conferons noz papiers: le Seigneur nous donra le meilleur aduis, que estimera estre expedient à sa gloire. De quelques iours en ça ay trouué icy quelques Portugalois, lesquels ont traffique en Espagne: et sont bien affectionez à fauoriser noz entreprinses en ce qu'ils pourront. Le moyen de distribuer les liures sera assez commode en ces quartiers d'ores en auant, ou la liberté de la religion, et predication de l'Euangile est publique. Reste seulement, que pour donner ordre à noz affaires, vous prenez la peine de venir part deça. Car sans legitime occasion et euidence d'icelle ie n'oseroye partir d'icy: ny donner las occasions de legereté qu'ay fait iusques icy: pensant d'un iour à autre uous aller trouuer. Mais quand vous viendries cela satisferoit à tout le monde, et on verra que la necessité me contraint à uous suyure: et non point la fastidie que i'aye prins de ce païs comme on l'estime pour le present. Du moyen commode pour vostre voyage vous y penserez. Mais à ce que m'ont dit ceux qui sont venus l'année passée de Londres, estiment que ce seroit le meilleur de descendre à la Royselle. la ou vous trouuerés vn ministre apellé monsieur de Nord, lequel est de mes amys, et vous acheminera vers Bordeaux: ou monsieur le Blanc vous receura fort voluntiers: et adressera au lieu de sa residence. En venant part deça noblies point de me porter quelques petis traités tels que vous aduiserez: ou me les enuoyeres par les lettres audit ministre Nord à la Roysselle: auquel i'aduertiray que me las face tenir: ou par la voye de Bourdeaux, las adressant au sire Pierre du Perray, marchand de Bourdeaux, pres du palais: ou par quelque autre voye que vous estimeres commode. Il à vn marchand à Tholose qu'on apelle Bernoye, lequel a des facteurs à Enuers, et à Londres. Si vous adressez vos lettres par lesditz facteurs: mettes leur une couuerte que s'adresse à madamoiselle de sainct Estienne espagnol, demeurant à la rue des Perolieres, à Tholose: et ladite damoiselle me las fera tenir. Jusques a ce que i'aye response de vous, mes lettres ne seront que le double de ceste icy.

Señor por otras abra V.M. recebido mi excusa de no iscreuirle en mi lengua ni de mi mano; ruegole que esto no sea ocasion de dexarme de escreuir lo mas presto que le sera possible. Salude de mi parte a todos esos señores y en especial a los señores sus padres. De . . . ssa çerca de Bergerac a 25 de Março de 1564.[10]

Si en absencia del Señor Cassiodoro otro alguno recebiere esta, ruegole que me responda por la uia que dira Syre Jaques Fichet.

Tuus ex animo si unquam
     Antonius Corranus, dit Belleriue.
[Endorsement in a different hand] Leîtres pour estre adressées au Sire Jacques Fichet Marchand de Londres pour les bailler à Monsieur Cassiodore Espagnol, ou en son absence à ses parents A Londres.

---

[10] Hessels was unable to decipher the place of origin of this letter, but MacFadden, p. 205, shews that it was Boesse, about fourteen miles south-east of Bergerac, the home of Sieur Jean d'Escodéca.

# Appendix III

# Depositions Concerning Reina Laid Before the Bishop's Commissioners

This is the text of the depositions concerning the doctrine and morals of Casiodoro de Reina laid before the Bishop of London's commissioners soon after Reina's flight from England in 1563. The documents from which the following is taken consist of copies made from the originals by Reina himself, an interesting feature of which is the underlining of certain phrases by Reina, shewn here in italics. These autograph transcripts by Reina are preserved in Frankfurt City Archives (Sammelband Kirchendokumente B, Französisch-reformierte Kirche 195, fols. 589-602). They have suffered a certain amount of damage, with the resultant loss of some words on every page, and whole sentences on a few pages. Since Reina's handwriting is a very legible italic, omission marks in the text indicate this damage.

[fol. 589] Ce mercredi 15 de Septemb. 1563, nous les commissayres assemblez par le commandement de Monsr. l'Evesque avons resceu les tesmoignages suyvans sur la cause de Cassiodore.
[The deposition by Gaspar Zapata]

Viri optimi ac integerrimi. Quandoquidem ab Illmo. Domino Episcopo Lond. est vobis tradita ex provincia cog . . . doctrinæ vitæ et morum D. Cassiodori, et ego autoritate vestra sum vocatus ut exponam id quod sentiam de eius doctrina, primum profiteor coram Domino Deo et Angelis eius, atque coram vobis, viri iudices, qui Dei personam representatis, me hui non accedere tanquam accusatorem aut calumniatorem D. Cassiodori. vt ille falso mihi et aliis imponit: quod quidem pernego atque in hoc conscientiam ipsius requiro, et illius familiarium, ac præsertim conscientiam Balthasaris Sanchez, et Angeli Victorii, et Francisci de Abrego et Aliorum: qui omnes optimè norunt me post confessionem quam edidit adolescentulus illa de flagitio nefando, me inquit exhortatum esse omnes qui rei conscii erant, vt nos gereremus in hac causa ex verba Dei, corrigentes dum taxat eum fraternè: si quidem erat crimen adhuc occultum, et ne permitteremus diuulgari, quo vitaretur scandalum. quod ita factum est. Accedo igitur coram vobis tanquam Dei organum, quo illi visum est vti in hac inquisitione, vt reddam dum taxat testimonium verum et incorruptum de iis quæ scio de doctrina et vita Cassiodori. Anterim Deum opt. max. precor, vt mihi adsit virtute Spiritus sui cælestis, qui me ducat in omnem veritatem.

Quod ad doctrinam attinet, non est mihi suspectus Cassiodorus ante confessionem Adolescentuli, licet aliqua audiuerim, quae possunt mihi gignere suspitionem: et maximè Italus quidem machinis bellicis præfectus mihi dixit Aureliae tempore obsidionis. prox[a] præteritæ, Londini habetis (inquit) ministrum Hispanum apprimè doctum et pium, quem scio non confiteri nisi vnicum Deum, non duos, vt vos qui asseritis, Christum esse verum Deum. Tamen his verbis non fui inductus, vt hoc de Cassiodoro crederem at verò intellecta confessione adolescentuli, mentem meam . . . Deum erigens dixi Deus omnipotens quid hoc est? quomodo isto . . . batur, traditus sit in tam reprobum sensum, vt præter . . . et . . . sui oblitus, perpeteauerit? scelus tam prodigiosum? et quis hoc patefecisset, nisi tu: Domine, cuius admirabilis est prouidentia et curam in gubernanda tua Ecclesia? qui ex ore illius adolescentuli extorseris hanc confessionem? Certè domine, hoc admirabili iudicio tuo aliquid maius tentas. Fortassè impiè hic sentit de Eterno filio tuo: proinde hoc indigno scelere multò aliud indignius patefacere vis, atque ita cum ad resipiscentiam adducere.

Tunc paulo post cepi confessionem fidei, quam ille suo nomine et aliorum Hispanorum obtulerat. Ecclesiæ Gallicanæ, considerare, et in ea annotaui quædam, quæ in animo meo grauem suspitionem gignunt. Ea igitur (viri docti et pii) pono discutienda et examinanda. Primùm in tota eius confessione non inuenio, vbi fateatur, Christum Dominum esse æternum filium Dei ab eterno genitum a Patre: nec vbi discutis verbis fateatur duas naturas, nempè diuinam et humanam hypostaticà esse vnitas in Christo, quod est suspectum in confessione fidei: maximè eorum qui erant tunc suspecti hereseos Serueti . . . in hac vrbe.

In primo cap. sect. 2. suæ confessionis descriptio personæ filii est mihi suspecta: quia etsi dicat esse representationem ex expressam imaginem substantiæ Patris, et hæc de diuina Christi essentia prædicatur: tamen loquutio est translatio, et potius ad nos relationem habet, quàm ad Patrem, vt sciamus quid in Christo quærendum sit. neque Apostoli consilium fuit tradere ibi quid simile intus habeat Pater cum filio, sed qualiter Deus nobis patefit in Christo. Ergo in descriptione personarum antequam indueret carnem diserte et clarè dicendum erat, Jesum Christum, quatenus Deus est, esse Filium Patris vnicum ab Eterno genitum, non factum, verum Deum cum Patre et Spiritu Sancto, coeternum, consubstantialem et Patri equalem. Porro si nomen substantiæ Cassiodoro denotet essentiam, absurdè dicitur Filium, quatenus Deus est, esse expressam imaginem substantiæ Patris, cum eadem sit, et quidem [fol. 590] simplex vtriusque essentia. Sectione 5 eiusdem cap. dicit sic, vel auferat à Christo . . . Spiritu Sancto dignitatem Dei. nam multi sunt qui illi attribuunt dignitatem Dei, et auferunt essentiam et eternitatem. Tertio. mihi est valde suspectus propterea quod non solum fatetur Christi esse Filium naturalem Dei, sed asserit, et sic docet, omnes regenitos per verbum et fidem esse filios Dei naturales quia illis datur Spiritus Sanctus et communicatur seu infunditur natura diuina, iuxta illu . . . Petri, Sumus consortes naturæ diuinæ. At verò si regeniti sunt filii naturales, ergo sunt filii essentiales. argumento à natura ad essentiam. Igitur sunt eiusdem essentiæ et substantiæ cum Deo, quod est nimis absurdum. Inquo videtur assertiri hæreticis nostri temporis qui asserunt, filium Dei esse Deum essentialem, quos refutat D. Calvinus in libello qui inscribitur, Impietas Valentini etcetera. Quarto, ego audiui a Cassiodoro hanc propositionem, Pater producit filium per verbum quæ quidem propositio auget mihi suspitionem. Nam cum quæsiissem ab eo, an crederet Christum esse Filium Dei Eternem (sunt enim qui dicunt tunc cepisse cum verbum caro factum est) respondit, Quemadmodum nos sumus præcogniti a Deo ab eterno, postea aut cum tempore sumus regenti per verbum et fidem, ita Pater (inquit ille) producit filium per verbum. et cum ego intulissem, Ergo filius est aliquid distinctum a verbo tunc expediuit se nec affirmando nec negando dicens, Ego credo cum omnibus piis et cum ipso Athanasio. Proinde suspicor illum habere cum Serueto Christum esse Eternum filium, quin præcognitus, et non quia sit ab eterno genitus à Patre.

Quinto. Capit. 8. sect. 1. cum agit de natura et persona Christi, dicit, Confitemur et credimur firmiter, Authorem nostræ salutis, nempe Christum, quod ad naturam et personam illius attinet, esse verum hominem . . . ptum. etcetera. vbi nomen naturæ simpliciter posit mihi suspitio . . . quia . . . bus naturis vnitis in Christo hypostaticè. Et quoniam . . . Deum, quid mirum? Idem Arriani, Seruet. et Val. fatentur.

Sexto. Cap. 9. Sect. 2. dicit, Dedit item nobis non solum nomen filiorum, sed etiam vt realiter sinus, communicans nobis virtute sui spiritus naturam diuinam: Vbi asserit quod superius tetigi.

Septimo. Cap. 10. Sect. 2. partitur iustificationem hominis inter hominem et Deum.

dicit enim hominem iustificari, ex parte hominis (inquit) per veram pœnitentiam et fidem, et ex parte Dei per suam solam misericordiam et liberalitatem. At Scriptura in solidum attribuit gratuiter misericordiæ Dei iustificationem, et docet, fidem, quæ iustitiam Christi apprehendimus, domum Spiritus Sancti esse, et similiter Pœnitentiam.

Octauo. Capt. 21. sect. 2. dicit, Credimus, quod omnis caro resurget tam bonorum, quam malorum, licet quemadmodum ad diuersos fines ita etiam diuersis principiis. Pii enim. quia eorum resurrectio pendet à Christi resurrectione vt a prima causa, resurgent in eadem carne ad vitam eternam virtute seminis diuinitatis quod in ipsis seminatum fuit per diuinum verbum et fidem. Ratione cuius seminis est impossibile eos perpetuo detineri vinculis mortis, eadem ratione qua Christus non potuit detineri. In cuius resurrectione habent pignus certissimum suæ resurrectionis et probationem experimentalem de eo quod in hoc casu poterit natura diuina cuius per spiritum Dei iam sunt participes. Doctrina hæc est mihi suspecta.

Atque superiora, viri iudices, suspecta sunt, a me non odio aut maleuolentia dicta, sed iussi vestro, amore religionis, et veræ pietatis ad gloriam omnipo tentis Dei et Christi filii sui Eterni Domini nostri ecclesiæ suæ.

[fol. 591] Illud etiam non est omittendum Cassiodorum adiunctum Ecclesiæ Gallicæ et Flandricæ non interfuisse congregationibus et conciliis initis singulis mensibus vt eum vtràque Ecclesia conferret, declaretque charitatis, religionis et doctrinæ vnitatem ac vinculum, quin potius, vt intellexi, semper hæc neglexit, licet fuerit prouocatus. Contra, eos intimos habuit, qui vel aduersentur, vel excisi erant, vt schismatici et hæretici ab vtrique ecclesia. Hoc est testimonium quo ad doctrinam Cassiodori.

Gaspar Çapata.

## La deposition d'Angelus.

Tres honnorez Seigneurs. Puisque vous m'avez commandé par ordre du Reverendissime Euesque de Londres de dire ce que je scay et soubçonne de la doctrine de Cassiodore, je protest devant Dieu et ses anges et vous de dire simplement la verite.

1. Premierement. donques je scay que luy tout incontinent qu'il eut a frankfort vng livre de Seruet, le baisa, et dict, que jamais il ne cognust bien Dieu iusques ace qu'il eut ce liure-la, et que Seruet seul auoit entendu le mistere de la Trinite. ceci m'a dict Lion et Cortes de Luy.

2. Que Seruet auoit esté bruslé iniustement. Ceci m'a dict Lion, Cortes, et Herrere qu'il disoit.

3. Que Jesus Christ estoit la Parolle eternelle de Dieu, non pas fils eternel: mais que l'hors il commença d'estre fils quand il print chair humaine. allegoit le passage Verbum caro factum est . . . Ceci ont dit les autres de luy.

4. Qu'on pouvoit bien tenir secrete . . . sans mourir pour elle pour ce qu'elle estoit dangereuse et scandaleuse. Ceci m'a dict Lion de luy.

5. Qu'il disoit n'y auoit point de charité a Geneue. et que lá on ne preschoit point de la mortification ne de la charité. sinon tout contre les moynes. ceci m'a dict Lion de luy.

6. Qu'il n'estoit pas bon de fayre eglise Espagnole à Geneue pour la crainte du Magistrat.

7. Qu'il a escript vne letre a Castalio le suscript de laquelle estoit Docto et pio viro Sebastiano Castalioni. Je l'ay veüe es mains de Cortez à Losanne laquelle Cassiodore envoyoit de Geneue.

8 Que nuos sommes non seulement enfans adoptiffs de Dieu mais aussi naturels pourtant que Dieu nous communique sa nature diuine. allegoit le passage de S. Pierre, Sumus consortes diuinæ naturæ. et adioustoit que c'estoit doctrine de grande consolation, et l'aultre imparfaicte et a demi. ceci je ay ouy deux foix en ses sermons.

9. Que nous pouuons enfreindre l'election de Dieu eternelle, perdre la foy, et l'esprit de Dieu. Je luy dis que beaucoup de meschans perdent le goust de la misericorde de

Dieu, non pas les vrayment esleus. Il respondit que Dauid estoit vrayement esleu: mais neantmoins dict Spiritum rectum tuum ne auferas à me. par lequel declare qu'on peut perdre la grace. ceci m'a dict luy mesme. [fol. 592]

10. Qu'il a admi Acontio non seulement aux sermons, mais il l'a faict cheff des congregations et assemblees secretes.

11. Qu'il a fauorisé a Adrian qui fut banni.

12. Qu'on debuoit fayre la cene comme S. Paul dict, Que les Corinthiens la faisoint. C'est en prenant vng repas tous ensemble, et non pas ainsi qu'on l'administre a Geneue. Ceci m'a dict Herrere de luy.

13. Finalement Sa confession de foy m'est fort suspecte en l'article de la Trinité et des troys personnes lesquelles il n'admet rondement, mais pour se conformer avecque les eglises. Le mesme dict du Baptesme des enfans. Ce qu'il ne debuoit pas fayre, comm'il semble, en vne petite confession de foy on debuoit estre brieff, clair et rond.

Angelus Victorius Sardres.

Le tesmoignage de Francisco Abrego de la doctrine de Cassiodore et de ses compagnons.

il nous apelle faux freres, pour tant que nous ne nous accordions a leurs opinions. Lion m'a dict, que les Anabaptistes font bien de n'admettre point la Trinite ne troys personnes ce qu'il louoit fort. Item, qu'vng Espagnol puni pour Anabaptiste a Anuers fut sauué, et ne fut condamné pour cela combien qu'il mourut pour tell'opinion.

Item, il loua Seruet disant que depuis les Apostres null n'à parlé mieux. et qu'il ne fut point entendu.

Item Herrere me dict le mesme du dict Seruet, lequel estoit avecque le mesme Lion.

Item le mesme Herrere me dict en presence de Gaspar Çapata que conbien que les Anabaptistes le creussent que Jesus Christ . . . sauueur n'auoit point prins chair de la vierge les tenoit pour . . .

Item François de la . . . point d'authorité en l'escripture par laquelle conste que les enfans doibuent estre baptizés. et que plusieurs croyent par songes et non par autorité de l'escripture: pour monstrer qu'ils ne doibuent estre baptizés.

Item je soubçonne de Cassiodore, a scauoyr de sa foy, de ce que ses compagnons m'ont dict, et aussi bien pource que je scay de sa vie, et pour sa confession de foy qu'il a faicte, et pource qu'il a caché ce qu'il à traduict de la Bible en Espagnol.

Franciscus Abrego.

Tesmoignage de Balthasar Sanchez.

Messieurs puisque vous m'auez demandé de rendre tesmoignage dela doctrine de Cassiodore, je vous proteste deuant Dieu de confesser la verite de ce que je soubçonne de luy.

Premierement Cortes et Lion incontinent qu'ils vindrent ace pays, me dirent que Cassiodore disoit que les noms de Trinité et de Personnes ne vauloint rien: mais qu'ils estoint forgez des hommes contre la parolle de Dieu.

Item Lion m'a dict que les Juiffs et les Turques ne se convertissent point a nostre religion pour autant que nous faisons trois dieus. ce que luy auoit dict Cassiodore.

Item le mesme Lion apporta a ma maison vng liure imprimé lequel traictoit, qu'on ne debuoit point brusler les heretiques.[1] ce que Lion defendoit et me fit a croyre.

Item le mesme Lion me dict incontinent apres, que mons<sup>r</sup> Caluin fit brusler Seruet a

---

[1] The book referred to was probably one of three published in 1554 by Sébastien Castellion and his friends against Calvin's action in permitting and defending the burning of Servetus, viz. *De Hæreticis an sint persequendi* (Basle), *Traité des Hérétiques A savoir si on les doit persécuter* (Lyons), and *Contra Libellum Calvini in quo ostendere conatur Hæreticos jure gladij coercendos esse* (Basle).

Geneue iniustement et par enuie: pource que Seruet disoit qu'incontinent qu'il sortiroit dela prison donneroit à cognoistre qui estoit Mons^r Caluin.

[fol. 593] Item Lion et Cortez me dirent que Mons^r Caluin n'entendit point Seruet, et qu'ils croyent qu'il se repentoit de l'auoyr brusler contre sa conscience, et qu'il n'en feroit brusler plus jamais ce qu'ils auuoint ouy dire a Cassiodore.

Item le dict Lion me dict que Mons^r Caluin fit vng liure de ne point brusler les heretiques puis estant prins Seruet en fit vng aultre tout contrayre de brusler les heretiques.[2]

Pour ma certitude et repos de ma conscience je demanday à Cassiodore incontinent qu'il vint d'Almayne, pourquoy Seruet auoit esté bruslé, respondit, Par fault de charité.

Item, que Seruet estoit vng grand homme, et que s'il eust vescu, il eust faict grand profit à nostre nation.

Item, qu'en Espagne auoit dict des messes qui firent plus grand profit qu'aucuns sermons de Londres.

Item, que quand il passoit a Geneue par le lieu ou il fut bruslé, les larmes luy tomboit des yeulx.

Item, qu'il croyoit que si l'euangile venoit a France, Geneue seroit vn aultre Rome, ce qu'il disoit pour la iustice de Geneue.

Item, qu'à Geneue on ne prechoit d'autre chose que contre le pape et les moynes et non pas des choses d'edification.

Item, il a tenu grande familiarite avecque les ennemis de l'eglise Flamande.

Item, il à esleu pour estre cheff de nostre consistoyre Aconcio.

Item, il envoyoit secrets messages a Adrian banny.

Item il me semble qu'il a faict mal de cacher ce qu'il a traduict de la bible en Espagnol il seroit bon qu'on l'examinast bien.

Balthasar Sanchez.

Testimonium Jer . . . versum a Germanice à Joanne Wttenhou . . .

De Confessione Hispanica Cassiodori del . . . meam sententiam grauia pun . . . deprehendi quæ mihi malam sus . . . am gignunt, cum antea haberent occasionem in eam inquirendi.

Primum. cap. 1. vbi scribit de diuinitate Filii, minus dicit quoque par est, iuxta meam opinionem, posteaque non scribit Filium esse sine principio sicut et Patrem.

Eodem cap. præbat suspitionem omittendo verbum Personæ, cuius loco vtitur res: sit enim, istæ tres res.

Eodem cap. vtitur his verbis, Trinitas est Persona, scribit enim, quo nos conformemus ecclesiis fidelium, ideo admittimus hæc nomine Trinitas et Persona. Hæc paulo ante dicit quod captus humanus non possit comprehendere neque intelligere.

Cap. 21. de resurrectione mortuorum scribit quod fideles resurgent virtute diuini seminis quod in ipsis seminatum est per verbum Dei et fidem: et quod impii etiam resurgent non quidem virtute diuinitatis, sed virtute Dei, qui ipsos suscitabit.

In articulo fidei scribit ipse Jesum Christum filium Dei vnicum Dominum nostrum, sed non vnicum seu vnigenitum filium.

Atque sunt præcipua puncta quæ habeo ex ipsis confessione, tametsi et innumera sunt alia vnde suspitionem capere liceat: rerum ea iudicio vestro relinquo, quippe qui maioribus domis dotati estis hûque iudices commissi estis.

Tempore excommunicationis Adriani Haemsteri ad ipsum postulans ab ipso consilium, nimirum quid facturus essem in ea causa quaternas ad consensum eiusdem excommunicationis attineret. Tinc suasit ipse mihi omnino silerem, neque me ei rei commiscerem, et casu qua [fol. 594] hic interrogarer, dicerem, me adeo non sapere, vt quiquem in ea re agitare possem: et posteaque ipsi coepissent, etiam absoluerent. Ipso quoque Bartholomei die nuper præterito loquens cum D^no Capata, agnoscebat

[2] See note 5 to Chapter IV.

ipse in mea præsentia quod fideles essent naturales filii Dei, quemadmodum et Christus Jesus vnde intelligo Christum esse filium Dei. adoptione quemadmodum et nos. similiter leo redarguit me ante annum vnum dicens crassam esse hæresim credere, Christum esse a semine mariæ, dicens quoque omnes comburi debere qui hoc dicerent et crederent. Atque verba frequenter conspuebat probrosissimeque ac plane contemptim se gerebat.

Cassiodorus quoque mihi suspectus est quod versionem suam Bibliorum absconderit suppresseritque. similiter quod se Ministerio ipse abdicaverit.

Ita subscriptum Jeremias Ackerman.

Ce Mardi 21 de Septembre nous les commissaires estans assemblez auuons reseu la deposition des tesmoins par escript touchant la vie de Cassiodore comm'on leur auoit enioinct.
[Deposition of Gaspar Zapata.]

Viri iudices, Dicturo iussu vestro de crimine quod Ioannes filius Ioannis de Vayona sponte confessus est Cassiodorum a Reina perpetrasse, mihi inprimis præfandum est coram vobis (viri integerrimi) me ante hac semper voluisse atque nunc velle hanc rem omnino sepultam, et in eo totis viribus incubuisse ne patefieret, ob gravissimas considerationes quin hoc prætextu narrationem rei extenuasse, quoties cum familiaribus Cassiodori, quibus eam libuit communicare, in eum sermonem incidissem. Sed quando Domini prouidentia factu, est, vt præter votum . . . vobis sit exponenda, idque instantia illius, cuius maxime opo . . . n ingenue ac bona fide quod mihi compertum . . .
Deum aut suppremum iudicem precor mihi spiritu suo adsit sincero et candido effectu eum inuocanti quo reddam testimonium veritati, neque et illo pacto me sinet deuiare, neque ab ea discedere. Omissis igitur aliis quæ possent non mediocriter Cassiodorum grauare, *à quibus libenter abstineo,* ita se res habet.
Quadam die mensis Julii. proximè præteriti accessit ad me Franciscus de Abrego, et nuntiauit intellexisse se a Joanne filio Joannis de Vayona adolescentulo annis nato decem et septem. Cassiodorum eo veluti scorto fuisse abusum. *quod mihi denuntiauit Franciscus de Abrego, ex declaratione ipsius licebit cognoscere. proinde non opus est hîc interseratur.* Ego verò respondi me nullo pacto posse credere de Cassiodoro tam prodigiosum scelus. Admoneo hominem vt taceat, ac nemine dicat. Ille autem, si mihi non adhibes fidem, adolescentulum conueni: ex eo comperies rem ita se habere. Tunc Franciscus adducit adolescentulum nescio quo praetextu ad templum D. Pauli me ibi expectante: et salutato adolescentulo dixi, Adeo stultus est Joannes vt rem gravissimam et periculi et detrimenti maximi plenam quam oporteret in tenebris esse sepultam palam feceris? et obiurgans eum tace (inquit) et obmutesce: nam magnum cum tibi tum maxime Cassiodoro poteris dare damnum. At ille, Domine (inquit) nemini patefeci, nisi huic Francisco, cui asserenti et mihi et aliis duobus Flandris patefecisti, vt nudius tertius significasti, Joannes assentit, addiditque non declarasse nomen, neque unde Cassiodorus fecerit, respondit verecunde et nimis pudore suffusus, abusum esse eo, cum simul eodem in lecto dormirent. Hîc mihi veniam dabunt castissimæ vestrum omnium aures, si obscœnitate verborum offensæ, atque argumento imputabitis rei et turpissimæ et indignissimæ.
[fol. 595] Interrogatus igitur an intromiserit membrum, affirmauit ita esse, atque digito suo indice ostendit mensuram. Interrogatus an tum senserit aliquam dolorem, respondit non, sed postridie illius diei laborauit (inquit) fluxu ventris. Interrogatus quoties eum esset aggressus Cassiodorus, respondit primo in cubiculo inferiore quod est in scala edium semel. deinde in superiore vbi quinquies aut sexies et pluries etiam donec me superauerim a lecto. Interrogatus an fuerint frequentes illi congressus. Respondit a primo congressus qui fuit in cubiculo scalæ ad secundum qui fuit in superiore, præteriere, vt mihi videtur, 30. aut 40. dies. posthunc frequenter me est aggressus, aliquando

duabus solum interiectis noctibusque, aliisque quatuor. Interrogatus, cur sinebat se violari, respondit, Is me amplexabatur retro adeo arcte vt non possem effugere. Interrogatus quanto tempore durabat ille actus, respondit quarta parte horæ, vt mihi videbatur. Interrogatus an Cassiodorus dicere ei quicquam, respondit, Cassiodorus quærebat à me se aliquid senserem aut mali quicquam passus essem; et ego respondebam, non domine. nihilo minus is dicebat, Da mihi veniam Joannes, da mihi veniam. atque orante et precibus efflagitanti vt tacerem, nil ei respondebam eram enim animo consternatus, et extra me ipsum, ac proinde nil morabar. Hoc aiebat esse factum post primam illam coniunctionem. Interrogatus an parentes eius essent rei conscii. Respondit, minime. quin precatus est me ne quicquam dicerem. Cassiodoro neque parientibus. Iterum cum iuueni occurrerem et eum in superiorem sermonem conducerem, conatus sum variis quæstionibus eius animum explorare, vt mihi certo posset de eius constantia vel inconstantia constare. at iuuenis constanter perstitit in criminis confessione, neque dimotus est vel pilum de substantia facti. Porro Franciscus de Abrego quo die me huius rei fecerat certiorem, communicauerit item eam Balthasaro Sanchez et Angelo Victorio. proinde opus fuit cum eos referre quod de confessione adolescentulis e . . . quod factum est ac decretum adire qu . . . prudenter et considerate . . . gereremus. Considerat . . . enim esse et maximi et ponderis, ob idque non temere procendendum. *Consilio igitur huius viri visum fuit nobis facturum optimum si res iudicaretur patri adolescentuli vt* pietate et conspectu commotus filius depromerat purius rei veritatem. ex pectore. Tum petii a Vayona vt filium in agrum educeret, atque ibi prius *inuocato Domino* simulque eius indicio ob oculo posito iuueni, pater ad eum sic, Capio fili mi abste scire quid rei tibi cum Cassiodoro contigerit. Caue autem fili ne falsum contra proximum proferas, neque viro immerenti falsi criminis notam inuras. Time ergo Deum, et eius iudicium, et fatere veritatem, filius autem copiose lacrymas effundens et pollicitus se eum dicturum, confessione coram matre edita non absimili a superiore confirmauit eam et ratam bel . . . fecit. Vayona (credo) attestabitur mihi, examinetur. Sed interim videre erat lamentabili patris et filii spæctaculum. Uterque profuse lacrymabatur: hic quidem interram defixis oculis semiuiuus: ille verò in coelum, inuocansque Deum, in haec verba prorupit, Domine elargire mihi quæso tollerantiam qua possim sustinere hanc secundam iniuriam mihi ab homine isto factum, longe profecto grauiorem priore. Significabat autem scandalum suscitatum ob nimiam hominis tum familiaritatem tum consociationem cum uxore.

Tandem adii Cassiodorum, nam mihi seniori tradita fuit hæc prouintia vt fraterne eum corrigerem et simul etiam acriter reprehenderim, quo resipisceret et daret gloriam Deo. Id erat enim nostrum votum, necque aliud quicquam requirebatur. Sed quid ego hac mea diligentia sim consequutus, experientia testater. Traducor enim ab homine et iam male audio cum nihil minus sim promeritus. Attamen hoc me consolatur, quod iudicio Dei sistimur. Christus enim Dominus per vos iudicium exercet. Alocutus igitur Cassiodorum, dixi, Aspice me Cassiodore non vt Gasparum Capatam sed tanquam Angelum e cœlo ad te missum. Turpitudo tua [fol. 596] est iam reuelata. Constat te confessione cuiusdam iuuenis peccatum sodomiæ perpetrasse. Resipisce igitur et de gloriam Deo Altissimo. Id solum remedii est tibi reliquum. Sin minus neque effugies iram Dei neque magistratus vindictam. Interea dum ego hunc sermonem facerem, ille vultu, gestu, et totius corporis habitu, animi sibi mali conscii edidit significationem, ita à quouis vel stupido posset facile intelligi. Et Correptus ingenti pauore et sensu iudicii Dei profecto, sine me (inquit) respirare. et quum nudasset et aperuisset pectus, animo aliquantul . . . recepto pollicetur se dicturum veritatem. et fassus est se quinque aut sex pollutiones habuisse cum lateri adhæret adolescentulus ille filius Ioannis de Vayona. primam quidem in cubiculo ab illo annotato, reliquas autem in superiore: sed sibi euenisse dormienti absque consensu voluntatis, ac proinde citra culpam. Cum autem intellexisset rei huius esse conscios Balthasarum, Angelum, et Franciscum, præterea et patrem iuuenis, precatus est vt illos congregarent quod ilicò factum est. Conuenimus igitur vnà in agro, Vayona cum filio, Balthazar, Angelus et Franciscus, similiter et Cassiodorus. Ibi autem eorum confessionibus, vtique perstitit in sententia. Sed interrogatus vlterius adolescentulus *an dormiret Cassiodorus* quando ille abutebatur, nam propter confessionem Cassiodori opus fuit vt expediretur haec quaestio, respondit, se nescire. Verum est (inquit) Cassiodorus me admonuisse, vt si quid sentirem, cum euigilassem. *quod quidem a me semel factum est vltimo* cum speraui me ab illius lecto. nam tentanti me illo congressu dormire. Tunc adstantes dixerunt adolescentulo et praesertim Angelus, Vide quid dicas et caue ne falso loquaris. Si verum non est hactenus assensisti, dicito, non. Si verum est, dicito, si. Cui adolescens coram omnibus cum multis lacrymis respondit Hispanice, si que me lo hizo. quod Gallice sonet, Ouy, ouy, qu'il m'a faict cela. Tunc ego cum Cassiodoro seorsum aliquantulum separatus ab aliis, dixi, Opus est . . . vt veritatem fatearis, . . . *gatiua, quia quoad ex animis istorum coniic . . .* Magistratum. at ille respondit, nullam . . . it iuuenem à lecto cum primum contigisset ille primo . . . habuisse tunc inspirationem diuinam quam postea nihili habuit. Cæterum videns se vrgari ab aliis vt agnosceret culpam et gloriam daret Deo, quorum sermones non repetam, nisi Joannes de Vayona qui dicebat, Agnosce Cassiodore cum Dauide, esto Dauid, esto Dauid. Tunc Cassiodorus, Optimè video (inquit) excusationes meas apud vos nullius esse momenti, *Proinde ego me constituo omnino reum.* ac è vestigio prostratus humi tantus quantus est (vsus est cæremonia quadam monastica mihi nunquam visa) osculatus est terram (semel atque iterum precatus veniam. et cum eum erigeremus, et oraret vt tacerem), promisimus.

Posthoc dominica proxima destitit a ministerio, habita oratione ad omnes Hispanos dicens se esse inhabilem ad illud . . ., atque habere testimonium propiæ conscientiæ voluntatem Dei esse vt disisteret.

Post aliquot dies rogauit me vt rem istam exponerent familiaribus et intimis suis, ita enim sibi expedire. Causabatur autem Franciscum de Abrego non posse se continere, quin aliquid effutiret vnde possent amici rem suspicari. Ego verò respondi, minime opus esse illa diligentia : me daturam operam vt Franciscus taceret. Sed eo instante et precibus postulante vt sibi hanc rem gratissimam facerem polliceor me præsiturum quod ipse efflagitabat. Itaque congregatis eius amicis *exposui eis confessionem adolescentuli et Cassiodori* : et cum finem narrandi fecissem, dixi, Hæc res modo est occulta, et necessè est ob grauissimas causas ab omnibus nobis occultari et sepeliri, proinde opus est silentio nobis imposito eam præterire. Quod ad me attinet, quia non sum in ea constitutus index praeripiendi Deo iudicium non est animus. *Adolescens asserit, Cassiodorus negat, nitamur* nunc negatiua dum peccatum est occultum, quod erit tutius, quamuis scio affirmationem in hoc casu potiorem esse negatione quae nihil probat in iure. Tunc conuersus ad Franciscum [fol. 597] de Farias (is erat in Hispania monasterii prior) dixi, Domine Farias si causa haec agitaretur in Hispania, non ignoras procedendam esse ad torturam. *nam adolescentis testimonium in hoc casu sufficiens est.* Et ille respondit, ita esse.

Hæc sunt quæ de hac re mihi sunt comperta bona fide a me recitata ad gloriam Dei Dominj nostri et ecclesiae suæ bonum.

Gaspar Capata.

Testimonium Balthasaris Sanchez de Vita Cassiodori Latine redditum.

Quod ad filium Joannis de Vayona attinet, cum id detectum fuit, ego eram tum Cantabrigiae *proinde profiteor mihi esse significatum nihil penitus agitanti* : neque credebam cum nuntiaretur. Porro postquam redii Cantabrigia proficiscor in templum more meo, et cum finita contione aliqui ex fratribus ad me accederunt et gratulati essent reditum, accessit et Franciscus de Abrego aliquantulum sub tristis et cogitabundus, ac mihi statim dixit, Domine nescio quid sim facturus, putabam enim me huc venisse vt inter probos viros agerem, et credo me frustratum. Ego vero respondi, Quid rei est? euenitne tibi? Tunc ille, Quendam ex nostris qui et præfertur cæteris tum dignitate tum sanctitate arbitror satanam esse. Et ego contrario petii vt significare mihi vellet quisnam esset. Ille autem, Cassiodorus (inquit) is est. nam comperio esse sodomitam, et non audeo eum adire reprehendendi causa absque consilio aliquorum fratrum, quia minister est, et præstat authoritate. Tunc me magna tenuit admiratio, et nolebam id de Cassiodoro credere: quære tum à Francisco, cuinam communicauerat illud. Respondit, Domino Gaspari Çapatæ. Et quid tibi dixit, inquam? Is vero (inquit Franciscus) dicit se nolle credere, donec conueniet iuuenem atque serutetur illius animum. Optime inquit, Tu ergo interim face et nemini dicas atque caue . . . ne rem Flandriæ quibuscum verseris, palam feceris. nam si quid ia . . . Posthæc venit ad me D. Çap[ata] . . . qui quidam fa . . . ingenuè ad tutum, quod ei in F . . . plus: si volebam conuenire eum, se credere non recusaturum iuuenem eandem coram me edere confessionem. At ego dixi, *me nolle cum iuuene loqui,* et ita decretum fuit donec eum possem conuenire coram Cassiodoro facie ad faciem. Tunc item intellexi eandem rem Angelo Victorio esse cognitam. quapropter nos quatuor conuenimus deliberaturi quo pacto res nobis esset gerenda, vt hominem adduceremus ad proprii defectus confessionem alii nemini præbentos scandalum. Tunc dixi, me habere cognitam perspectumque ingenium Cassiodori, proinde opus esse vt optimo consilio et christiano in ea re procederemus. Quare decretum est adire consilii capiendi gratia virum quendam et pium et orthodoxum, cui rem aperuimus nominibus personarum suppressis. Is verò dixit, quare non conuenitis de hac re ministrum vestrum? cui ego respondi, Me credere Cassiodorus de hac re potius nociturum quam adiuturum, ac proinde nolle adire eum. Is tunc primum adhortatus est, vt in re procederemus vt Christianos viros decet: cui respondimus, nihil aliud a nobis quæri. Addidimusque, *illum qui illud crimen admisisset, esse hominem vafrum, et sophistam, vt pote qui* monachus fuisset. Tunc ille dixit, O monachus fuit, et vafer est, vt dicitis: ergo opus est vt caute vos geratis: nam qui huic vitio assueti sunt, in  procinctu habent paratum responsum cum deprehenduntur. Proinde cauete vobis, ne is postea oneret vos aliquo calumnia. Itaque consilium meum est, vt vobiscum assumetis patrem iuuenis, videatisque an coram patre velit filius crimen fateri, et ita maiore vi muniti eritis, qua possitis resistere malefactori et calumniatori. Tunc discessimus: et D. Çapata duxit patrem et filium in agrum. *Quid ibi adhuc sit, is et pater referent.* Item D. Çapata solus conuenit Cassiodorum cum esset in sua bibliotheca. *Is etiam referet, quae ibi fuerunt acta.* [fol. 598] illo eodem die sumus omnes congregati in agro *rogati a Cassiodoro.* Scilicet D. Çapata, Angelus, Franciscus, et ego: tum etiam Vayona cum filio. *Voluit aut Cassiodorus* vt in agro esset conuentus, ne quid pater suus aut alii, si domi essent, olfacerent. Ibi examinatus fuit Cassiodorus seorsum, et sponte fassus est quicquid cum iuuene sibi euenisse dormienti sibi euenisse. Se habuisse nescio quot pollutiones nocturnas et somnia turpia, cum esse aliquoties calidior solito. Se dicere iuueni, quod si quid sentiret, eum euigilaret. Tunc vocatus adolescens, et coram omnibus interrogatus, constanter perstitit dicens cum lacrymis, Ita est, cum mecum rem habuit, repetens ter eadem verba. Tunc ego dixi Cassiodoro, Noli veritatem obscurare, quin potius fatere, considerans adolescentulum in hoc casu esse fide dignum. Ergo fatere,  ingenue nihil simulans: hoc pacto ingoscet tibi *Dominus Deus.* Multis aliis terminibus fuit admonitus, ab aliis dicentibus *nos non quærere ruinam,* quin potius salutem. Vide quid adolescens dicat: nempe *te eum constrictum tenuisse retro: se voluisse euadere et non posse.* Ad quae Cassiodorus respondens, dixit, *fieri potuisse se eum tenere complexum, membroque suo in vas adolescentuli intromisso, tamen se non eiecisse intus semen:* quia inueniebar (inquit) experrectus, quando effluebat. De eo aut quod homo dormiens committat ei culpam non imputatum iri. Cæterum Angelus Victorius, qui loquutus est cum eo omnium postremus, Video te (inquit) domine, *nolle veritatem ingenue fateri.* At qui Deus ex ore tuo, uel te inuito, sermonem veritatis extorquet. Si res hæc discutienda esset coram Gallis aut Flandris, æderent profecto horrendum spectaculum de te. *Nam quas fassus es pollutiones* nimis satis sunt vt condemnationem meritam subires. Cui Cassiodorus respondit, *Verum est Domine.* Tunc prosequutus Angelus dixit, Agnosce igitur culpam, et da gloriam Deo, quod solum a te requirimus, et nil al . . . ille lacrymis obortis, dixit, Video meas ex . . . lt . . . *reddo omnino reum.* et continuò . . . tum propter culpam, tum scandalum p . . . bis. Post rodauit nos necui quicquam diceremus, vt vitaretur scandalum . . . quod promissimus hac lega, si signa pœnitentiae ostenderet. Ille vero dixit, nos visuros in eo signorum pœnitentiae satis.

Dominica sequenti distitit sponte non inuitus a ministerio dicens publice, se sentire quod voluntas Dei erat vt relinqueret contionandi munus: hoc enim testimonium ei reddere propriam ipsius conscientiam, *quod quidem consideratione dignum mihi visum fuit, propterea quod dominica præterita orationem habuerat de eligandis senioribus.* Postea voluit hinc descendere Francofordiam versus, *nemine cogente neque vlla causa necessaria intercedente.* Item constat adolescentulum mansisse in vrbe 30. aut 40. dies post reuelatum crimen, quo tempore neque verbum fecit Cassiodorus de hac re: quin submissione et deiectione animi veram pœnitentiam simulauit. Hæc est, quod meminisse licet, veritas coram Dea et Angelis eius. *Iterumque profiteor ne merique istius hominis quæsisse neque quærere ruinam* aut infamiam, quin potius si qua afficitur, ipsummet esse authorem alioqui credo Deum velle eum patefactum, et quemadmodum dixi initio huius testimonii mei, quando haec re reuelata fuit, non eram in vrbe: neque unquam cogitassem *in tanto viro* tam indignum scelus deprehendi posse.

Balthasar Sanchez.

Testimonium Francisci Abrego Latine redditum.

Quum paucis diebus a nuptia Cassiodori a Reyna irem cubitum in hospitium Joannis de Vayona vt solitus eram, et ego et Joannes filius eius exutis vestibus conscenderemus lectum dormituri, is quæsiuit a me, vt valeret uxor Cassiodori, Cui respondi bone valere. At ille, Credo (inquit) nam poterit sibi gratulari quod nacta sit virum qui ei optimi satisfaciet, quippe qui magna vi et potentia sit præditus. Ex his verbis conieci [fol. 599] iuuenem aliquid scire de Cassiodoro, sed nihil minus quam quod postea exposuit. Ego igitur eum, vt declaret quo esum id dicaret, et quam ob causam. at ille recusare. ego vero instare: Dic mihi quæso quam ob rem, scisne quicquam bene poteris fidei meæ committere. seruabo depositum. Ille vero, Nihil est (inquit) ac si quid sit, scire tua non refert: desine obtundere. Ego aut nimis iam accensus rei cognoscendæ, signæ esset, instantius vegebam iuuenem, donec is victus, vel potius imminente iam hora tanto sceleri detegendo præordinata, incipit rem exponere. Dormiebamus (inquit) ego et dominus Cassiodorus simul in eodem lecto. Optime scio quid is valeat. Quid (inquam) scis, dic iam. Tunc Joannes, Quid sum dicturus, Hizomelo, id est, mecum rem habuit. At ego, Que te hizo? id est, quid tibi fecit? Jocaris Joannes. Tunc ille affirmauit Cassiodorum abusum fuisse eo retro, narrans fere omnia quæ in congressibus, et post interueneant. Ego aut vix poteram credere. tenebar enim magna admiratione: nihilominus tamen, interrogavi eum, quoties vbi et quando id factum esset: et respondit, *Quinquies, aut sexies et pluries etiam* congressus est mecum intromisso membro, quod signauit suo indice. *Post primum congressum aiebat se laborasse fluxu ventris.* et Cassiodorum arripere eum dormientum et tenere complexum *retro vt non posset euadere*: et mane rogare eum cum lacrymis vt nemini diceret. Id enim euenisse cum dormiret, *et multa alia addidit quæ non prosequor.* Id autem factum esse aiebat in cubiculo quod est in scala ædium Cassiodori, et in alio superiora. Quando vero id contigerat, Dominus de Saula qui fuit minister in hac Ecclesia, habitabat in eisdem ædibus: et tunc Cassiodorus discesserat in contabernio parentum propterea Joannes iste inseruiebat ei, ac dormiebat cum eo. Posthæc, cum semper obuersaretur animo tam indignum scelus, nihil aliud agebam quatuor aut quinque noctes cum essemus vna in lecto . . . are Joannes . . . vt viderem . . . staret dictis. Is vero consta . . . alios duos Flandros præter . . . pressisse et Flandros esse . . . communicaret rem hanc sumpta occasione ab alia quam illi narrarunt. Ea  quidem res magnum mihi peperit scandalum, propterea quod recens veneram ex Flandris aliquantula luce perditus, ex maximo desiderio cognoscendæ veritatem Euangelii, ac parum abfuit quin redirem ad papatum, nisi Dominus me donasset maiore fide. Tunc decretum est rem deferre ad Dominum Gasparem Capatam, et simul ad alios duos ex fratribus, quos visum est mihi ei adiungere, vt quid in ea opus esset facto, mecum perspicarent. Quod si obtemperandum esset animi mei affectui, recta ilico me ad Magistratum conferrem. nam quid facerem commotus graui punitione digno scelere? Præterea volui renegare ascitis aliquot sociis, quo maior esset authoritas, et indubitata fides. *Intellexerem enim Cassiodorum esse hominem, qui raro aut nunquam agnoscere vult proprios defectus*; ac si corrigendi eum assumerem potestatem grauaturum aliqua calumnia. Adii igitur Çapatam, et exposita re, ille noluit mihi credere, quin addidit, nullam se fidem ad habiturum, nisi audito prius iuuene atque sufficienter examinato. Et constituto sequenti die conueniendo iuueni iuimus ad templum D. Pauli, quo adducto et salutato, dixit ei Çapata, Cur esset adeo insanus, qui secreta sua aliis reuelaret tam temere: iniunxitque ei ne posthac cuique dicaret: quia tum sibi cum Cassiodoro magnum posset adferre detrimentum. Joannes quæsiuit, sciretne Cassiodorus se eam rem patefecisse: cui Çapata, Minime (inquit) neque nunc quicquam ei dicemus. Sed dic Joannes, quid tibi Cassiodorus fecit, et quomodo. nam licet Franciscus narrauerit, tu potius in hoc casu audiendus et credendus. Tunc coram me et Çapata nimis verecunde exposuit quod intea mihi soli, *et cum pluribus aliis circumstantiis* de quibus eum Çapata interrogauerat.

[fol. 60o] Audita igitur iuuenis confessione distincta et clare deliberauimus ego et Çapata, Item Balthasar Sanchez et Angelus Victorius (ii enim erant quos asciueram in testimonium huius rei, *alii aut erant familiares Cassiodoro,* vt pote monachi eiusdem monasterii) conuenire quendam *virum doctrina et pietate insignem* vt nobis consuleret ex Dei verbo quomodo nos gerere debebamus in hac re citra noxam nostram ex proximi. Concilio igitur istius viri (cui profecto hoc nomine multam debemus gratiam alioque procederamus in causa vt imprudentes et inconsiderati homines) decretum fuit assumere nobiscum patrem adolescentuli. nam reputabamus plurimum in hac re momenti habiturum conspectum paternum et authoritatem ergo filium. et confessionem coram patre edita delinquentem aptius conuictum iri de crimine, vt agnosceret culpam et *daret gloriam Deo*: tum etiam ansam ei ereptam, ne postea insurgeret in nos insolenter, vt solent qui tergiversationibus et calumnis perpetrant scelera, nimis impudenter, contegunt. Çapata aut fuit commissum vt exequendo consilio operam præstaret suam: *vt quando ex eius declaratione et Joannis de Vayona constabit de confessione adolescentuli quam coram patre edidit in agro, supersedeo ab ea, tum etiam ab ea quam fecit Cassiodorus domi suæ priusquam adduceretur in* agrum. Vbi postea congregati sumus omnes, nempe Çapata, Balthasar, Angelus et ego: item Joannes de Vayona cum filio. Et Çapata adduxit secum Cassiodorum, atque in omnium praesentia constanter perseuerauit adolescens in suis confessionibus. Item Cassiodorus fassus est se habuisse quinque aut sex pollutiones dormiens cum iuuene Joannis de Vayona. et cum obiiceretur quae iuuenis fatebatur, dixit, se dormientem commisisse, si quid commiserit, absque determinatione: et quod dormienti non erat imputanda culpa. quod responsum mihi visum est esse prius excogitatum quando se pollueret cum adolescentulo. Tandem cum ei cum Balthasar, Angelus et Vayona dicerent, ne tergiversaretur, sed agnitione culpæ *daret gloriam Deo,* dixit lacrymis obortis, Video mihi non valituras apud vos quas adduco excusationes, *proinde confiteor . . . omnino*. nam prius dicebat, se non agnoscere . . . ulum separare a suo lecto post primam . . . eam bis osculatus est, petiitque veniam . . . igitur eum iussimus homo animo esse . . . quia rogauit . . . pr . . .fuit.†††

Hoc est testimonium Francisci de Abrego, quod quidem constanter assero esse verum coram Domino Deo et Angelis eius.

†††Postea sequenti dominica abdicauit se ministerio. et quoniam ignori eorum quae agebuntur eum rogabant magnis precibus, ne vellet desistere, dixit in omnium consessu se esse ineptum in praesentiorum ad id munus testimonio propriæ conscientiæ.

Testimonium Jeremiæ Ackerman de vita Cassiodori latine redditum à Joanne Wtenhouio rogatu fratrum.

In isthac re nihil habeo peculiare quod tester, cum nihil norim præterque ab iis qui ipsum iuuenem ipsum inquisiuerunt, ad peccati agnitionem adduxerunt, quod ipsum ipsimet melius testari poterunt, quam ipse possim. Hoc tantum habeo, quod puerum meum qui est frater ipsius iuuenis interrogaui, qui mihi dixit quod ipsius frater agnouisset quod Cassiodorus ei tule quippiam *sex aut septem vicibus* fecisset, idque diuersis temporibus. Interrogaui quoque iuuenem meum, cur non ex templo indicasset, respondit metum obstitisse. Adhæc ait quoque puer meus, quod sit satis pecuniarum semper habuerit quamdiu apud eum esset, quam Cassiodorus illius dominus ei daret, neque unquam interrogaret in quem vsum eam collocaret. *Vnde mihi videtur quod ipsum seduxerit.*
Ita subscriptum Jeremias Ackerman.

Le tesmoignage d'Angelus Victorius.

Il me semble qu'il à faict mal contre le vouloyr des Anciens de tracter si familierement banquetant en compagnie plusiers foix et demorant tout seul auecque la femme de Jan de Vayone en sa chambre, comme Je l'ay trouue auecque elle deux foiz, ce qui est mal et scandaleux en vng ministre, Espagnol, et jeune.
[fol. 601] Il me semble qu'ayant promis de vouloyr prescher pour rien au commencement, comm'aussi il prescheá pres d'un an pour neant, debuoit aussi continuer sans demander apres salayre lequel il refusá au commencement.
Item, il m'a offensé en ce qu'il proposa qu'il ne vouloit point prescher, mais qu'il en faulloit apeller vng aultre qui est en Nauarre, et que pour ce faire il seroit bon qu'on luy constituast des-ja vng bon salayre, lequel il prendroit iusques a cequ'il vint.[3] mais neantmoins peu apres qu'il eust le salayre, il voulust auuoyr le ministere.
Item il m'a offense enceque sans fayre prieres, ne sans donner espace, mais tout soudainement proposa en consistoyre qu'on ne luy donnast point ne comme a ceux qui ont beaucoup, ne a ceux qui ont peu. et que Monsr de Saules auoit cinquante liures, et qu'ils regardassent qu'il ne peuuoit auuoyr moins de 40 liures, ce qui luy fut facile d'impetrer de dix qu'ils estoyent, desquels n'eust honte de demander 40 liures.
Item il m'a offensé de ce qu'oultre cela prennoit les presents lesquels on luy bailloit pensant qu'il n'auuoit rien.
Item il me semble qu'il a dissipé l'eglise des Espagnols de Geneue solicitant ceux qu'il a peu a s'endepartir, tellement qu'on l'appelloit la le Moise des Espagnols. Monsieur Pierius[4] aussi qui jamais ne luy a escript ne rescript il me semble aussi bien que les autres Espagnols qui sont à Geneue, en est fort offensé. Voyre il en a eu des grandes querelles.
Item le fils de Jan de Vayone a confessé clairement comment il a esté abusé de luy du vice abominable de sodomie. Et . . . se retiroit . . . le suiuoit et estrignoit entre ses bras. Et que le matin . . . fit quelquechose en dormant, qu'il . . . foix plus chault qu'il ne souloit . . . auecque l'enfant et qu'incontinent il s'ensueilloit, . . . quoy . . . respondis, que la chose estoit a iuger des François et Flamencs, qu'on en fairoit horrible espectacle de luy: combien qu'il ne confessast la chose mais seulement ce qu'il disoit des pollu-

---

[3] This would, of course, be Antonio del Corro.
[4] Pierius was the latinized form of the name of Juan Pérez.

tions. Tant i a que Dieu qui ne veut nulle chose cachee luy arrachoit ce parolles-la contre son vouloyr, les quelles estoyent àsez souffisantes pour le condemner. combien qu'a la verité le jeune garson estoit ence cas-la croyble, et que l'on ne penseroit point que quand il l'estraignoit entre ses bras et qu'il le suiuoit de pres quand il s'enfuyoit, qu'il l'enseignast le pater-noster. Pourtant (dis-je) cognoissez vostre faulte, *et donnez gloire a Dieu.* Alhors il dict, Je voy que mes excuses ne me seruent de rien, *pourtant je me rend coupable* de tout. Alhors il se jettá par terre deux foys, et demandá perdon a Dieu et a nous. Ce faict il nous pria de n'endire rien à personne pour euiter l'escandale, et nous luy prometismes *par serment,* s'il se repentoit de bon coeur.

Deux ou trois jours apres desistá de prescher de soy mesme disant qu'il ne se sentoit souffisant, et autres choses de sa conscience, com'il m'a esté dict.

Apres Je n'en sçay combien de jours contre ce qu'il nous auoit prie de n'endire rien il pria Mons^r Çapata qu'il manifestast le cas comm'il auoit esté aux aultres Espagnols ses familiers et qui auuoint esté en vng mesme monastere en Espagne. Je soubçonne qu'il faisoit cela pour fayre que le dict Mons^r Çapata (*qui est noble, lequel à esté secretayre du Vice-Roy de Naples* et pourtant son tesmoignage vault beaucoup) amoindrit la chose: mais *il dit la verité.*

Deus optimus maximus, qui vindicauit à doloribus mortis vnigenitum filium suum vindicet etiam Cassiodorum, si fuerit innocens; sin aliter, ita illum puniat, vt eius anima incolumis saluaque sit.

Angelus Victorius.

[fol. 602] Le tesmoignage de Paschasius dela Motte Flamend membre de l'eglise Flamende de Londres.

Moy allant de Londres a Grauelines de Flandres pour les affayres d'vng mien parent en compagnie de Christofle Marischal[5] ministre de l'Euangile, lequel alloit pour les mesmes affayres, passant de Grauelines pour aller à Cassel par Barbourg,[6] *par fortune et sans y penser* Je rencontray en Barbourg Jean fils de Jean de Vayone, ce quel ie cognoissoy bien a Londres: et il me demandé de son pere s'il estoit viff ou mort de la peste. Et l'homme qui le tenoit en sa maison me donna deux lettres pour la mere du jeune garson et pour vn'aultre personne: et le jeune garson sortit de Bourburg auec moy parlant iusques à demi lieue plus ou moins, et moy ayant entendu l'affayre que l'on disoit qu'il auuoit confessé en Londres deuant quatr'ou cinq personnages, qu'il me le disse, et qu'il regardast bien de dire la verite, car ce n'estoit chose de peu d'importance de dire cela d'vng ministre. et il me respondit que ce qu'il auuoit confessé en Londres estoit vray. *Alhors Je luy demanday de me dire comme* la chose auoit esté, et combien de temps il estoit que cela auuoit esté, et le jeune garson tout honteux me dict que Cassiodore l'auoit abusé du peché qui est contre nature, et je luy demanday s'il auuoit senti quand Cassiodore luy fit celá, et il me respondit qu'ouy, sur tout deux foix il se sentit mal, et qu'acheué l'affayre *luy sortoit dela* villenie par derriere. et qu'il s'en vouloit fuyr, mais ne pouuoit point, d'aultant qu'il le tenoit embracé par derriere. et aussi bien avecque sa grande honte il me *dict d'aultres particuliertez que mes oureilles ne pouuoint point endurer.* Tout ceci il dict à moy seul parlant par le chemin. Apres je me retiray vng peu auec luy et Christofle Marischal *afinque n'ouyssent point les propos les femmes* qui venoyent en nostre compagnie et deuant C . . . repetá et confirmá le jeune garson le mesme . . . et la verité deuant Dieu et ses Anges . . . *de sa volonté sans estre induict* ne co . . . Aussi bien me par . . . Bourburg l'homme qui

---

[5] Otherwise known by his latinized name of Christophorus Fabricius.

[6] That is Bourbourg (Département du Nord), about half-way between Gravelines and Cassel.

tenoit le jeune garson, et il me contá tout cest'affayre, me disant qu'il l'auuoit ainsi entendu du jeune garson *car il le luy auoit demandé* par plusieurs foix.

The text of the certificate given to Reina by the ministers of the French Refugee Church of Frankfurt, Jean Salvard and Théophile de Banos. This has hitherto remained unpublished. It is to be found on fol. 607 of the Frankfurt documents.

Nous soubsignez a present Ministres du S$^t$. Evangile en lEglise francoise recuillie en ceste ville de francfort ayans veu, et leu la suscrite declaration a nous presentée par ledict M. Cassiodore de Reyne parlaquelle Il nous proteste de la purete de sa doctrine sur les points dont il auoit este par nous requis. Auons accepté et approuuè sadicte declaration la recognoissans pour pure et conforme a la parolle de Dieu ET en signe de nostre approbation auons adiousté icy nos signatures declairans en estre bien satisfaictz et contens. Et ce en nom de nostre compagnie qui nous en a donnè la charge.[7]

faict a francfort ce 12 de Juillet 1571

[signed] J. Salvard   T. De Banos

---

[7] Regarding the declaration made by Reina on the same day, see above, note 9 to Chapter IV.

# Appendix IV

# Two Letters of Jean Cousin Concerning the Affair of Reina

Below is the text of two hitherto unpublished letters of Jean Cousin, the minister of the French Protestant Church of London, written to Jean Salvard and Théophile de Banos, the ministers of the French Refugee Church of Frankfurt, in answer to their request for information about Casiodoro de Reina. The original letters, written on successive days, 8 & 9 August 1572, are preserved in Frankfurt City Archives (Sammelband Kirchendokumente B, Französisch-reformierte Kirche 195, fols. 627-30 & 631-3 respectively). They have suffered damage in the same way as other documents in this collection, and, in addition, Cousin's extremely poor handwriting makes difficult the task of reading them. These letters establish the exact date of Casiodoro's flight from England, about which there have been many wild guesses, and they give many interesting details concerning the events which led up to it.

Monsieur et frere Ayant receu vos lettres sur la fin du mois de mars, et que les marchans estoyent partis pour vostre foire ie nay eu moyen de vous donner response iusques a present. Quant a la cause de Cassiodore ie la croyé [?] pour du tout enseueli, et ie ne m'en puis souuenir que ie n'aye horreur du scandale qui en est advenu. Quant au discours des choses, il seroit fort prolixe de le vous escriptre, mais seulement ie vous toucheray aucuns points. Vous dittes avoir veu quelque extrait de nostre Consistoire. ie ne scay bonnement que cest, mais il me souuient bien den auoir escrit quelque chose a mon beau frere Mr. Raymond Channet [?] ung an ou deux apres le departement de Cassiodore de ce pais que ie fis estant requis, comme ie suis maintenant de vous, non que iaye prins plaisir de diuulguer ce scandale car il n'a esté que trop enarome et trop cognu pour en ouvrir les bouches aux adversaires. Quant aux depositions des tesmoins envoyées a Geneue il ne se sont arrester a la main, ni a la plume, de celuy qui a escrit, mais aux parolles, desquelles iay les originaux signez des tesmoins suyuant le commandement de Monsieur levesque de Londres, et ie n'estime auoir rien envoyé quil ne soit fidelement collationé. Le commencement de ceste cause fut tel. Le mardy 31 dAoust 1563 Monsr. Cassiodore se presenta a nostre Consistoire mettant en avant les propos suyuans La verite iay veu grande chose a proposer. Jay chante les louanges du Sr. iusques aujourdhuy, mais iay maintenant vne chanson bien lourde. Il y a vn cas qui ne se peut celer et ne doit. Jay esté blasmé de terribles crimes dheresies meschantes & d'vn crime fort nephand : et iay cognu que cela estoit diuulgué. Jay pensé apres auoir inuoqué le Sr. et iay deliberé de mettre le cas deuant le magistrat, non pas que si vous le traitiez, il ne fust bien traité, mais pourtant que faudra user de constrainte pour faire venir les personnes, le magistrat fera mieux cela. touteffois ce ne sera point sans auoir vostre conseil. Jay proposé cecy a ceux de ma compagnie lesquels mont donné leur aduis ie veux aussy auoir le vostre et de Monsr. leuesque, sur ce ie me proposeray aux questions a fin quon trouue la verite. L'histoire est telle vng homme nous a fait du nostre [?] dune main et nous empesche de lautre. cest Balthasar. Il a commencé a me blasmer disant que iestoye glorieux. vn superbe que ie me vouloye faire adorer. Il a passé plus outre que iauoye resceu plus de 200 livres sterling que

113

ie n'auoye point distribué comme il falloit. Jl dis que iauoye eu a faire a la femme
dun de nostre compagnie. Il a tellement poursuyvy son mauvais vouloir contre moy
que si quelcun venoit à nostre compagnie il lattiroit a soy par argent ou par banquet
et gaignoit ainsy les personnes, lors il mexposoit en blasmes disant de moy ce qui bien
luy sembloit, de tout cela ie donneray les tesmoins. Un ieune compagnon vient ung
iour de flandres lequel ie retiray pour quelques iours en ma maison. Balthasar la rentra
et luy a donné a entendre comme aux autres et aussy sest separé de moy. Ce compagnon auec le garçon de Jean de Bayonne ont tenu propos de moy, le filz de Jean
de Bayonne disoit de moy: Cassiodore a bien fait de se marier il a eu a faire auec
moy. Cela est venu de luy alentour iusques a Balthasar . . . eglise, et puis a vn gentilhomme, qui est en nostre maison. Lvn . . . l'autre au Consistoire mais le gentilhomme
obtaint quon deuoit parler . . . et apres auoir parlé ensemble ilz vindrent au pere, en
lenfant depose quil estoit ainsy sur ce le gentilhomme parla a moy. Je luy confessay
tout ce qui en estoit. Je me suis bien apperceu vn iour, dy ie, lenfant couchant auec
moy: car iestoye poure et nauoye quvne couche: iapperceu vne chose qui a donné
occasion a lenfant de parler de moy. Je diray la chose, conbien que ien aye honte, pour
monstrer que ie ne suis coupable comme on pense. Il mest aduenu que moy estant
endormy, iay eu quelque pollution iusques a 4. ou 5. fois. Je cogne [?] lors que lenfant
lauoit apperceu, et ie luy dis sil apperceuoit plus que telle chose maduinst en dormant
quil me resueillast. Et moy ayant honte de ma poureté iay achepté vng lict pour le
separer dauec moy: Apres mes parolles le gentilhomme vouloit amener lenfant mais
doutant que dautres le sauoyent ie fus daduis que ceux qui estoyent aduertis y fussent
et sortis somes [?] aux champs. On a appelé lenfant a part et moy apart. Je dy au
garçon: Garde que tu ne dye plus outre que la verité. ?ay ie fait telle chose! Il res-
pond Ouy. On luy dit nommément ?a il fait cela! ouy. As tu senti quelque chose!
Je ne say. il me semble quouy. Puis ie me retiray et le gentilhomme vient a moy, disant
si ie croyé [?] mercy quil me seroit pardonne. Je dy que si i'auoye fait cela, iadoreroye
le Sr. en sa prouideuce. Sur ce vsoyent de menaces dung coste a dautre. Confessez
dit il la chose. Non dy ie. Je ne lay fait ne par volonte ne par consentement, mais
estant endormy cela mest aduenu. Et deuant Dieu ie say que iay nulle excuse mais il
nest pas ainsy deuant les hommes. Je leur dis que ie me deporteroye de mon ministere
iusques ace que ceste honte seroit osté de moy. Et ilz promirent de sen taire. Depuis il
est aduenu quilz sont allez vers ceux qui hantoynt mes presches. Sauez vous pourquoy
Cassiodore sest demis ce nest point pour la translation de la Bible mais ce sont les
heresies et crimes que le retiennent. Jay trouué en la fin que ce gentilhomme ne va
point droitement en cest affaire. Quant aux heresies ie les remettray deuant vous autres
et eux les proposeront mais touchant le reste ie remettray le tout deuant le magistrat.
touteffois ie ne veux rien faire sans vostre conseil pour nestre redargué de temerité:
Voila comme de mot a mot la harenge que Cassiodore fit deuant le Consistoire comme
les Anciens quy vivent encore en ont souuenue. et comme la chose est escritte au
registre. On dit a Cassiodore quon luy feroit response au prochain iour de Consistoyre,
quy fut le ieudy suyvant. Nostre response fut quil deuoit prendre le conseil de Maonsr.
leuesque deuant que den parler au magistrat. il dit quil suyuroit nostre aduis. Il fit vne
requeste que nous ninpostissions sur [?] ce aceux qui diuulgoyent la blasme contre luy
por euiter le scandale des eglises estrangieres et bailla leurs noms. Au mesme iour Cassiodore demanda conseil touchant la cene quy de deuoit faire le dimanche prochain.
Il disoit: Jay bien besoin de me fortifier vng foy pour soustenir laffliction qui mest
suruenue, mais ie ne say comment me presenter auec ceux qui ostent ma renommée.
On luy respondit en ces parolles, Dautant que ceste cause nest encore mise en cognoissance, nous remettons la chose a vostre conscience et comme nous ne voulons vous
deffendre la cene, aussi nous ne pouuons deffendre aux autres sans auoir plus ample
information du fait.

114

Le mardy suyvant 7. de septembre Monsr. Cassiodore se presenta a nostre Consistoire disant que Monsr. leuesque ayant entendu sa complainte luy auoit donné liberté de choyr certains hommes pour prendre cognoissance de sa cause. Jay deliberé disoit il, de prier Monsr. Couverdal, Monsr. Witinguen et Monsr. Withenne et vous prie de me donner vng de vostre assemblée. On luy dit, vous cognoissez ceux de lassemblée, puis que leuesque vous a donné le choix, ce nest pourtant a nous de vous en nommer.

Le lendemain 8<sup>m</sup>. lettres nous furent enuoyées de la part de Monsr. leuesque. La superscription estoit. Dilectis mihi in hom . . . D. Joanni Cognato ecclesiae gallicanae pastori, D. Joannj Utenhovio ecclesiae germanicae seniori, D. Roberto Crowleo pastorj ad Sanctum Petrum, D. Jacobo yongo ad Sanctum Bartholomeum, ministro, Antonio Capelle et Joanni Hettié ecclesiae gallicanae senioribus. Londinij. La somme des lettres estoit, qu'ayant ouy la complainte de Cassiodore et que pour certaines raisons il ne pouuoit vaquer pour en cognoistre, il nous en donnoit la charge pour oyr les parties, de luy en faire relat [ion] . . . estant vne remonstrance en latin bien prolixe que Cassiodore luy auoit presenté. Le lendemain qui estoit Jeudy 9. de Septembre les six personnes se trouuoynt en nostre temple. Les lettres de leuesque furent leües. Cassiodore fut ouy qui nous opposa les mesmes quil auoit dit a leuesque. Il nous donna les noms de ceux quil appeloit ses accusateurs et calomniateurs. Le lundy suyvant fut assigné pour oyr les parties de Cassiodore. Le lundy donc 13. dudit mois comparurent deuant nous six, deputez, Çapate, Balthasar, Angelus, Abrego, & Jeremias. Leur fut declaré en quelle authorité et pourquoy, nous les auions fait venir. On leur commanda de respondre sur deux points, quelle faulse doctrine ilz trouuoyent en Cassiodore pour vng, et quel crime enorme ilz cognoissoyent en sa vie. mais que premierement ilz respondissent de la doctrine.

Lesdicts Çapate et ses compagnons respondirent que comme accusateurs, diffamateurs ou calomniateurs quilz n'auoyent rien a dire de Cassiodore, fuste de sa doctrine, ou de sa vie, mais silz estoyent interoguez de ce quilz cognoissoyent de luy, quilz mettroyent en auant choses sur telles evidences, que par confrontation auec ledit Cassiodore ilz esperoyent que la partie se trouueroit de leur costé. Mais les deputez après plusiers parolles auec les susdits et considerans lauthorité que leuesque nous donnoit par ses lettres (desquelles iay encore la copie) nous prinsmes aduis ensemble de dire ausdits Çapate et a ses compagnons quilz nous exhiberoyent par escrit ce quilz cognoissoyent dela doctrine et vie de Cassiodore, pour donner lieu a Cassiodore de respondre, et le confronter auec eux. On leur assigna le mercredy suyvant a 3. heures apres midi pour nous informer dela doctrine. Le mercredy qui estoit le 15. ilz donnerent leurs escripts touchant la doctrine. On leur commanda de retourner deuant les deputez a vendredy enuiron 2. heures apres midi. ce quilz feirent et furent ouys touchent le crime de sodomie. Il leur fut commandé dexhiber par escrit ce quilz auoyent depose, chacun sa deposition, pour mardy quj seroit le 21 de septembre 1563. Le iour venu les escripts furent exhibez. Ce mesme iour charge fur donné alun des commis de dire a Cassiodore quil eust a venir Lapres disner deuant les deputez pour respondre de sa cause. Mais Cassiodore ne se trouua point et on ne sauoit quil estoit deuenu.

Le Jeudy suyvant quj estoit le 23. de Septembre. on seut pour certain que Cassiodore sen estoit fuj le mardy precedent de grand matin pour passer la mer et depuis na esté veu en Angleterre. Cestoit le iour proprement auquel il deuoit estre confronté. Le vendredy 24. de Septembre les deputez prindrent aduis ensemble de rescripre a Monsr. leuesque et luy demander ung iour pour luy faire entendre ce quilz auoyent negotié en la cause de Cassiodore. Le mesme jour se trouua le pere de Cassiodore deuant les deputez voulant excuser labsence de son fils. Ung autre nommé Pharias fit tout effort de bailler des escripts aux deputez tant en son nom que de Cassiodore: mais on leur respondit quon n'auoit rien a faire auec eux. Plusiers autres choses sont ensuyvies comme diverses depositions du garçon en flandres deuant Jacques de la Croix Espagnol et autres. Il eu vng examen signé du garçon (nommé Jean de Bayonne) et des ministres quj estoyent en Anvers. Plusiers autres choses appertenantes a nostre cause se pourront trouuer en temps et lieu. Si Cassiodore vouloit comparoistre deuant iuge competant comme il semble protester en cest escrit que vous nous avez enuoyé auec vos lettres, mais il est bien tard, pour recommencer vne telle cause.

Voila messrs. et freres le discours le plus bref que iay peu faire et le plus simple sans amplifications. et dequoy ie puis rendre raison deuant ung chacun par les memoires quj se trouueront quand besoin sera. Je ne vous mande point les copies des escripts de ceux quj ont deposé, La chose seroit trop prolixe.

Au reste quant a lescrit de Cassiodore que mavez enuoyé, outre plusiers choses qui me semblent bien stupides [?] et sans fondement, ie trouue fort estrange quil se vante d'auoir esté ala cene avec nous pour quelques fois sans nulle contradiction survenant [?]. Au plus il ny sauroit auoir esté quvne seule fois, et encore estoint remis asa conscience que vous pouvez veoir par ce qui est escrit cy dessus.

Icy faisant fin prieray nostre bon Dieu Messrs. et freres donner a Cassiodore ung vray sentiment de ses fautes auec pardon et remission dicelles, a vous accroissant de ses graces et sa benediction sus vos labeurs.

De Londres ce 8. dAoust 1572

Vostre entier frere et humble serviteur
Jean Cousin
ministre de leglise françoise

[Endorsement]
La procedure de la cause de Cassiodore enuoyé de Londres.

Messieurs et honnores freres Je vous ay envoye a mon aduis ce que vous requeriez touchant la cause de Cassiodore. Il me deplait bien fort que ledit personnage na suyuj melieur conseil, ce que ie passe le plus pour raison des graces que Dieu luy auoit fait, dont leglise en pouvoit recevoir vtilite. mais sans une doute cest vng artifice de Sathan de donner telles bricolles aux pouvres hommes quj pouuoyent seruir a Dieu et a son eglise plus que dautres. Il les amorse par ses illusions aux concupiscences vilaines et puis Dieu exerçant son iuste iugement les laisse trebuscher en sens reprouué ou bien les veut humilier et esprouuer a fin quilz se recognoissent quelz ilz sont en eux mesmes, pour ne se glorifier sinon en celuy seul duquel procede tout ce que nous auons du bien. Quant a ce personnage luy estant en ce pais, sil est comme on ma dit, iamais homme de son estat ne fut plus caressé, ne mieux aimé quil estoit, non seulement il auoit moyen de se bien entretenir, mas aussi de faire beaucoup de bien a dautres de sa nation, et il commençoit le plus a prosperer ce malheur est advenu. Lequel en son commencement estoit petit et aisé á remedier, mais il sest escarmouché et na point recogneu celuy qui le frappoit, mais il sest irrité le plus contre ceux qui (comme ie croy) procuroyent son bien, son honneur, et son salut. Quant a moy ayant consideré souvent toutes les procedures de ce personnage, et tout ce que iay apperceu en sa cause, ie ne me puis persuader autrement sinon quil est grandement coupable de tout ce qui a esté deposé contre luy. Les raisons Quant au garson qui luy auoit esté serviteur, qui est ce qui iamais leust induit a inuenter si vilaines choses, ales dire et repeter devant tant de gens, auec vne perseuerance incredible. Il se trouuera pres dune demi-douzaine dexamens et tousiours est demeuré constant. Je dy examens deuant gens notables. Le pere de lenfant a esté effrayé des parolles de son filz pour estre examiné de deputez, encor que leuesque lasseuroit quil ny auoit aucun danger, car il ny auoit pourtant eu de loy capitale en Angleterre contre le peché de Sodome, sinon depuis cest esclandre, cela faut il notter que le pere enuoya incontinent son filz outre la mer quand il vit que le fait venoit en lumiere.[1] Quant aux deportemens de Cassiodore plusiers choses sont a remarquer, des la premiere heure quon luy parle de cest affaire il fut espouuanté en soymesme et depuis a continué. Tous estoyent ses amis, ou ie suis grandement trompé, Lenfant, le pere, ceux qui lont admonesté des premiers, son assemblee, nostre Consistoire, Leuesque homme humain sil y en a en Angleterre, amateur des eglises estrangeres, et quj desiroit de supporter Cassiodore comme ses lettres le tesmoignent. Quant aux deputez, luy mesme Cassiodore les auoit choisis, comme ie croy, du nombre de ses amis, et ie say que tous auoyent tresbonne affection que ce scandale ne vinst en lumiere, ie le dy de tous, et lafferme de mon costé specialement. Cassiodore na seu appliquer toutes ces choses a son prouffit et ie ne puis penser quj en ayt esté la principale cause sinon quil a voulu ouurir par moyens illicites ce que Dieu instamment vouloit reveler. et ainsy il sest precipité en plusieurs endrois. Je trouue fort mauuais quil sest deposé de son ministere de son authorité particuliere. cela me fait penser que sa conscience estoit fort troublee audedans puis quil abbandonnoit vne chose si sainte au dehors, cela nest pas la constance des serviteurs de Dieu quand tout le monde conspire contre eux. Il y a vng second point La remonstrance quil presenta a monsr. leuesque par escrit est pleine de grande inuectiues contre ceux qui deuoyent parler de son affaire et qui fraternellement lauoyent admonestez selon la regle de Jesus Christ. Math. 18. Il y a vng autre point Le propre iour quil deuoit estre confronté, quil deuoit respondre pour soy mesme et soutenir son innocence, voire si innocence estoit en luy, il quitta son droit et senfuit honteusement, Je ne pense pourtant quil y ayt homme sage qui puisse aprouuer une telle lascheté, et en chose de si grande importance, en esgard a la personne quil soustenoit considéré immesurement [?] quil auoit vsé de ces parolles forsant sa complainte a leuesque. *Quod si vel leuiter tam tetro crimine* contaminatus resertus fuero, non recuso subire vim acerrimus supplicium; neque (quod ipso a supplicio longé grauius existimo) infame ad posteros nomen *turpissimj* criminis nota conspurcatam. Si vere ob gravissima alioquj mea [?] puncta [?] quæ et multa et gravia autem coram Deo agnosco, aut ob fidej et constantiæ meæ per ... aut ob quod ius aliud, arcanum providentiæ suæ consilium, ad tam turpe incendium usque negligere constituerit Deus innocentiam meam eamque permiserit tam *grauj* calomnia ad tempus superiori: nihilominus contumeliosissime in oculis hominum mors aio sibj bene conscio fidele coram Deo testimonium innocentiæ suæ ferentj [?] ad gloriam nominis suj speciosissima erit. Neque me iam multum detenet alterius partis, etsi turpissimum ad distinctum rej examen discensurum, quj et vetera et noua exempla in pijs hominibus ob oculos habeam vindicatæ a Deo innocentiæ, etsi validioribus falsis attestationibus impetite. Et quidem si tantj criminis aliqua ex parte mihi essem male conscius prodire in lucem non contenderem, quin potius abirem, consulerem turpi fuga turpissimæ vitæ. Si quidem iam sunt amplius duo menses, quod huic sentinae habeo admotas nares. Vnde neque tempus, neque rationes, ad subtrahendum meo periculo defererunt. Sed Christo gratia, cui toto animj, et corporis mei conatu inseruiuj hactenus, nuncque inseruio, quj vires atque animum suppeditat, ne impuris calumniatoribus terga vertum, etsi tam impotenti calomniæ, tam asserto testimonio, tam obfirmatis adversarijs sit resistendum. Il y a aussi plusiers indices et pratiques dezquelles Cassiodore a vsé pour effacer ce blasme depuis sa retraite de Londres, mais auec peu de prouffit comme les issues le monstrent Le sieur Jacques de la Croix, que iestime estre vng homme de bonne pieté, en peut bien sauoir quelquechose, et autres quj ont signé auec luy certaines lettres attestatoires de linnocence de Cassiodore quj furent enuoyées a Monsr. leuesque de Londres, auec vng examen Lan 1564. Quel besoin estoit il daller mendier des attestations pour le temps passé, ou il falloit respondre du present. et de

---

[1] It is a fact that at the time of Reina's alleged offence and the enquiry into it sodomy was not a criminal offence. Cousin's claim concerning its becoming so may well be true. See Appendix V for an examination of this point.

courrir si loing iusques a mettre en peine leglise Italienne de Geneue comme il se
conste par vng escrit signe de la iustice; la ou il pouuoit respondre sans danger au lieu
duquel il sestoit retire sans constrainte. Finalement en escrit quil vous a presente rend
assez ample tesmoignage que le pouure homme na point consideré les absurditéz desquelles facilement on le pourroit contrairier sil nestoit point transporté en sa propre
cause. Je vous prie seulement de considerer ce quil dit des pollutions, iamais on na
douté des pollutions reales, ne luy mesme aussi, mais il sexcusoit que cestoit en dormant, maintenant il dit ie n'entens point de quelque effusion de semence, de laquelle
ie suis bien certain que iamais ne mest aduenu alentour. Sa harangue deuant nostre
Consistoire porte que lenfant lauoit bien apperceu, dont il auoit en honte. Ladmonesta
de le resueiller, achepta vng lict pour le separer. Toutes les depositions de lenfant
mesme, celle quil fit deuant Jaques de la Croix et laquelle a esté enuoyée de Francfort a Londres que seroit ce de tout cela sinon des imaginations reales fondées sur les
pollutions spermelles de Cassiodore?

Je ne me veux amuser plus auant sur ces choses. Il me suffit de vous auoir touché
aucuns points, Lesquelz se pourroit notter en la cause de Cassiodore. Cest vng dormir
vrayment pernicieux quand lhomme ne se peut resueiller en son vice, cest pour neant
que nous cerchons des fueilles auec Adam, Dieu a plus de moyens de descouurir nostre
turpitude, quil ny a de fueilles au bois pour la cacher. Cependant Dieu vueille garder
a chacun son droit, et a son eglise le sien : et descouurir les hypocrites en leurs dissimu-
lations. Icy faisant fin ie prie nostre bon Dieu Messieurs et freres de vous remplir des
dons de son saint Esprit de zele prudence et charité pour vous employer vertueusement
en vostre St. ministere, a la gloire de son nom et edification de son eglise. De Londres
ce 9 dAoust 1572.

Si lopportunité m'eust esté donné ie vous eusse mandé quelque chose des nouuelles
quj voltigent, ie me suis arresté a choses plus serieuses, et vous prie freres de vous
employer enuers Cassiodore sil y a moyen de le redresser, autrement gardez vous et
veillez sur vostre troupeau. [Here there is a line very carefully crossed out.]

Monsieur de Banos Jay souuent eu de vos lettres vous estant a Paris : ie vous prie
de continuer pour le moins es foires et ie respondray de mon costé.

Quant a vous Monsr. Saluart Jay ouy beaucoup de bien de vous par Monsr. Cheualier
quj sest retiré a Caen en Normandie, si vous luy escriuez ie feray tenir [?] vos dedans
[?] si a moy, ie vous en sauray gré.

Quant a ces escripts ie les remets a vostre prudence vous sauez a quj nous seruons,
et de quj nous deuons nous garder.

Vostre affectionné frere et seruiteur

Jean Cousin.

# Appendix V

## The Offence of Sodomy in England and the Case of Casiodoro de Reina

Casiodoro de Reina fled from England on 21 September 1563 firmly convinced that the sodomy of which he was accused was a hanging matter. It is conceivable that he would have remained to face the court of enquiry had he not had this erroneous idea. Both his accusers and his defender, Farías, in the Refugees' Churches seem to have been under the same misapprehension, and thought also that the sole evidence of the youth allegedly concerned would be enough to secure conviction and execution. The fear that the offence was punishable by death was also shared by Jean de Bayonne Sr, in spite of assurances by the Bishop of London that this was not the case, and he sent his son away across the Channel to imagined safety. Jean Cousin's letter of 9 August 1572 indicates that sodomy was not a capital offence at the time of Reina's alleged offence and the enquiry into it, and that it only became so because of the scandal caused by the Reina affair. An examination of the history of the law concerned shews that Reina, de Bayonne, and the other refugees were wrongly informed (or, more likely, were making assumptions based on the continental practice), and also that Cousin may well have been at least partly correct. In any case, the dates accord with his statement.

Sodomy (otherwise called buggery) anciently came under ecclesiastical jurisdiction in England, and was apparently an offence that was not very severely punished. As part of Henry VIII's policy of progressive reduction of the jurisdiction of the ecclesiastical courts, the right to try the offence was transferred to the temporal courts, and, by an Act of 1533 (25 Henry 8 c.6), it became a felony punishable by death. The statute was re-enacted three times in Henry VIII's reign, in 1536, 1539, and 1541. It was repealed by Edward VI's first parliament in 1547, but was replaced on the statute book in 1548. Mary Tudor's first action was to repeal all statutes passed in the previous reign, the intention in this case being presumably to return the offence to the ecclesiastical jurisdiction. It was not put back into the statute book till 1563, when, by Statute 5 Eliz. c.17, it once more became a felony punishable by death.[1] A consideration of the extract from the relevant Act given below will shew that the Parliament which enacted 5 Eliz. c.17 was held at Westminster on 12 January 1563/4, that is, four months after Reina's flight, and that the Act was not to come into force till 1 June following (viz., 1 June 1564).

[1] H. Montgomery Hyde, *The Other Love: an Historical and Contemporary Survey of Homosexuality in Britain* (London, 1970), pp. 38ff. The following extract from Hyde's book throws interesting light on the case of Casiodoro, since he was accused jointly of heresy and sodomy:

> *Bougre* derived from the Latin *Bulgarus* meaning native of Bulgaria, where the Albigensian and Manichaean heresies were known to flourish. The term Bulgar or *bougre,* was gradually applied to all heretics, and from being an abusive term for heresy in general *bougrerie* became the common appellation for the supposed sexual habits of heretics and usurers. No doubt some of the Albigensians were homosexuals, as also were some Knights Templars, who were suppressed by the Inquisition, many of the

*Anno Quinto Reginæ Elizabethæ. At the Parliament held at Westminster on the .xii. of January, in the fifthe yeere of the raigne of our Soueraigne Lady Elizabeth, by the grace of God, of England, Fraunce, & Ireland Queene, defender of the fayth, &c ... were enacted as followeth.* [London], (1563/4), fol. 54ʳ⁻ᵛ

An Acte for the punishment of the vice of Buggerie. The .xvii. Chapter Where in the Parliament begun at London, the third day of November, in the .xxi. yeare of the late kyng of most famous memory, King Henry the eyght, and after by prorogation holden ... in the twenty and five yeare ... there was one acte and statute made, entituled: An Acte for the punishment of the vice of Buggerie, whereby the sayde detestable vyce was made Felony ... Forasmuch as the sayde estatute ... standeth at this present repealed and voyde, by vertue of the statute of repeale, made in the fyrste yeare of the late Queene Marie: sythen which repeale ... dyuers euyl disposed persons haue been the more bold to commit the sayd most horrible and detestable vyce of Buggery aforesayde, to the hygh displeasure of almyghtie God: Be it enacted, ordeyned, and established, by the Queene ... by the assent of the Lords spiritual and temporal and the Commons ... that the sayde statute ... made in the .xxv. yeare of ... King Henrie the eyght ... every branch, clause, article and sentence therein conteyned, shal from and after the fyrst day of June next commyng, be reuiued, and from thenceforth shal stand, remayn and be in ful force, strength and effect for euer.

---

Knights confessing their practices in the torture chambers of the Holy Office. But by and large the charge of homosexuality seems to have been part of a general 'smear' campaign employed by the Inquisition against its enemies ... It was always open to the Church to 'relinquish' offenders to the secular power for punishment, as was so often done by the Inquisition in Spain, and there may well have been some who felt that, as with sorcerers, sodomists convicted by the ecclesiastical courts ought to be handed over to the civil authorities for burning. It is extremely improbable that in England they were thus 'relinquished' and that their offence was ever penalized in this way (pp. 36ff).

# Appendix VI

## Reina's Letter to Diego Lopez

This letter is to be found in the Bibliothèque Nationale in Paris, MS Dupuy 103, MS latin 8582, fol. 103ʳff. It was discovered by E. Boehmer, and published by him, 'Ein Brief von Cassiodoro de Reyna', *Romanische Studien*, 4 (1880), pp. 483-6.

Al sᵒʳ y hr° charissᵒ en Chrᵗᵒ Diego Lopez Español. En Paris.

Señor y hr° muy amado en Christo.

La paz del Señor sea con V.m. Esta feria de Francafort recebi vna de V.m. en que haze mencion de otras dos que me ha escripto delas quales yo no he recebido ninguna que me era harto estraña cosa pensar que se descuydasse tanto en escreuirme y dar me noticia muy amenudo desu estado sabiendo quanta parte tomaria yo o de su prosperidad o de su aduersidad por la cõmunicacion que tenemos en el cuerpo mystico del Señor alqual sea gloria eternalmente por auernos hecho detal manera participes de si y de su substancia que enel todos los q̃ verdaderamente son suyos lo seamos los vnos delos otros como (ala fin) miembros de vn mismo cuerpo. Esta communicacion de Sanctos tanto quanto mas es incognita àlos que nunca tuuieron parte en Christo, tãto es mas biua y operosa entre los que por gracia del Padre Eterno participaron del con la qual ansi como gozan sin cessar delas influencias de aquella diuina Cabeça, ansi estan siempre sollicitos los vnos por los otros dando enesta biua sollicitud fiel testimonio y irrefragable del espiritu del Señor de que participan. Los que (hermano) se glorian con razon del titulo de Christianos, en esta sola señal (quando otra ninguna ouiesse) se declaran y disciernen delos que vanamente lo vsurpan porque lo que los otros hazen en esta parte por la communicacion que tienen con Christo, estos o nunca lo hazen o si alguna communicacion tienen es o por sus prouechos particulares o por sus amistades humanas.

De auerle el Señor encaminado en sus negocios de tal manera q̃ no pierda su tiempo me huelgo mucho, y hago gracias al Señor q̃ mantiene con el su palabra y promessa en esta parte en lo qual le obliga de nueuo a emplearse todo en su seruicio: ni yo esperé menos dela piedad de essos señores sino que le assistirian en todo lo que pudies- sen y ansi creo que lo haran en lo por venir.

Enloq̃ toca àla disposicion de nuestros negocios, aca estamos determinados confauor del Señor de poner la mano en la impression dela Biblia dentro de vn mes en q̃ nos acomodaremos quanto nos sera possible a las condiciones y parecer que estos señores y V.m. me escriuieron los dias passados. Esta ya el concierto hecho con Oporino Im- pressor de Basilea donde sera necessario q̃ yo me halle. Esta concertado q̃ imprimira 1100 exemplares delos quales el tomara asu cuenta 200 y nos dexara 900. Estos 900 creese que no costaran arriba de 500 escudos. moderaronse los que hizieron el concierto ansi con el dinero que tienen, como con la opportunidad dela distribucion del libro que se cree que por algunos años no sera muy buena, ni aun para la de tan pocos como han acordado de hazer.

Para este negocio nos vendria bien alproprosito el ayuda del hr° Bartholome Gomez la qual el me prometio quando estuue alla. con esta va vna para el enq̃ le ruego que lomas presto q̃ pudiere venga a Basilea para este effecto assegurandole q̃ enloq̃ toca ala recompensa de su trabaio se hara conel muy bien y creo que estara occupado dessos señores en su Nueuo testamento lo qual (si ansi es) visto que el Nueuo testamento esta ya tan al cabo y q̃ para loq̃ resta se podran ayudar de componedor frances, no le estoruara esso de venirnos aayudar en tiempo. Si por ventura no esta ay V.m. le embiara esta letra con buen recaudo donde quiera que estuuiere y o ay o en otra parte le persuadira quanto pudiere a que nos haga a todos y a toda la nacion este bien.

Si ouiesse alguna manera conque embiarme vn exemplar delo q̃ esta impresso del Nueuo Testamento me hara muy gran merced de embiarme hasta donde la impression llega. Creo que Monss^ur Languet (que es el portador deesta) le podra dar auiso por q̃ medio melo podra encaminar: al qual tambien me hara md de acordarle vn libro q̃ me ha prometido de embiarme de alla que se llama Vetera noua etc.

Si el s^or Bartholome determinare de venir, como le rogamos, V.m. procurara de saber loque alla gana para que por essa via sepamos lo q̃ aca se le dara por su salario.

Por aora no tengo mas q̃ escreuir a V.m. de encargarle q̃ tenga memoria de orar al Señor por nosotros y especialmente supplicarle que prospere esta obra contra todo aduersario q̃ se le leuantare pues el sabe q̃ lo q̃ en ella pretendemos y auemos pretendido hasta aora no es otra cosa q̃ la propagacion desu conocimiento y el consuelo desu Iglesia. El señor sea con V.m. de Strasburg 27 de Septiembre 1567.

Hr° de V.m. en Christo

Cassiodoro.

Los misterios dela Inquisicion estan empressos en latin creo q̃ por alla los veran.

# Appendix VII

# The Letters of Casiodoro de Reina

A list of the extant letters of Reina is given below. Many of these exist in autograph copies; others are known only from contemporary or later manuscript copies, whilst others are known by printed copies, for which the present whereabouts of the manuscript concerned has not been traced, although it is not inconceivable that it is still extant. Against each letter are symbols to indicate the source(s) as follows:

| | |
|---|---|
| * | indicates where the autograph copy is to be found, if known |
| B | Basle City Library |
| BM | British Museum |
| BW | published by Boehmer in *Bibliotheca Wiffeniana* |
| F | Frankfurt City Archives |
| G | Geneva City Archives |
| L | parts of this letter are to be found in Lehnemann |
| MHR | Musée Historique de la Réformation, Geneva |
| MP | parts of this letter are quoted by Menéndez Pelayo in *Heterodoxos* |
| P | Bibliothèque Nationale, Paris |
| Q | published by Boehmer, *Q.F.F.Q.S. . . . Ioanni Friderico Buch . . . Insunt Epistolæ quædam . . . Hispanorum qui Argentorati degerunt* (Strassburg, 1872). This *festschrift* appears to be the publication that Boehmer (and after him Menéndez Pelayo) confusingly refers to as his 'University Programme'. |
| S | Strassburg Public Library |
| Z | published by Boehmer, *ZHT* 50 (1870), pp. 285-307. The reference for these is given as 'Predigerminsterium, Frankfurt', but all attempts to identify this have so far failed. |

### LIST OF EXTANT LETTERS BY CASIODORO DE REINA

1560, London, Request to Queen Elizabeth and Cecil for a church   BM*, BW

21 September 1563, London, Protestation of innocence to the Bishop of London   F[1]

24 March 1565, Strassburg, to the Strangers' Church of Strassburg concerning doctrine (short form)   G*, BW

24 March 1565, Strassburg, to the Strangers' Church of Strassburg concerning doctrine (long form)   G*, BW

22 April 1565, Frankfurt, to Beza   G*, BW

22 April 1565, Frankfurt, to Marbach   L[2]

12 November 1565, Strassburg, to the Scholarchs requesting the right to live in Strassburg   S*

---

[1] This letter is known from two transcripts of it made by Jean Cousin. One is quoted in a letter of Cousin preserved in Frankfurt City Archives, and here given in Appendix IV. The other is printed in Hessels, III, 1, 36.

[2] J. Fecht, *Historiæ Ecclesiasticæ seculi A. N. C. XVI Supplementum* (Frankfurt/Speyer, 1684), pp. 195f.

28 January 1566, Frankfurt, Declaration on doctrine   G*, BW
1 March 1566, Strassburg, to Beza   G*, BW
29 March 1567, Strassburg, Reply to the Strassburg Church concerning the letter of Olevianus   G
9 April 1567, Strassburg, to Beza   P, MHR
27 September 1567, Basle, to López (and Gómes)   P*, MP[3]
28 October 1567, Basle, to Hubert   S*, Q
13 November 1567, Basle, to Hubert   S*, Q
4 August 1568, Basle, to Hubert   S*, Q
25 August 1568, Basle, to Hubert   S*, MP, Q
[1568], Basle, Request to the City Council for permission to print the Bible   B[4]
23 December 1568, Basle, to Hubert   S*, MP, Q
16 January 1569, Basle, to Hubert   S*, Q
15 May 1569, Basle, to Hubert   S*, Q
24 January 1569, Basle, to Hubert   S*, MP, Q
3 August 1569, Basle, to Hubert   S*, Q
6 August 1569, Basle, to Hubert   S*, MP, Q
8 December 1569, Basle, to Hubert   S*, Q
13 July, 1570, Strassburg, to Zwinger   B*, BW
7 August 1570, Frankfurt, to Hubert   S*, Q
12 July 1571, Frankfurt, Declaration to the French Church on doctrine   F*, G*, BW[5]
12 July 1571, Frankfurt, to Beza   F*, G*, BW[5]
21 August 1571, Frankfurt, to Beza   F*
22 August 1571, Frankfurt, Declaration on doctrine and morals   F*
25 November 1571, Frankfurt, Further declaration of innocence   F*, G*, BW[6]
25 November 1571, Frankfurt, to Beza   F*, G*, BW[6]
21 December 1571, Frankfurt, to Beza   F*
9 March 1574, Strassburg, to Zwinger and Adam Petri   B*, BW
12 April 1574, Frankfurt, to Hubert   S*, Q
24 September 1574, Frankfurt, to Zwinger   B*, BW
27 October 1574, Frankfurt, to Zwinger   B*, BW
23 November 1574, Frankfurt, to Zwinger   B*, BW
6 April 1575, Frankfurt, to Zwinger   B*, BW
7 April 1577, Frankfurt, to Zwinger   B*, BW
23 September 1577, Frankfurt, to Zwinger   B*, BW
1 April 1578, Frankfurt, to Zwinger   B*, BW
13 April 1578, Frankfurt, to Zwinger   B*, BW
6 November 1578, Antwerp, to Ritter   Z, L, MP
27 June 1579, Cologne, to Ritter   Z, MP
8 December 1579, Antwerp, to Ritter   Z, MP
18 December 1579, Antwerp, to Ritter   Z, L
11 January 1579, Antwerp, to Ritter   Z, L, MP
8 February 1580, Antwerp, to Ritter   Z, MP
1 March 1580, Antwerp, to Ritter   Z, L, MP
12 April 1580, Antwerp, to Ritter   Z, L
17 May 1580, Antwerp, to Ritter   Z, L

[3] E. Boehmer, 'Ein Brief von Cassiodoro de Reyna', *Romanische Studien*, 4 (1880), pp. 483-6.
[4] A. Fluri, 'Die Bärenbibel', *Gutenbergmuseum*, 9 (1923), pp. 88-90.
[5] Each of these letters exists in two copies, one in Frankfurt and one in Geneva. Both are Reina's autograph.
[6] As note 5.

17 August 1580, Antwerp, to Ritter   Z, L[7]
17 January 1581, Antwerp, to Zwinger   B*, BW
prid. Kal. M[?] 1581, Antwerp, to Ritter   Z
 9 January 1582, Antwerp, to Ritter   Z
 8 May 1593, Frankfurt, Declaration of orthodoxy made to the Lutheran Ministers
   of Frankfurt   L
10 February 1594, Frankfurt, to Adolf Fisscher   [8]
undated, no place of origin, to Ritter   Z

---

[7] Quoted in part by Tollin, p. 293.
[8] F. J. D. Nieuwenhuis, *Geschiedenis der Amsterdamsche Luthersche Gemeente* (Amsterdam, 1856), 19-22.

# Bibliography

PART I – MANUSCRIPT SOURCES, ARRANGED ALPHABETICALLY BY PLACES WHERE
THEY MAY BE FOUND

BASLE
*Üffentliche Bibliothek der Univeristät...*
Fr. Gryn. II. 26
    fol. 42   Letter of Reina to Zwinger, 13 July 1570.
    fol. 43   Letter of Reina to Zwinger, 9 March 1574.
    fol. 44   Letter of Reina to Zwinger, 24 September 1574.
    fol. 45   Letter of Reina to Zwinger, 27 October 1574.
    fol. 46   Letter of Reina to Zwinger, 23 November 1574.
    fol. 47   Letter of Reina to Zwinger, 6 April 1575.
    fol. 48   Letter of Reina to Zwinger, 23 September 1577.
    fol. 49   Letter of Reina to Zwinger, 13 April 1578.
    fol. 50   Letter of Reina to Zwinger, 17 January 1581.
Fr. Gryn. II. 27
    fol. 212   Letter of Reina to Zwinger, 22 April 1576.
    fol. 213   Letter of Reina to Zwinger, 7 April 1577.
G. II. 33
    fol. 241   Letter of Reina to Zwinger, 1 April 1578.

FRANKFURT AM MAIN
*Stadtarchiv*
Bürgerbuch 6, 1540-85, fol. 58$^v$, fol. 235$^r$.
Bürgerbuch 7, 1586-1607, fol. 179$^r$, fol. 288$^r$.
Sterbebuch 2, 1579-96.
Sterbebuch 4, 1612-26.
Judicialia Z 57 m.Anlage A-D, Acta Creditorum Jacob Cahnets contra Jacob Cahnets.
Judicialia W 236 II, List of the creditors of Dieterics von Beferfort.
Judicialia R 226 Acta Cassiodorij Reinij Contra Heliam von Offenbacs der Rechten-
    licentiater 1577.
Judicialia R 283 Acta Herr Cassiodori Reinig Clagers Contra Jacob Rasür zue Leiptzig
    Beclagten 1592
Sammelband Kirchendokumente B Französisch-reformierte Gemeinde 195.
    fol. 585-88   Specification of the documents relating to Reina.
    fol. 589-602$^r$   Depositions of various people regarding the doctrine and morals of
    Reina.
    fol. 602$^v$ff   Letter of Christophorus Fabritius to Johannes Utenhovius.
    fol. 605-8   Reina's explanation of parts of his Strassburg confession of faith of 24
    March 1565.
    fol. 609-12   Letter of Gaspar Olevianus to J. Salvard, August 1571.
    fol. 613f   Letter of Nicol. Balbani to J. Salvard, 20 August 1571.

fol. 615f  Declaration of Reina concerning the accusation of sodomy, 22 August 1571.

fol. 617-20  Copy of a letter of Reina to Beza, 21 December 1571.

fol. 621f  Copy of a letter of Beza to Reina, undated [1571].

fol. 623-6  Copy of a letter of Beza to Reina, 9 March 1572.

fol. 627-30  Letter of Jean Cousin to the French Church of Frankfurt, 8 August 1572.

fol. 631-4  Letter of Jean Cousin to the French Church of Frankfurt, 9 August 1572.

*Private Ownership*

Herr Georg Itzerott's transcripts of genealogical material relating to Frankfurt citizens, at present in Herr Itzerott's private possession.

GENEVA

*Bibliothèque publique et universitaire*

M.S. franç. 407 Correspondence ecclésiastique 1565-71.

fol. 2$^r$ff  Confession de foi de Cassiodore, Strassburg, 24 March 1565.

fol. 4$^r$f  Explication sur la dite, Strassburg, 28 January 1566.

fol. 6$^r$f  Letter of Olevianus, Sylvanus & Mosellanus, Heidelberg, 29 March 1565.

fol. 8$^r$-9$^v$  Response de Cassiodore de Reyna à l'église sur la lettre d'Olévianus, 29 March 1567.

fol. 10$^r$-11$^v$  additional chapters to the same.

fol. 12$^r$ff  Letter of Reina to Beza, 22 April 1565.

fol. 14$^r$-15$^v$  Copy of a letter of Beza to Reina, 9 Cal. Julii 1565.

fol. 16$^r$f  Letter of Reina to Beza, Strassburg, 1 March 1566.

fol. 18$^r$-19$^v$  Letter of Reina to Beza, Frankfurt, 12 July 1571.

fol. 20$^r$  Declaration et Protestation de Cassiodore sur le crime de sodomie dont il estoit accusé, Frankfurt, 25 November 1571.

fol. 21$^r$  Letter of Reina to Beza, Frankfurt, 25 November 1571.

fol. 24$^r$f  Notationes Cassiodori in Isaiam .

fol. 25$^r$  Notationes Cassiodori in Ezechiam.

fol. 31$^r$ff  Letter of Corro to Beza, London, 3 September 1568.

M.S. franç. 403 Correspondence ecclésiastique 1 C 1562-3 (formerly 197aaIII).

fol. 103$^r$ff  Copy of Corro's letter to Reina, Théobon, 24 December 1563.

M.S. latin 117

fol. 150$^r$ff  Letter of Beza to Reina, 9 March 1572.

M.S. supplémentaires 816 .

No. 8  Libro di Memorie Diverse Della Chiesa Italiana Racolte Dà Me Vicenzo Burlamachi In Geneva M.D.C.L. (De 1550 à 1669).

*Musée Historique de la Réformation*

Correspondence de Théodore de Bèze (inédite) 1564-1571.

Nos. 276, 656, 658, 679  Copies of letters between Reina and Beza.

LONDON

*British Museum*

B.M. Add. 48,096 (739c) – Yelverton 105 (Evetham Hall, Basingstoke).

Verbali della Chiesa Italiana di Londra 1570-1590.

Lansdowne Manuscripts

Vol. 4, art. 46  Petition of Reina to the Bishop of London for a church for Spanish Protestants (undated [1560]).

*City of London Guildhall Library*

Acta of the Consistory of the London Dutch Church

M 3 7397/1 SR 82.5  Vol. I 1 July 1560-18 August 1563.

M 3 7397/2 SR 83.5  Vol. II 18 August 1563-5 September 1569.

M 3 7397/3 SR 83.5    Vol. III 10 November 1569 - 2 September 1571.
M 3 7397/4 SR 100.1    Vol. IV 16 July 1573 - 5 June 1575.
M 3 7397/5 SR 83.5    Vol. V 4 September 1572 - 16 July 1573 & 26 June 1578 - 30 December 1585.

*Eglise Protestante Française de Soho Square*
Actes du Consistoire de l'Eglise Protestante Française de Threadneedle St.
    Vol. 1560-1565 & Vol. 1578-1588.

OXFORD
*Wadham College, Wiffen Collection*
Benjamin B. Wiffen's manuscripts and transcripts (unnumbered and uncatalogued).
Manuscript additions by B. B. Wiffen & Luis de Usoz y Río in various books.

PARIS
*Archives Nationales*
Archivo de Simancas, Secretario de Estado K 1509 - B 22 (microfilm only, original returned to Simancas) Carta del herege Marcos Perez al español que imprimé la Biblia en Paris.
*Bibliothèque Nationale*
M.S. Dupuy 103
    fol. 73   Copy of a letter of Reina to Beza, Strassburg, 9 April 1567.
M.S. latin 8582
    fol. 103$^r$f   Letter of Reina to Diego Lopez & Balthasar Gomes, Strassburg, 27 September 1567.

STRASSBURG
*Archives et Bibliothèque de la Ville de Strasbourg*
Archives St Thomas (AST)
    fol. 25/212   Copy of a letter of Beza to Reina, 9 Cal. Julii, 1565.
    fol. 48/29   Cassiodorus, espagnol aux scholarques (undated).
    fol. 161/83   Letter of Reina to Hubert, 28 October 1567.
    fol. 161/84   Letter of Reina to Hubert, 13 November 1567.
    fol. 161/85   Letter of Reina to Hubert, 4 August 1568.
    fol. 161/86   Letter of Reina to Hubert, 25 August 1568.
    fol. 161/87   Letter of Reina to Hubert, 23 December 1568.
    fol. 161/88   Letter of Reina to Hubert, 16 January 1569.
    fol. 161/90   Letter of Reina to Hubert, 24 June 1569.
    fol. 161/91   Letter of Reina to Hubert, 3 August 1569.
    fol. 161/92   Letter of Reina to Hubert, 6 August 1569.
    fol. 161/93   Letter of Reina to Hubert, 8 December 1569.
    fol. 161/94   Letter of Reina to Hubert, 7 August 1570.
Procès-verbaux des XXI, 1565
    fol. 397$^v$-398$^r$   Request of Reina to the City Council for the rights of 'habitation', 12 November 1565.
Epistolæ ad historiam ecclesiasticam VII O-P, Vol. 160
    fol. 188$^r$   Letter of Oporinus to Hubert, 10 December 1567.
    fol. 190$^r$   Letter of Oporinus to Hubert, 10 June 1567.
    fol. 191$^r$   Letter of Oporinus to Hubert, 15 November 1567.
    fol. 192$^r$f   Letter of Oporinus to Hubert, 22 December 1567.
    fol. 193$^r$   Letter of Oporinus to Hubert, 7 January 1568.
    fol. 194$^r$   Letter of Oporinus to Hubert, 15 January 1568.
    fol. 195$^r$f   Letter of Oporinus to Hubert, 12 January 1568.
    fol. 196$^r$   Letter of Oporinus to Hubert, 6 February 1568.

348 Université 25
fol. 92ʳff Letter of Antwerp Lutherans to Strassburg City Council, 20 March 1580.

PART II – WORKS OF CASIODORO DE REINA (INCORPORATING A FINDING-LIST FOR
SOME COPIES OF THE WORKS LISTED).

ORIGINAL WORKS

[*Declaracion, o confession de fe hecha por ciertos fieles Españoles, que huyendo los
abusos de la iglesia Romana, y la crueldad de la Inquisicion d'España hizieron a la
Iglesia de los fieles para ser en ella recebidos por hermanos en Christo. Declaranse
en este perqueño* [sic] *volumen los principales Fundamentos de la Fe y Religion
Christiana necessarios à la salud conforme a la Divina Escriptura de donde son
sacados con toda fidelidad y brevedad.* (Frankfurt, 1577)].
The only copy of this work ever to be noted (*Bib. Wif.*, II, 232) was reported missing
when sought in Frankfurt University Library in 1968.
*Confession de fe Christiana, hecha por ciertos fieles Espannoles, los quales huyendo
los abusos de la Iglesia Romana, y la crueldad de la Inquisition d'España, dexaron
su patria, para ser recebidos de la Iglesia de los fieles por hermanos en Christo . . .*
(Cassel, 1601).
Only known copy in Universitäts- und Landesbibliothek Sachsen-Anhalt, Halle.
*Christlich und in Gottes Wort wohlgegründtes Glaubenskanntnuß Der verfolgten
Evangelischen Kirchen in und ausser Hispanien gestellt durch etliche Christgläubige
Hispanier, welche wegen der Inquisition ihr Vaterland varlassen.* (Amberg, 1611).
Copy in British Museum.
*Evangelium Ioannis: hoc est, Iusta ac vetus apologia pro æterna Christi divinitate,
atque adeo, quatenus unum cum eo est, æqualitate cum Patre: adversus impietatem
Iudæorum, Cerinthi, Ebionitarum, Arrij, Mahumethis, & illorum scholæ, cum veteris,
tum novæ.* (Frankfurt, 1573).
*Expositio primæ partis capitis quarti Matthæi, commonefactoria ad ecclesiam Christi,
De periculis piorum Ministrorum Verbi in tempore cavendis.* (Frankfurt, 1573).
Copies of these two works (bound together) in Frankfurt University Library*; Bod-
leian; Cambridge University Library; Lambeth Palace Library†; St. John's College,
Cambridge; Peterhouse, Cambridge; Sidney Sussex College, Cambridge†; Emmanuel
College, Cambridge; Fitzwilliam Museum, Cambridge.
*Confessio in articulo de Coena, Cassiodori Reinii Hispani, Ministri in ea Ecclesia quæ
Antuerpiæ se Augustanam Confessionem profiteri dicit, quam si eius Symmistæ
sincere profitentur, sublata erit inter eos & Ecclesiarum reformatorum Ministros con-
troversia.* (Antwerp, [1578]).
Only known copy in Leyden University Library.

TRANSLATION
*La Biblia, que es, los sacros libros del vieio y nuevo testamento.* ([Basle], 1569).
Copies in British Museum; Frankfurt University Library*; Basle Public Library*;
British and Foreign Bible Society; John Rylands Library; Corpus Christi College,
Oxford; Queen's College, Oxford*; Cambridge University Library (two copies);
Trinity College, Cambridge; Queens' College, Cambridge; Pembroke College, Cam-
bridge; King's College, Cambridge; Fitzwilliam Museum, Cambridge; Magdalen
College, Oxford; Worcester College, Oxford; Hispanic Society of America (two
copies); Professor E M Wilson, Cambridge; Edinburgh University Library; Bodleian
(three copies); St Andrew's University Library

* Contains an autograph dedication by Reina.
† Marked as being a gift from the author.

WORKS EDITED BY REINA

CORRO, Antonio del, *Dialogus in epistolam D. Pauli ad Romanos,* Second edition (Frankfurt, 1587).
Copies in Bodleian; Queen's College, Oxford; Frankfurt University Library; Leyden University Library; Basle Public Library; Trinity College, Dublin.

SISTO DA SIENA (Sixtus Senensis), *Bibliotheca Sancta à F Sixto Senensi . . . ex præcipuis catholicæ ecclesiæ autoribus collecta,* Second edition (Frankfurt, 1575).
Copies in Bodleian; British Museum (both without the four leaves signed Qqq, which indicate Reina's connexion with this edition).


PART III – OTHER WORKS CONSULTED

*Actes du Consistoire de l'Eglise Française de Threadneedle Street, Londres,* Volume I, *1560-65, HSP,* 38 (Frome, 1937).

*Antwerpsche Archievenblad,* Volumes II, IX, X, XII, XIV (Antwerp, undated).

Architekten und Ingenieur Verein, *Frankfurt und seine Bauten* (Frankfurt, 1886).

*Articles et Conditions du Traicté fait et conclu entre l'Altesse du Prince de Parme, ...Pleasance, &c., Lieutenant, Gouveneur & Capitaine general és pays de pardeça au nom de sa Maiesté . . . d'une part, & la ville d'Anvers d'autre part, le xviij iour d'Aoust, l'an M.D.LXXXV* (Antwerp, 1588).

Asensio, Eugenio, 'El erasmismo y las corrientes espirituales afines', *Revista de filología española,* 36 (Madrid, 1952), 31-99.

Bataillon, Marcel, *Erasmo y España, estudios sobre la historia espiritual del Siglo XVI,* second edition, first Spanish edition, translated by Antonio Alatorre (Mexico, 1950).

———— *Erasmo y España, estudios sobre la historia espiritual del Siglo XVI,* third edition, second Spanish edition, translated by A. Alatorre (Mexico, 1966).

*Die Baudenkmäler in Frankfurt am Main,* 3 vols (Frankfurt, 1914).

Becker, Wilhelm, *Immanuel Tremellius. Ein Proselytenleben im Zeitalter der Reformation, Institutum Judaicum,* VIII (Leipzig, 1891).

Bernus, Auguste, 'Un laïque du seizième siècle: Marc Perez, ancien de l'Eglise réformée d'Anvers', *Revue religieuse de la Suisse romande,* 28 (Lausanne, 1895), No. 6, pp. 266-82, No. 7, pp. 324-7.

Besser, Gustav Adolf, *Geschichte der Frankfurter Flüchtlingsgemeinden 1554-1588* (Halle, 1906).

Beza, Theodore de, *Icones, id est, Veræ Imagines virorum doctrina simul et pietate illustrium, quorum præcipue ministerio partim bonarum literarum studia sunt restituta, partim vera Religio in variis urbis Christiani religionibus, nostra patrumque memoria fuit instaurata . . .* (Geneva, 1581).

———— *Epistolarum Theologicarum Theodori Bezæ Vezelii, liber unus, secunda editio* (Geneva, 1875).

————, eds. H. Aubert *et al., Correspondence de Théodore de Bèze,* Volume III, *1559-61,* Volume IV, *1562-5* (Geneva, 1963-70).

*Bilder zu Frankfurter Geschichte* (Frankfurt, 1950).

Blaes, J. B. & Alex Henner, *Mémoires anonymes sur les troubles des Pays-Bas 1565-1580,* 5 vols (Brussels/Ghent/Leipzig, 1859-66).

Blümmer, Franz, *Renata von Ferrara – ein Lebensbild aus der Zeit der Reformation* (Frankfurt, 1870).

Boehmer, Eduard, *Bibliotheca Wiffeniana – Spanish Reformers of Two Centuries from 1520 – Their Lives and Writings according to the late Benjamin B. Wiffen's Plan and with the use of his materials,* 3 vols (Strassburg/London, 1883-1904).

———— *Q.F.F.Q.S. Viro summæ venerando Ioanni Friderico Bruch . . . Primo rectori diem natalem octogesima vice . . . Insunt Epistolæ quædam Ioannis Sturmii et Hispanorum qui Argentorati degerunt* (Strassburg, 1872).

————'Ein Brief von Cassiodoro de Reyna', *Romanische Studien,* 4 (Bonn, 1880), 483-6.

———— 'Corro', *BSHPF,* 50 (Paris, 1901), 201-16.

———— 'Cassiodori Reinii epistolæ tredecim ad Matthiam Ritterum datæ', *Zeitschrift für die historische Theologie,* 50 (Gotha, 1870), 285-307.

Bonnant, Georges, 'Note sur quelques ouvrages en langue espagnole imprimés à Genève par Jean Crespin (1557-1560)', *BHR,* 24 (Geneva, 1962), 50-7.

———— 'Nouvelle note sur les imprimés genevois en langue espagnole dus aux presses de Jean Crespin (1557-1560)', *BHR,* 27 (Geneva, 1965), 318-21.

Boumans, René, 'Le dépeuplement d'Anvers dans le dernier quart du XVIᵉ siècle', *Revue du Nord,* 115 (Lille/Arras, 1947), 181-94.

British & Foreign Bible Society, eds. T. H. Darlow & H. F. Moule, *Historical Catalogue of the Printed Editions of Holy Scripture in the Library of the B. & F.B.S.,* with manuscript additions, 4 vols (London, 1903).

*Calendar of State Papers – Foreign Series – 1561-2* (London, 1866).

Castro, Américo, *Aspectos del vivir hispánico – espiritualismo, mesianismo, actitud personal en los siglos XIV al XVI* (Santiago de Chile, 1949).

Castro y Rossi, Adolfo, *Historia de los protestantes españoles y de su persecución por Felipe II* (Cadiz, 1851).

*Catechismus. Dat is Corte onderwijsinge vande voornemste Hooftstucken der Christelijker leere: Op Vraghe ende Antwoort ghestelt, Alsoo inde Christelijke Kerkē end scholen der nederduytscher landen de Confessie van Ausborch toe-gedaen synde, gheleert ende gheoffent wordt,* second edition (Antwerp, 1582).

*Catechismus, Dat is Onder-Wijsinghe van-de voorneemste hooft-stucken der Christelijker leere: Op Vraghe ende Antwoort ghestelt Door Franciscum Alardum, eertijts dineer des Godelijken woorts tot Antwerpen in-de Schure ...* (Antwerp, 1585).

*Colección de documentos inéditos para la historia de España,* vols XXV, XXVII, XCI (Madrid, 1854, etc.).

*Collection de Chroniques Belges – Relations politiques des Pays-Bas et de l'Angleterre sous le règne de Philippe II,* vols I & II (Brussels, 1958).

Corro, Antonio (Corranus), *Acta consistorii ecclesiæ Londinogallicæ, cvm responsio Antonii Corrani. Et quorvm lectione facile qvivs intelligere poterit statum controuersiæ inter Ioannem Cusinem ... et A.ᵐ Corranum Hispanorum peregrinorum Concionatorem* (London, 1571).

———— *Carta a Cassiodoro de Reina,* in *RAE,* VIII (Madrid, 1862).

———— *Lettre envoyée a la Maiesté du Roy des Espaignes, &c* (Antwerp, 1567).

Dechent, Hermann, *Kirchengeschichte von Frankfurt am Main seit der Reformation,* 2 vols (Leipzig/Frankfurt, 1913).

Denis, Philippe, 'Les Eglises d'étrangers à Londres jusqu'à la morte de Calvin. De l'Eglise de Jean Lasco à l'établissement du calvinisme' (unpublished *mémoire de licence,* University of Liége, 1974).

Dietz, Alexander, *Frankfurter Handelsgeschichte,* 3 vols (Frankfurt, 1910).

———— 'Cassiodorus Reinius, Gründer der hiesigen Niederländischen Gemeinde Augsburger Konfession, †15 März 1594, Zur Erinnerung an seinen 300jährigen Todestag', *Frankfurter evangelisch-Lutheraner Kirchen-Kalender,* Jahr 1894 (Frankfurt, 1894).

Diercxens, Jan Carl, *Antverpia Christo nascens et crescens seu Acta Ecclesiam Antverpensem* (Antwerp, 1773).

Droz, E, 'Note sur les impressions genevoises transportées par Hernández', *BHR Travaux et Documents,* 22 (Geneva, 1962), 119-32.

Fecht(ius), Johannes, *Historiæ Ecclesiasticæ Seculi A.N.C. XVI Supplementum; plurimum et celeberrimorum ex illo ævo Theologorum Epistolis ad Joannem, Erasmum et Philippum, Marbachios ante hac scriptis ...* (Frankfurt/Spires, 1684).

Férnandez Alvarez, Manuel, *Tres embajadores de Felipe II en Inglaterra* (Madrid, 1951).

Firpo, Luigi,, 'La chiesa italiana di Londra nel cinquecento e i suoi rapporti con Ginevra', *Ginevra e l'Italia*, Biblioteca Storica Sansoni, 34 (Florence, 1959).

Florian, Gebhard, *Der Welt-berühmten Freyen Reichs-Wahl- und Handels-Stadt Franckfurt am Mayn. Chronica* . . . vol. II ([Frankfurt], 1706).

Fluri, Adolf, 'Die Bärenbibel', *Gutenbergmuseum*, 9, I, 35-41, II, 82-90 (Berne, 1923).

Fournier-Marcigny, Fernand, *Genève au XVI^{me} siècle: La vie ardente du premier refuge français 1532-1602* (Geneva, 1942).

*Frankfurtische Religions-Handlungen Welche zwischen Einen Hoch-Edlen und Hochweisen Magistrat und denen Reformirten Bürgern und Einwohnern* . . ., 2 vols. (Frankfurt, 1735-45).

Fresenius, Johann Philip, *Kirchen-Geschichte von denen Reformirten in Franckfurt am Mayn worin derselben Ankunft, Aufnehm und Zuwuchs, des Gesuch einer besondern Kirche in der Stadt* . . . *vorgetragen werden* (Frankfurt, 1751).

Gaberel, Jean, *Histoire de l'eglise de Genève depuis le commencement de la Réformation jusqu'en 1815* (Geneva, 1853).

Galiffe, Jean Barthélemy Gaïfre, *Le Refuge italien de Genève au XVI^{me} & XVII^{me} siècles* (Geneva, 1881).

García Hernández, Adrian, *España y el Vizconde Palmerston, o sea defensa de la dignidad nacional en la cuestión de los pasaportes* (Appendix) (Madrid, 1848).

Geering, Traugott, *Handel und Industrie der Stadt Basel* (Basle, 1886).

Gerdes(ius), Daniel, *Florilegium Historico-criticum librorum rariorum cui Multa simul scitu jucunda intersperguntur, Historiam omnem Litterarium, & cumprimis Reformationis Ecclesiasticam illustrantia* (Groningen, 1740).

—— *Scrinium antiquarium sive Miscellanea Groningana nova ad Historiam Reformationis ecclesiasticam præcipue spectantia inseruntur tractatus varii generis,* 2 vols (Groningen/Bremen, 1749).

—— *Historia Reformationis sive Annales evangelii seculo XVI* . . . (Groningen/Bremen, 1749).

González, Jorge Augusto, 'Valera's Method for Revising the Old Testament in the Spanish Bible of 1602' (unpublished Ph.D. thesis, Emory University, Georgia, U.S.A., 1967).

—— *Casiodoro de Reina. Traductor de la Biblia en Español*, Monograph of the Sociedades Bíblicas Unidas (Mexico, 1969).

González Montes, Reginaldo (Gonsalvius Montanus), *Sanctæ Inquisitionis hispanicæ artes aliquot detectæ, ac palam traductæ* (Heidelberg, 1567).

Goris, J. A., *Etude sur les colonies marchandes méridionales (Portugais, Espagnols, Italiens) à Anvers de 1488 à 1567* (Louvain, 1925).

Grabau, Richard, *Das evangelisch-Lutherische Predigerministerium der Stadt Frankfurt a.M.* (Frankfurt/Liepzig, 1913).

Groote, Henry, L. V. de, 'De zestiende-eeuwse Antwerpse Schoolmesters', *Bijdragen tot de Geschiedenis,* 50^e Jaar (Antwerp/Ghent, no date), 179-318.

Grosart, Alexander B., ed., *The Towneley Hall MSS: The Spending of the Money of Robert Nowell of Reade Hall, Lancs.* (Blackburn/Manchester, 1877).

Grosheinz, Oscar, *L'Eglise italienne à Genève au temps de Calvin* (Lausanne, 1904).

Guaitta, Gottfried, *Merckwurdiges Verzeichniß derer von Zeit der Reformation allhier zu Franckfurt am Mayn gestandenen Evangelischen Predigern an der Zahl 188* . . . ([Frankfurt], 1774).

Guardia, J. M., 'L'Espagne protestante. Les écrivains réformistes', *Revue Germanique, française et étrangère,* 17 & 18 (Paris, 1861).

## Bibliography

Hauben, Paul J., *Three Spanish Heretics and the Reformation*, Etudes de Philologie et d'Histoire, 3 (Geneva, 1967).

────── 'A Spanish Calvinist Church in Elizabethan London 1559-1565', *Church History*. *American Society of Church History*, 34 (New York, 1965), 50-6.

────── 'In Pursuit of Heresy: Spanish diplomats versus Spanish Heretics in France and England during the wars of religion', *The Historical Journal*, 9 (London, 1966), 275-85.

────── 'Reform and Counter-reform: The Case of the Spanish Heretics', *Action and Conviction in Early Modern Europe*, ed. by T. K. Rabb & J. E. Seigal (Princeton, 1969), pp. 154-68.

Hennesy, George, *Novum Repertorium Ecclesiasticum Parochiale Londinense* (London, 1898).

Hessels, John Henry, *Ecclesiæ Londini-Bataviæ Archivum*, 3 vols (Cambridge, 1889).

Hume, M. A. S., ed., *Calendar of Letters and State Papers relating to English Affairs preserved principally in the Archives of Simancas*, vol. I, *Elizabeth 1558-1567*, vol. II, *Elizabeth 1568-1579*, vol. III, *Elizabeth 1587-1603* (London, 1892).

Illescas, Gonçalo de, *Historia pontifical y catholica* (Burgos, 1578).

Jacobi, F. J. Schultz, *Oud en Nieuw uit Geschiedenis der Nederlandsch-Luthersche Kerk* (Rotterdam, 1862).

────── & F. J. Domela Nieuwenhuis, *Bijdragen tot de Geschiedenis der Evang.-Luthersche Kerk in de Nederlanden*, 2 vols (Utrecht, 1843).

Kalkoff, Paul, 'Die Anfänge der Gegenreformation in den Niederlanden: Die Lutherische Bewegung in Antwerpen', *Schriften des Vereins für Reformationsgeschichte*, 1903 (Halle, 1903).

Kamen, Henry, *The Spanish Inquisition* (London, 1965).

Kervyn de Volkaersbeke, Philippe Auguste Chrétien & Isidore Lucien Antoine Diegerick, *Documents historiques inédits concernant les Troubles des Pays-Bas 1577-1584*, 2 vols (Ghent, 1847-9).

Kinder, Arthur Gordon, 'Cassiodoro de Reina and his Family in Frankfurt', *BHR*, 32 (Geneva, 1970), 427-31.

────── 'Two Unpublished Letters of Jean Cousin, Minister of the Threadneedle Street Church, concerning the Affair of Cassiodoro de Reina', *HSP*, 21 (London, 1971), 51-60.

──────'Cipriano de Valera (?1530-?1602)', *Bulletin of Hispanic Studies*, 46 (Liverpool, 1969), 109-19.

*Kirchenagend – oder Form und Gestalt, Wie es mit den Sakramenten und Ceremonien gehalten wird, in der Kirchen der Augspurgischen Confession zu Andorff* ([Frankfurt], 1567).

Kirk, R. E. G. & Ernest F. Kirk, *Returns of Aliens dwelling in the City & Suburbs of London from the Reign of Henry VIII to that of James I*, HSP, 10, 4 vols (Aberdeen, 1902-8).

Klipfel, H., *Le Colloque de Poissy* (Paris/Brussels/Leipzig, 1867).

Languet, Hubert, *Huberti Langveti Epistolæ ad Joachimum Camerarium Patrem & Filium* (Leipzig/Frankfurt, 1685).

Lea, Henry Charles, *Chapters from the Religious History of Spain connected with the Inquisition* (Philadelphia, 1890).

────── *History of the Inquisition of Spain*, 4 vols (New York/London, 1907).

Lecler, Joseph, *Histoire de la Tolérance au siècle de la Réforme*, *Théologie-Lyon*, 31 (Paris, 1955).

Lehnemann, Johannes, *Historische Nachricht von der vormahls im sechzehnten Jahrhundert berühmten Evangelisch-Lutherischen Kirche in Antorff und der daraus entstandenen Niederländischen Gemeinde Augspurgischer Konfession in Franckfurt am Mayn, aus beglaubten Urkunden mitgetheilet* (Frankfurt, 1725).

Léry, Jean de, *Historia navigationis in Brasiliam quæ et America dicitur . . .* ([Geneva], 1586).

Leuckfeld, Johann Georg, *Historia Spangenbergensis, Oder Historiche Nachricht Von den Leben, Lehre und Schrifften Cyriaci Spangenbergs . . .* (Quedlingen/Aschersleben, 1712).

Lindeboom, Johannes, *Austin Friars: History of the Dutch Reformed Church of London 1550-1950* (The Hague, 1950).

Linnhoff, Liselotte, *Spanische Protestanten und England* (Emsdetten, 1934).

Llorca, Bernardino, *Die Spanische Inquisition und die 'Alumbrados' (1509-1667) nach den Originalakten in Madrid und in anderen Archiven* (Berlin/Bonn, 1934).

Llorente, Juan Antonio, *Historia crítica de la Inquisición de España,* 10 vols (Madrid, 1822).

—— translated by Alexis Pelletier, *Histoire Critique de l'Inquisition d'Espagne depuis l'époque de son établissement par Ferdinand V jusqu'au règne de Ferdinand VII . . .* (Paris, 1817).

—— *A History of the Inquisition of Spain from the time of its establishment to the reign of Ferdinand VII* (London, 1826).

Longhurst, John E., 'Julián Hernández, Protestant Martyr', *BHR Travaux et Documents,* 22 (Geneva, 1960), 90-118.

—— *Erasmus and the Spanish Inquisition. The Case of Juan de Valdés,* University of New Mexico Publications in History, 1 (Albuquerque, 1950).

McCrie, Thomas, *Works,* Volume III, *History of the Progress and Suppression of the Reformation in Spain* (London/Edinburgh, 1856).

MacFadden, William, 'Life and Works of Antonio del Corro (1527-1591)' (unpublished Ph.D. thesis, Queen's University, Belfast, 1953).

Mansilla, Christoval, *Inuectiua contra el heresiarcha Luthero. Cõpuesta por el muy reuerẽdo padre fray Christoual Mãsilla, de la orden de los predicadores. Dirigida al muy Illustre señor dõ Pedro fernãdez de Cordoua, cõde de feria* (Burgos, 1552), facsimile reprint edited by Antonio Pérez y Goméz, *El ayre de la almena,* IV (Cieza, 1961).

Márquez, Antonio, *Los Alumbrados: orígenes y filosofía 1525-1559* (Madrid, 1972).

Marroquín, Hazael T., ed., *Versiones castellanas de la Biblia* (Mexico, 1959).

*A Memoriam. Relics of the Spanish Inquisition (Seville)* (no place or date).

Menéndez Pelayo, Marcelino, *Historia de los heterodoxos españoles,* 3 vols (Madrid, 1880-1).

—— *Historia de los heterodoxos españoles,* second edition, 5 vols (Buenos Aires, 1945).

Mertens, F. H. & K. L. Torfs, *Geschiedenis van Antwerpen* (Antwerp, 1849).

Moorrees, F. D. J., translated by Edmond Durand, *Scènes et tableaux de la Réformation en Belgique 1520-1830* (Nessonvaux, 1909).

Moreau, E. de, *Histoire de l'Eglise en Belgique,* Volume V, *L'Eglise des Pays-Bas* (Brussels, 1952).

*Naamroll der Predikanten, In de Gemeentens, de Onveranderde Augsburgsche Geloofsbeleidenisse Toegedaan: In de Zeven Verëenigde Nederlandsche Provintiën . . . Waar onder ook die, welke te Antwerpen, &c. gestaan hebben.* (Amsterdam, 1777).

Nieto, José C., *Juan de Valdés and the Origins of the Spanish and Italian Reformation,* *BHR Travaux,* 108 (Geneva, 1970).

Nieuwenhuis, F. J. Domela, *Geschiedenis der Amsterdamsche Luthersche Gemeente* Amsterdam, 1856).

# Bibliography

Peeters-Fontainas, Jean, *Bibliographie des impressions espagnoles des Pays-Bas Méridionaux 1520-1799* (Louvain/Antwerp, 1933).

—— *Bibliographie des impressions espagnoles des Pays-Bas Méridionaux 1520-1799*, second ed., 2 vols (Nieuwkoop, 1965).

Pellicer y Saforcada, Juan Antonio, *Ensayo de una bibliotheca de traductores españoles – donde se da noticia de las traducciones que hay en castellano de la Sagrada Escritura, santos padres, filosofos, historiadores, medicos, oradores, poetas, asi griegos como latinos: y de otros autores que han florecido antes de la invencion de la imprenta* (Madrid, 1778).

Pfandl, Ludwig, 'Das Spanische Lutherbild des 16. Jahrhunderts. Studien und Vorarbeiten', *Historiches Jahrbuch der Görresgesellschaft*, 50 (Munich, 1930), 464-97.

Pinta Llorente, Miguel de la, *La Inquisición española y los problemas de la cultura y de la intolerancia* (Madrid, 1948-58).

Ponce de la Fuente, Constantino, *Doctrina Christiana, en que esta comprehendida toda la informacion que pertenece al hombre que quiere seruir a Dios . . . Parte primera delos articulos dela fe* (Antwerp, 1555).

—— *Suma de Doctrina Christiana, Sermon de Nuestro Redemptor en el Monte, Catecismo Christiano, Confession del Pecador por Constantino Ponce de la Fuente i ahora fielmente reimpresos, RAE, XIX* (Madrid, 1863).

Pont, Johann Wilhelm, 'De Belijdenis van de Luthersche Gemeente te Antwerpen over de Erfzonde 1579', *Nieuwe Bijdragen tot Kennis van de Geschiedenis en het Wezen van het Lutheranisme in de Nederlanden*, I, pp. 119-64 (Schiedam, 1907).

—— 'De Luthersche Gemeenten in de Zuidelijke Nederlanden (1556-1585)', *Nieuwe Bijdragen tot Kennis van de Geschiedenis en het Wezen van het Lutheranisme in de Nederlanden*, III (Haarlem, 1911), 395-436.

—— 'De Catechismus van Franciscus Alardus', *Nieuwe Bijdragen tot Kennis van de Geschiedenis en het Wezen van het Lutheranisme in de Nederlanden*, II (Amsterdam, 1909), 1-146.

Prims, Floris, *De Groote Cultuurstrijd*, Volume I, *De Religionsvrede 1578-1581*, Volume II, *De Christelijke Republik 1581-1585* ([Antwerp], no date).

—— 'Een incident uit de Religionsvrede 1580', *Bijdragen tot de Geschiedenis*, 3, No. 1 (Antwerp/Ghent, 1953).

——, ed., *Register der Commissie tot Onderhoud van de Religionsvrede te Antwerpen 1579-1581*, Commission Royale d'Histoire (Brussels, 1954).

*Protest vande Christelijcke Ghemeynte binnen Antwerpen, toeghedaen der Confessien van Ausborch, op de Articulen vande Pacificatie van Nederlant, Ghemaect tot Ceulen den xviij. Julij, etc.* (Antwerp, 1579).

*Protestation des fideles en la ville d'Anvers dediez a la Confession D'Ausbourg, presentée au Conseil des Estatz, sur les Articles de la Pacification du [sic] Païs-Bas: Faict à Cologne le xviij. Juillet. &c.* (Antwerp, 1579).

Puigblanch, Antonio, *La Inquisición sin máscara* (Cadiz, 1811).

*Reformistas Antiguos Españoles*, 20 vols., edited by Benjamin B. Wiffen & Luis de Usoz y Río (San Sebastián/Madrid/London, 1848-65).

Rahlenbeck, Charles, *L'Inquisition et la Réforme en Belgique (Anvers)* (Brussels, 1857).

Ramus, Petrus (Pierre de la Ramée), *Petri Rami Basilea ad Senatvm Popvlvmque Basiliensem* ([Lausanne?], 1571).

Redondo, Agustín, 'Luther et l'Espagne de 1520 à 1536', *Mélanges de la Casa de Velázquez*, 1 (Madrid/Paris, 1965), 109-65.

Ritter, Johann Balthasar, *Evangelisches Denkmal der Stadt Franckfurth am Mayn, Oder, Ausführlicher Bericht von der daselbst im XVI. Jahrhundert ergangenen Kirchen-Reformation . . .* (Frankfurt, 1726).

Rodocanachi, E.P., 'Renée de France, un roman dans l'histoire', *Nouvelle Revue,* 94 (Paris, 1895), 117-40, 334-59; 95 (Paris, 1895), 764-87.

Roy, Charles, 'L'école française de Montbéliard', *BSHPF,* 32 (Paris, 1883), 515-21.

Schäfer, Ernst H. J., *Beiträge zur Geschichte des Spanischen Protestantismus und der Inquisition im sechzehnten Jahrhundert,* 3 vols (Gütersloh, 1902).

―――― 'Sevilla und Valladolid: die evangelischen Gemeinden Spaniens im Reformationszeitalter', *Schriften des Vereins für Reformationsgeschichte,* 78, Part I (Halle, 1903).

Scharff, Friedrich, 'Die Niederländischen und die Französischen Gemeinde in Frankfurt a.M.', *Archiv für Frankfurts Geschichte und Kunst,* New Series, 2 (Frankfurt, 1862), 245-317.

Schickler, Fernand de, *Les Eglises du refuge en Angleterre,* 3 vols (Paris, 1892).

Schmidt, Charles, *La vie et les travaux de Jean Sturm, premier Recteur du Gymnase et de l'Académie de Strasbourg* (Strassburg, 1855).

Schlüsselburg, Conrad, *Conradi Schlusselburgii theologi Lutherani . . . studium . . . Epistolarum clarissimorum quorundam theologorum . . . volumen* (Rostock, 1624).

Schrevel, A.-C. de, *Recueil de documents relatifs aux troubles religieux en Flandres 1577-1584,* Société d'Emulation de Bruges, *Mélanges,* 8 (Bruges, 1921).

Selke de Sánchez, Angela, 'Algunos datos nuevos sobre los primeros Alumbrados – El Edicto de 1525 y su relación con el proceso de Alcaraz', *BH,* 54 (Bordeaux, 1952), 125-52.

Sepp, Christian, *Kerkhistorische Studiën* (Leyden, 1885).

――――*Geschiedkundige Nasporingen* (Leyden, 1872).

―――― *Polemische en Irenische Theologie – Bijdragen tot hare Geschiedenis* (Leyden, 1881).

Serrano y Sanz, Manuel, 'Pedro Ruiz de Alcaraz, iluminado alcarreño del siglo XVI', *Revista de Bibliotecas y Museos,* 7 (Madrid, 1903), 1-16, 126-39.

―――― 'Francisca Hernández y el Bachiller Antonio de Madrano, sus procesos por la Inquisición (1512 á 1532)', *Boletín de la Real Academia de la Historia,* 41 (Madrid, 1902), 105-38.

Sierra Corella, Antonio, *La censura de libros y papeles en España y los índices y catálogos de libros prohibidos y expurgados* (Madrid, 1947).

Sigüenza, José de, *Historia de la Orden de San Jerónimo,* 2 vols (Madrid, 1907).

Steinmann, Martin, *Johannes Oporinus: Ein Basler Buchdrucker um die Mitte des 16. Jahrhunderts,* Basler Beiträge zur Geschichtswissenschaft, 15 (Basle/Stuttgart, 1967).

Steitz, Georg-Edward & Herman Dechent, *Geschichte der von Antwerpen nach Frankfurt am Main verpflanzten Niederländischen Gemeinde Augsburger Confession* (Frankfurt, 1885).

Stockwell, B. Foster, *Prefacios a las Biblias castellanas del siglo XVI,* 2nd ed., (Buenos Aires/Mexico, 1951).

Stoughton, John, *The Spanish Reformers: their Memories and Dwelling-places* (London, 1883).

Strype, John, *Annals of the Reformation & establishment of religion & other various occurrences in the Church of England during Queen Elizabeth's happy reign* (Oxford, 1824).

―――― *Life of Edmund Grindal* (Oxford, 1821).

―――― *Memorials of Archbishop Cranmer* (Oxford, 1812).

Tablante Garrido, P. N., *Itálicas en los Nuevos Testamentos de Torres Amat y Reina y Valera* (St Louis, 1950).

―――― 'La Biblia del Oso y su foliatura', *Universidad,* 6 (Mérida, Venezuela, 1957), 3-7.

―――― 'Del Nuevo Testamento traducido por el Doctor Juan Pérez', *Humanidades,* 3-4 (Mérida, 1959), 1-15.

Tellechea Idígoras, J. Ignacio, 'Biblias publicadas fuera de España secuestradas por la Inquisición de Sevilla', BH, 44 (Bordeaux, 1962), 236-47.

Texeda, Francisco de, *Scrutamini Scripturas: The Exhortation of a Spanish converted Monke* . . . (London, 1624).

Tollin, Nathaniel, 'Cassiodore de Reina', *BSHPF*, 31 (Paris, 1882), 386-97; 32 (Paris, 1883), 289-98.

Valera, Cipriano de, *Dos Tratados. El primero es del Papa y de su autoridad . . . El segundo es de la Missa recopilado de los Doctores y Concilios y de la sagrada Escritura* ([London], 1588).

—— *Dos Tratados. El primero es del Papa y de su autoridad . . . El segundo es de la Missa . . . Segunda edicion augmentada por el mismo autor* ([London], 1599).

Van der Essen, Léon, 'Episodes de l'histoire religieuse et commerciale d'Anvers dans la seconde moitié du XVI^e siècle', *Bulletin de la Commission Royale d'Histoire*, 80 (Brussels, 1911).

—— 'Les progrès du Luthéranisme et du calvinisme dans le monde commercial d'Anvers', *Vierteljahrschrift für Sozial- und Wirtschaftsgeschichte*, 12 (Berlin/Leipzig, 1914), 152-234.

Van Gelder, H. A. Enno, *Revolutionnaire Reformatie* (Amsterdam, 1943).

Van Lennep, M. F., *De Hervorming in Spanje in de zestiende eeuw* (Haarlem, 1901).

Van Roosbroeck, Rob., ed., *De Kroniek van Godevaert van Haecht over de Troubelen van 1565 tot 1574 te Antwerpen en elders*, 2 vols (Antwerp, 1929).

Van Schelven, Aart Arnout, 'Cassiodorus de Reyna, Christophorus Fabricius en Gaspar Olevianus', *Nederlandsch Archief voor Kerkgeschiedenis*, 8 (The Hague, 1911), 311-32.

Verheyden, A. L. E., *De Hervorming in de Zuidelijke Nederlanden in de XVI^e Eeuw* (Brussels, 1949).

Von Lersner, Georg Augustus & Achille Augustus von Lersner, *Nachgeholte vermehrte und continuierte Chronica Der Weitberühmten freyen Reichs-Wal- und Handels-Stadt Franckfurth am Mayn . . . oder Zweyter Theil* (Frankfurt, 1734).

Von Mosheim, Johann Laurentius, *Dissertationum ad Historiam Ecclesiasticam pertinentium volumen accedit Mich. Gerdesii Martyrologium Protestantium Hispanorum Latine versum ex Anglico* (Altona, 1733).

—— *Dissertationum ad Historiam ecclesiasticam*, 2nd ed., 2 vols (Altona/Flensburg, 1743).

Wilkens, C. A., *Geschichte des Spanischen Protestantismus im sechzehnten Jahrhundert* (Gütersloh, 1880).

Williams, George Huntston, *The Radical Reformation* (London, 1962).

Zülch, Walter Karl, *Frankfurter Kunstler 1223-1700* (Frankfurt, 1935).

*Zurich Letters (Second Series): Comprising the Correspondence of several English Bishops & others with some of the Helvetian Reformers . . .*, Publication of the Parker Society (Cambridge, 1845).

# Index

Ábrego, Francisco de, 28-34, 99, 102, 104-10, 115.
Ábrego, Luis de, 10.
Ackerman, Jeremias, 31, 103f, 110, 115.
Acontius (Giacomo Concio), 23, 26, 34, 84, 96, 102f.
Alcalá de Henares, University of, 1, 4ff.
Albret, Jeanne d', 40, 97.
Alcocer, Diego de, 3.
Allard, François, Lutheran pastor in Antwerp, 76.
Alumbrados, Illuminists, Illuminism, 2ff, 6f, 14.
Alva, Duke of, 67.
Amboise, Pacification of, 40f.
Anabaptists, 23n, 38, 84, 102.
Angel Victor Sardius, 19, 22, 29-36, 84, 99, 101f, 105, 107, 109.
Antwerp, 13f, 25, 34, 38f, 49, 63-71. depopulation of, 67, 76.
Apiarius (Samuel Biener), 52.
Arellano, Cristóbal de, 16.
Arias, García, 11f, 16.
Arnoldi, Bernard, 74.
Austin Friars Flemish Church, London, 20.
Autos de fe in Seville, 1559 : 16; 1560 : 9, 16; 1562 : 16, 19.

Baena, Isabel de, 10, 16.
Balbani, Nicolas, Italian pastor in Geneva, 58.
Banos, Théophile de, French pastor in Frankfurt, 57f, 80, 112, 118.
Baptism, 84, 102.
Baptista, Alonso, 16.
Bärfüsserkirche, Frankfurt, 79f.
Basle, 46-57, 121f.
Bassée, Nicolas, printer in Frankfurt, 61, 78.
Bayonne, Jean de, father, son, wife of, 28-37, 104-111, 114f, 118f.
Béarn, 25ff.
Bedford, Earl of, 24.
Beferfort, Dieterich von, 80.
Benito, monk of San Isidro, 16.

Bergerac, 26, 40f, 97.
Bernuy, —, or Bernouilli, 71, 98.
Beza (Théodore de Bèze), 13, 20, 24f, 34, 43, 45f, 57ff, 66n, 84, 87, 96n.
Bible, Complutensian Polyglot, 1.
  Enzinas's New Testament, 13.
  Reina's version, 46-56, 102ff.
  Servetus's edition, 55n.
  Sanctes Pagninus's version, 79n.
  Valera's revision of Reina's version, 55f.
Blois, 14.
Boazius, Augustijn, 39.
Bode, Jacques, 74.
Bode, Johan, 63.
Bode, Michel, 70f, 74, 80f.
Boesse, 98.
Bohórquez, Juana & Maria de, 10, 19.
Boquinius, 42.
Bourbourg, 111.
Brabant, Duke of, 76.
Brentius (Johan Brenz), 97.
Broikius, 40.
Brussels, 33.
  New Union of, 67, 70.
Bucer (Martin Butzer), 61, 86f.
Bugenhagen, Johan, 6.
Bullinger, Henry, 12, 14.
Burie, M.de, 41.

Calvin, Jean, 13f, 19, 82, 85f, 100, 102f.
  Catechisme, 14.
  Institution, 39.
Cando, (or Cardo), Gian Francesco, 32f.
Canto, Alonso de, 25.
Capelle, Antoine, 30, 115.
Capito, Wolfgang, 87.
Cárdenas, Francisco de, 16.
Carmelite Convent, Antwerp, 69, 75.
Carpintero, Miguel, 16.
Castellio, Sébastian, 19, 46n, 82ff, 101, 102n.
Catechism, Spanish of 1550, 13f.
  Strassburg, 73.
  Antwerp Lutheran, 73.
Cecil, Lord William, Secretary to Queen Elizabeth, 21, 24, 54, 93.

# Index

Cehnets, Jacob, 80.
*Censura de Biblias,* 9.
Charles V, 4f, 7f.
Chaves, Francisca, 10.
Chemnitz, Martin, 73f.
Churruca, Domingo, 16.
Chytraeus, David, 75f.
　*Histoire de la Confession d'Auxpurg,*
　76.
Cisneros, Cardinal, 1, 9.
Coetus of Refugee Churches in London,
　21, 24.
Colegio de los Niños de la Doctrina,
　Seville, 10.
Cologne, 57, 68, 70.
Commission of Enquiry on Casiodoro de
　Reina, 30-4, Appx. III.
Conejo, María de, 10.
*Confessio in Articulo de Cœna,* 65n, 70,
　80, 88.
Consubstantiation, 86.
Cop, Luc le, 76.
Corro, Antonio del, 12, 14ff, 19f, 22,
　25ff, 39ff, 59, 65, 85, 110.
　*Lettre envoyée au Roy,* 12.
　*Dialogus Theologicus,* 78.
Corro, Antonio del, Grand Inquisitor of
　Seville, 8.
Cortés, Lope, 16, 19, 101.
Cousin, Jean (Cognatus), minister of the
　French Reformed Church in London,
　27-37, 57f, 64, 113-9.
Cousturier, Jacques, 35.
Coverdale, Miles, 30, 115.
Crisóstomo, Juan, 16.
Crowley, Dr Robert, 30, 115.
Cruz, Diego de la (Jacques de la Croix),
　7, 34, 115, 117f.
Cruz, Isabel de la, 4.

Diaz, Bartolomeo, 83.

Eggerdes, Peter, 73.
Elizabeth, Queen, 20, 24, 53ff, 119f.
Enzinas, Francisco de, 13.
Erasmus, Desiderius, 3f, 6, 9, 11.
Escobar, —, 10, 12.
Escodéca, Jean d', Seigneur de Boesse,
　40, 98.
Eucharist, 42, 44f, 64, 66, 75f, 84, 86,
　88.

Farías, Francisco, Prior of San Isidro,
　16, 31f, 35, 65, 106, 115, 119.
Fehr, P., painter of Frankfurt, 77n.
Fernández, Alonso, Archdeacon of
　Alcor, 3.

Ferrara, Renée, Duchess of – see Renée.
Feure, Thomas le, 25.
Fichet, Jacques, 27, 96, 98.
Firlei family in Poland, 62.
Fisscher, Adolf, Lutheran pastor in
　Amsterdam, 79, 84, 89.
Flaccius Illyricus, Matthias, 50, 72f.
Fouet, Pierre & Jeanne, 31, 35.
Frankfurt am Main, 14, 19, 21n, 28, 37,
　39f, 77.
　*Agenda,* 70ff.
'French Fury' in Antwerp, 76.

Gallars, Nicolas des, Sieur de Saules,
　French pastor in London, 24f, 27,
　34, 40, 43, 46, 57, 59, 108, 110.
Geneva, 12-16, 19f.
Giblon, Jean, 35.
Gil, Juan (Egidio), 6-12.
Giustiniano, Antonio, 65f.
Gomes, Bartholomé, 48, 50, 53, 121f.
Gonsalvius Montanus, Reginaldus, 6, 9ff,
　16f, 47n.
González, Juan, 10, 12, 16.
Gregory IX, Pope, 10.
Greiff, Nicholas, 69.
Grindal, Edmund, Bishop of London/
　Archbishop of Canterbury, 20f, 30-7,
　61, 64, 66, 93, 99, 113, 117, 119.
Guarin, Thomas, printer in Basle, 51f.
Guzmán, Enrique de, 11.

Haemstede, Adriaan, 23, 26n, 34, 84,
　102f.
Haus Braunfels, Frankfurt, 63.
Haus der Groll, Frankfurt, 63.
Heidelberg 41-4.
Heidelberger, Joseph, 57.
Henry VIII, 119f.
Hernández, Julián, 13f, 16, 19, 39.
Hernández del Castillo, Luis, 7.
Herrera, —, 101f.
Heshusius, 74.
Hesse-Cassel, Landgrave of, 78.
Hettié, Jean, 30, 115.
Holy Ghost Church, Heidelberg, 42.
Honestis, M. d', 42f.
Hubert, Conrad, pastor in Strassburg,
　46-54, 57, 61.

*Imagen del Antechristo,* 13f.
Impanation, 66, 86.
*Index,* 9.
Inquisition, Spanish, 4-7, 9f, 12ff, 16, 20,
　24, 27, 34f, 47.
Italians, in Geneva, 20, 118, in London,
　65, in Antwerp, 32ff.

Jan van Nassau, 68.
Jerome, St., 10f.
Jesuits, 9, 11, 68.
Jews, 1f, 12, 38, 60, 102.
John of Austria, 67.

Koechlin, Huldrich (Coccius), 46, 48ff, 60, 83.
Krautwald, Valentin, 26, 96f, 100.

Legrand, Augustin, 14, 51, 59, 63.
Leon, Abraham, 25, 39.
León, Hernando de, 16, 101f.
León, Juan de, 16, 20, 27.
Léry, Jean de, 78.
Lewin, William (Luinius), 64.
Loiseleur de Villiers, 71.
London, French Refugee Church, 20f, 23-7, 65f, Flemish Refugee Church, 20f, 23, Spanish Refugee Church, 20, 24, 65, Italian Refugee Church, 20f, 65.
López, Diego, 16, 47f, 50, 121f.
López, Ursula, wife of Marcos Pérez, 70.
Losada, Cristóbal de, 10, 16.
Luther & Lutheranism, 5-9, 11f, 14, 87ff.

Maçon de la Fontaine, Robert le, 64, 66n.
Málaga, Andrés de, 16.
Manrique, Alonso, Archbishop of Toledo, 3f.
Marbach, Johan, 42, 43n, 45, 48n, 61.
Marche-en-Famenne, 67.
Marell, Servas, 62.
Marischal, Christoffle (Fabricius), 32, 111.
Martin V, Pope, 11.
Martínez, Isabel, 9.
Martyr, Peter, 24, 26, 96.
Mary Tudor, Queen, 119f.
Matthias, Archduke, 67f, 70, 73.
Maurice of Nassau, 67f.
Medina de Rioseco, 4.
Melanchthon, Philip, 6, 14, 87.
Mendoza, Bernardo de, Spanish Ambassador to England, 64.
Miguel, monk of San Isidro, 16.
Molina, Juan de, 16.
Montargis, 14, 41.
Montbéliard, 74, 78, 83.
Montemolín, 18.
Morzillo, Francisco, 42f.
Mosellanus, Franciscus, 42f.
Moslems, 1ff, 12, 60.
Motte, Paschasius de la, 32, 111.

Nowell, Alexander, 65.

Nowell, Robert, 65.
Nuestra Señora de Barrameda, Sanlúcar, 7.
Nuestra Señora del Valle, Écija, convent, 11, 14f.

Observantine Hieronymites, Order of, 10f, 18f.
Œcolampadius, 6, 87.
Offenbacs, Elias von, 62f.
Olevianus, Gaspar, 41-4, 46, 57f.
Olmedo, Lope de, 10f.
Oporinus, printer of Basle, 46n, 47-52, 61, 83, 121.
Original sin, 73, 79, 89.
Orleans, 34, 40f, 99.
Osiander, 26, 96.

Pablo, Pedro, 16.
Pacification of Ghent, 67, 70.
Parma, Alexander Farnese, Duke of, 76.
Parma, Marguerite de, 38n.
Pascual, Mateo, 5.
Patiens, Petrus, 72.
Paz, Peregrino de, 16.
Pérez, Juan, secretary to Charles V, 3.
Pérez de Pineda, Juan, 13ff, 19f, 39, 41, 48, 51, 79, 82, 110.
    Sumario breve de la doctrina, 13.
    New Testament, 13.
    Psalms, 13.
    Carta a Felipe, 14.
    Catecismo, 14.
    Epistola Consolatoria, 14.
Pérez, Marcos, 39, 49ff, 53, 57, 67, 70.
Perpetual Edict, 67, 70.
Perray, Pierre du, 27, 96, 98.
Peschard, Michiel, 74.
Petri, Adam, 61.
Philip II, 8, 67.
Poissy, Colloquy of, 20, 24f, 30n, 40.
Poland, 62,
Ponce de la Fuente, Constantino, 6-9, 12, 16.
    Exposicion del Primer Psalmo, 8.
    Suma de Doctrina, 8, 13.
Ponce de León, Juan, 10, 16.
Populerius, 79, 89f.
Porres, Gaspar de, 16.
Puerta, Francisco de la, 16.

Quadra, Álvaro de la, Spanish Ambassador to England, 22, 24f.

Real presence, 87f.
Reina (Extremadura), 18.

Reina, Anna, 25, 34, 45, 49f, 70, 72, 74f, 80f.

Reina, Augustin, 59.

Reina, Casiodoro de, flight from San Isidro, 16, 19, birth(place), 18, monk, 18f, in Geneva, 19f, 82f, 85, 110, in Frankfurt, 20, 33, 37, 39ff, 45f, 57-63, 66, 77-80, 108, in London, 20-37, 64ff, Spanish Confession of London, 21, requests a church in London, 21f, Appx.I, at Colloquy of Poissy, 24f, marriage, 25, case against, 27-37, Appx.III, Appx.IV, flight from London, 31, in Antwerp, 34, 38f, 63-77, in Orleans, 40, in Bergerac, 40f, in Montargis, 41, in Strassburg, 41-6, 50f, 61, in Heidelberg, 41-3, 85, in Basle, 46-57, cleared of charges, 64ff, becomes a Lutheran, 65, in Cologne, 68, sets up a charity in Frankfurt, 77, portrait of, frontispiece, 77, 92, in Hesse-Cassel, 78, death, 80.

publications, Bible 1569, 46-56, Spanish Confession of London, 62, notes on Isaiah, 46, notes on Ezekiel, 46, *Evangelium Ioannis,* 56, 59-61, 85, 90f, *Expositio primæ partis capitis quarti Matthæi,* 56, 59-61, 91.

letters, list of, Appx.VII.

Reina, Johan, 63.

Reina, Marcus, 50, 57.

Reina, Margarethe, 59.

Reina, Servas, 62.

Reina, parents of Casiodoro de, 19, 24, 115.

Renée de France, Duchess of Ferrara, 14, 41.

Richelius, Theodosius, 61.

Ritter, Matthias the Younger, pastor & Superintendent of foreign congregations in Frankfurt, 46, 61, 63-77, 88.

Ruiz de Alcaraz, Pedro, 4.

St Anthony's Church, Threadneedle Street, London, 20.

St Bartholomew's Church, London, 30.

Sainte-Foy-la-Grande, 96.

St Germain temple, Geneva, 20.

Santa Isabel convent, Seville, 10.

San Isidro del Campo convent, Seville, 10-16.

San Jerónimo, Bernardo de, 16.

San Juan, Fernando de, 10.

St Mary Axe Church, London, 22.

St Nicholas Church, Frankfurt, 79.

St Paul's Church, Frankfurt, 79n.

St Peter's-le Poor Church, London, 30.

Salvard, Jean-François, French pastor in Frankfurt, 42, 57f, 112, 118.

Sánchez, Balthasar, 28-34, 65, 99, 102f, 105-9, 113ff.

Sanctes Pagninus, 55n, 90.

Saravia, Adrian, 85.

Sastre, Juan, 16.

Savonarola, 11.

Schadeus, 79.

Schlüsselberg, Conrad, 75.

Schwenkfeld, Caspar, 26, 96f.

Serrarius (Antoine Serray), 74, 76, 78ff.

Servetus, 19f, 22f, 27, 36, 55n, 82-7, 100-3.

Seville, 6-12.

Simony, Jean, 35.

Sixtus Senensis, *Bibliotheca Sacra,* 61.

Sleidanus, 14.

Socinus, 23.

Sodomy, 27f, 30f, 36, 58, 104-18, Appx.V.

Sosa, Luis de, 16.

Spanish Confession of London, 21, 23, 30, 36, 62, 83, 85f, 103.

'Spanish Fury' in Antwerp, 67.

Spitalkirche, Frankfurt, 78.

Strassburg, 41-57.

Sturm, Johan, 43, 45f, 48f, 53f, 60f, 64.

Sulzer, Simon, 46, 48ff, 60, 63.

Sylvanus, Johannes, 42.

Taffin, Jean, 68, 75.

Texeda, Francisco de, 85.

Théobon, 26f, 95ff.

Throckmorton, Sir Nicholas, 24f.

Toledo, 4.

Transubstantiation, 86.

Tremellius, John Emmanuel, 59f.

Trent, Council of, 1.

Trinity, Holy, 21f, 36, 44, 60, 83ff, 88, 100-3.

Ubiquity, Doctrine of, 27, 42, 66.

Uceda, Diego de, 4.

Ulrich, Duke of Wurttemberg, 78.

Unitarianism, 23.

Urbanus Regius, 14.

Ursinus (Zacharias Beer), 42f, 85.

Utenhovius, Joannes, Flemish minister in London, 32n, 34, 36f, 40, 64, 103, 110, 115.

Valdés, Alfonso de, 4f.

Valdés Bernardino, 16.

Valdés Juan de, 4f, 13.
Valer, Rodrigo de, 6f, 9.
Valera, Cipriano de, 6, 10, 16f, 19ff, 35, 55f, 60f, 79, 82, 92n, 96.
Valladolid, 3, 6.
Vargas, Francisco de, 6, 10.
Velsius, Justus, 26, 34, 96.
Versasca, Bartolomeo, 53f.
Virués, María de, 10.

Wandanabelle, Hans, 52.
Weissfrauenkirche, Frankfurt, 80.

Whittingham, William, 30, 115.
Withenne, —, 30, 115.

Young, James, 30, 115.

Zanchi, Girolamo, 46, 50.
Zapata, Francisco, 25, 29n.
Zapata, Gaspar, 7, 29-36, 99-105, 107, 109, 111, 115.
Zayas, Gabriel de, 64.
Zwinger, Thomas, 46, 49, 53, 57, 61ff, 83.
Zwingli, 27n.